MILFORD HAVEN

THROUGH TIME

Patricia Swales Barker

AMBERLEY PUBLISHING

First published 2013

Amberley Publishing
The Hill, Stroud, Gloucestershire, GL5 4EP
www.amberley-books.com

Copyright © Patricia Swales Barker, 2013

The right of Patricia Swales Barker to be identified as the
Author of this work has been asserted in accordance with
the Copyrights, Designs and Patents Act 1988.

ISBN 978 1 4456 2073 2 (print)
ISBN 978 1 4456 2078 7 (ebook)

British Library Cataloguing in Publication Data.
A catalogue record for this book is available from the
British Library.

Typesetting by Amberley Publishing.
Printed in Great Britain.

Appointed GPSR EU Representative: Easy Access System
Europe Oü, 16879218
Address: Mustamäe tee 50, 10621, Tallinn, Estonia
Contact Details: gpsr.requests@easproject.com, +358 40
500 3575

Introduction

Milford Haven has been described as the finest natural harbour in the country. It is immediately accessible to the Atlantic Ocean; in fact it is arguably the nearest British port to the United States and the Panama Canal. The advantages of the Haven had long been recognised, even by Shakespeare in *Cymbeline*.

Although the town of Milford Haven celebrated its bicentenary in 1990, the areas of Hubberston and Steynton are medieval parishes. The area was probably visited by the Viking fleets as early as the ninth century. Hakin, within Hubberston parish, was an active fishing village and the terminus of the Irish Mail Packet ship. The Steynton parish boundary included the town of Milford until 1891.

Sir William Hamilton acquired the Manor of Pill and Hubberston, a large area of land along the waterfront, through his marriage in 1758 to Catherine Barlow. His agent was his nephew Charles Francis Greville, who identified the potential of the area. In 1790 an Act of Parliament allowed the owner to 'make and provide quays, docks, piers and other erections and to establish a market, with proper roads and avenues thereto respectively, within the Manor or Lordship of Hubberston and Pill in the County of Pembroke'. The new town was called Milford. The Navy Board began shipbuilding on a site at the location in 1797. One of the naval architects there was Jean-Louis Barrallier, who worked with Greville to draw up a plan for the proposed development of the town. This included a port facility at the inlet of Hubberston Pill and a new town to its east along the waterway. The town would be laid out simply in a grid plan with three long, parallel streets interconnected by shorter, steep streets rising up the hill overlooking the waterway. Front Street (later named Hamilton Terrace) was designed with impressive and prominent houses, Middle Street (Charles Street) was to be the shopping street and Third Street (Robert Street) would comprise relatively simple terrace housing.

A number of Quaker whalers from Nantucket Island, Massachusetts, settled in the new town in 1792, and their influence can be seen in the architecture of Hamilton Terrace. This connection is also recalled in the street names of Nantucket Avenue, Fulke Street and Starbuck Road. Their main market was London, where whale oil was used as fuel for street lamps.

The first two large buildings in the town were built at either end of Hamilton Terrace, St Katharine's church and the New Inn, which opened in 1800. This was renamed the Lord Nelson Hotel following the Admiral's visit to the town in 1802. On his visit, Nelson was impressed by the magnificent harbour and recommended its use for shipbuilding to the

Admiralty. Unfortunately, this early optimism was misplaced as the town grew very slowly. A setback was the removal in 1814 of the Navy Dockyard to a new base at Paterchurch, on the other side of the waterway, despite seven royal vessels having being launched from the dockyard, including HMS *Milford*. Some years later, the transfer of the Irish Packet service from Hubberston to Hobbs Point at Pembroke Dock was a further blow to the town's prosperity.

In 1811, Fenton wrote,

> The situation of the town of Milford is most singularly beautiful, as occupying a point of land with a gentle slope on all sides towards the water which almost surrounds it, with an exception to the north. To the south it has the main haven, here spreading into a spacious reach, having all the appearance of a fine lake, with its boundaries endlessly varied, and its surface, when I last saw it in the summer of 1808, unruffled and of the purest azure, on the east Prix Pill, and on the west the Priory Pill. Nothing can exceed the luxury of this scene altogether, and it is to be lamented that it is not more alive with traffic.

Shipbuilding and repairs in small yards along Hubberston Pill and the waterfront were the backbone of local industry. The first bridge to link Hubberston and Hakin with Milford was constructed in 1859, replacing stepping stones and wooden boards. The railway reached Milford by 1863 and in the next year the foundation stone of a new dock, situated in the central part of the seafront, was laid. The aim was to create a dock that would establish Milford as a major port. The dock was eventually opened in 1888, operated by the Milford Docks Company.

During the 1880s, Brixham and Hull ships brought in catches of prime fish to Milford. Their success inspired many East Coast trawler owners to move their ships from Yarmouth, Hull, and Scarborough to Milford. In 1888, *Sybil*, a steam trawler, was the first ship to enter the newly opened docks and her catch was sent to Billingsgate, London. Rich harvests of hake were found around the Smalls about 20 miles off Milford, and herring also became a major catch.

Hopes that Milford could be a port for transatlantic liners failed to materialise, but it did begin to prosper as a fishing port. This was due to its proximity to good fishing grounds, a safe anchorage and good rail links. Investment in ice factories, the fish market, a dry dock facility, chandleries, offices, smokehouses and other essential ancillary trades also drove the success.

In 1912, the *Pembrokeshire Herald* wrote, 'The fish trade is Milford's sole industry and everything and everyone in the town depends upon it. Directly or indirectly between 1,500 and 2,000 people are engaged in it. The population of the town has doubled by means of it and thousands of pounds worth of house property has been erected as an outcome of its prosperity.'

During both World Wars, many Milford trawlers were commandeered for minesweeping but some fishing continued. The town suffered many losses. At its height the fishing industry at Milford Haven involved 130 vessels and provided work for around 4,000 people. Annual catches averaged 40,000 thousand tons of herring and mackerel, with the record year being 1946 when 58,000 thousand tons were landed. The population of Milford increased from about 4,000 in the 1880s to 6,399 in 1911. Employment was provided for many in the town and surrounding area and Milford became the fifth-largest fishing port in the UK.

By the mid-1960s, the annual catch sold through the Milford Fish Market had reduced to 10,000 tons and continued to decline. By 2001, around 6,000 tons was landed, mostly by French, Belgian and Spanish vessels, and then exported in refrigerated lorries. Activity in the port reduced and the dock, the original nucleus of the town, became increasingly derelict as buildings fell into disrepair and were demolished.

Government of the town from 1857 was placed in the hands of fifteen Improvement Commissioners, appointed as a result of the passing of the Milford Improvement Bill by Parliament. Their area covered from Gellyswick in the west to Castle Pill in the east, and so included Hubberston, Hakin, and the town of Milford. The commissioners were responsible for raising rates to maintain the two bridges (Victoria and Black Bridge), roads, street lighting, and a gasworks. In 1894, administration of the town passed from the Commissioners to the Milford Haven Urban District Council. This was the first time the town was named Milford Haven. The success of the fishing and allied trades led to an expansion of the population and so housing needs increased. The council revived the Saturday market, improved the paving and lighting of the streets, and developed the water and gas supplies to the town. The council was considered to be one of the most progressive in the country, at the forefront of the development of the town. The shopping centre in and around Charles Street thrived, new chapels opened and extra housing was provided. By 1939, the population exceeded 11,000. By 1952, the UDC had built 1,000 houses and in 1974, when Preseli District Council was established as the first tier of local government, there were over 2,000 council-owned homes in the town.

The Milford Haven Conservancy Board was established in 1958, taking control in 1960 of the waterway, previously the responsibility of the Royal Navy. In 1986, it was renamed Milford Haven Port Authority and remains responsible for regulating the Haven, as well as managing and operating many of the marine and port activities.

Because the deep water harbour was able to take the largest tankers, Milford Haven developed during the 1960s and 1970s into a major world oil port with four large refineries and jetties located on the Haven. The new industry, although located on the waterway, had some effect on the fortunes of the town as the construction of the oil refineries and their support services boosted the economy. It provided significant employment for local workers and brought into the area many workers who then settled in the county. Construction of the Esso Refinery and jetty extending out into the deep water, located between Hakin and Herbrandston, began in 1957. By 1970, Milford Haven had become the largest oil port in Europe.

The population had risen to almost 14,000 by 1981 and the town continued to be the largest in the county. But the mid-1980s saw almost 25 per cent unemployment in the town, mainly due to the continued decline of the fishing industry. The development of light industry was encouraged and the Thornton Trading Estate took on an important role. In 1984, the Milford Haven Waterway Enterprise Zone was established to encourage economic regeneration.

Two events in the early 1990s were pivotal in redefining the direction for the future of Milford Haven. The 1990 bicentenary celebrations and the 1991 Tall Ships Race allowed the tourist and leisure potential of the town and its port to be tested. The success of the events led to the recognition that tourism is now a vital factor in the local economy. The coastal path, panoramic views of the Haven from the town, yachting and other leisure facilities, the town's heritage as expressed in the Milford Museum, the conservation and wildlife of the Haven (designated as a Special Area of Conservation) and other tourist attractions have to be a vital part of the future prosperity of the town.

The Milford 2000 plan, launched in 1990, projected the conversion of the derelict docks into a leisure-orientated marina, as well as light industrial units and retail space. By the year 2000, a massive visual change had occurred in the dock area as the Milford Marina was constructed. Up to 360 yachts and pleasure boats now line the pontoons alongside the new Nelson Quay, where there are a number of attractions including cafés, restaurants and retail outlets. Smoke House Quay is a modern waterside development of apartments and penthouses. Some light industry units can be found north of the Victoria Bridge and a retail park and commercial centre at Havens Head.

A new fish market was built on the Hakin side of the dock. Milford is still the largest fishing port in Wales, and the Port of Milford Haven's Milford Dock Master Plan is set to regenerate the Dock Basin in Milford Haven and attract further business related to the fishing sector.

The Esso oil refinery, which was at the forefront of the oil industry investment in the Waterway, closed in 1984. The large site lay empty for many years before being transformed into a LNG site. Now there are two LNG receiving terminals on the waterway and the Port of Milford Haven is one of the largest in the UK in terms of tonnage.

In their Master Plan, the Milford Haven Port Authority see development at Milford Dock as an opportunity to provide a new waterfront destination that will benefit the marina and fishing industry as well as the centre of Milford and the wider community.

The town of Milford Haven has experienced over 200 years of contrasting fortunes. Its history has been well documented in many publications. This book, which confines itself to the town of Milford Haven rather than the Waterway of the same name, provides an opportunity to compare old (and not so old) and new views. In some instances, very little has changed; in others the new view bears little or no relation to the old. Most of the old photographs and postcards I have used were collected by my Hakin-born husband. Just before the dock area began to be dismantled and transformed he took many photographs, and although these are only just over twenty years old, they demonstrate the immense changes the town has undergone.

I am grateful to Tom Andrews, Bryan Jones, Norman Jones, Anne Leney, Brenda Munt and Rosalie Stephens, who kindly lent me pictures. I am also indebted to my late husband Alan, who invested in an excellent camera and equipment, which I have used to take the contemporary photographs.

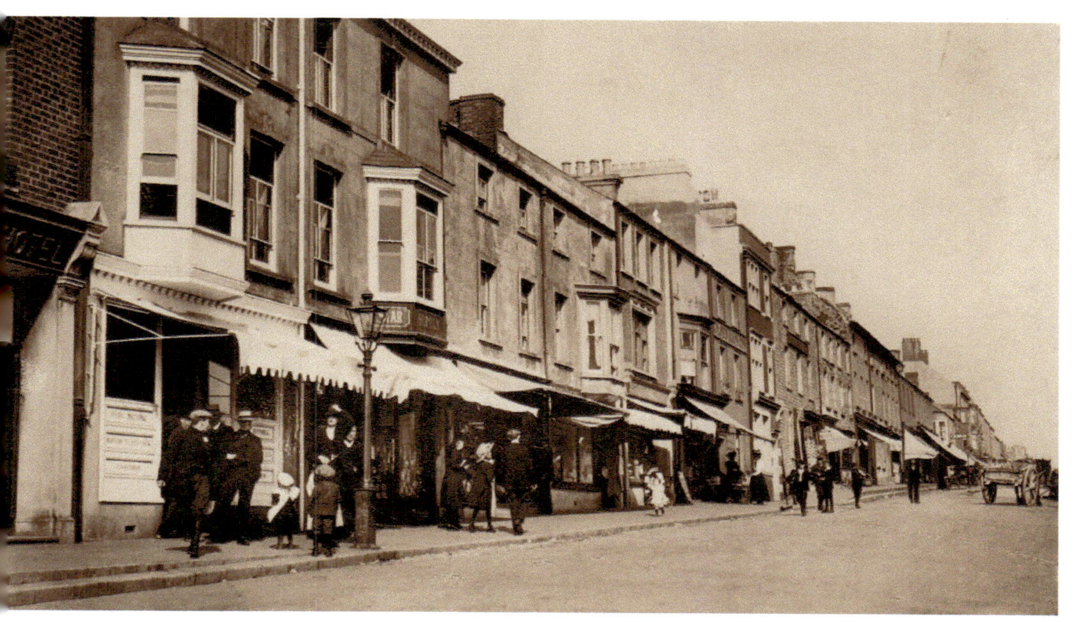

Charles Street

Charles Fulke Greville, designer of Milford, intended Middle Street (later named after its creator) to be the town's main shopping street, with a market at the west end. This view was taken in the early years of the twentieth century from the market end. The market building was later used as a cinema and bingo hall. In 1911, the population of Charles Street was 500. Most of the street's fifty-five shops, usually with the shopkeeper's family living above the shop, were at the western end, while at the eastern end there were private houses. The Star Supply Store, one of the first national shops to come to the town, is behind the lamp post, and just at the left of the picture is the edge of the Lord Kitchener Hotel, which is still in existence.

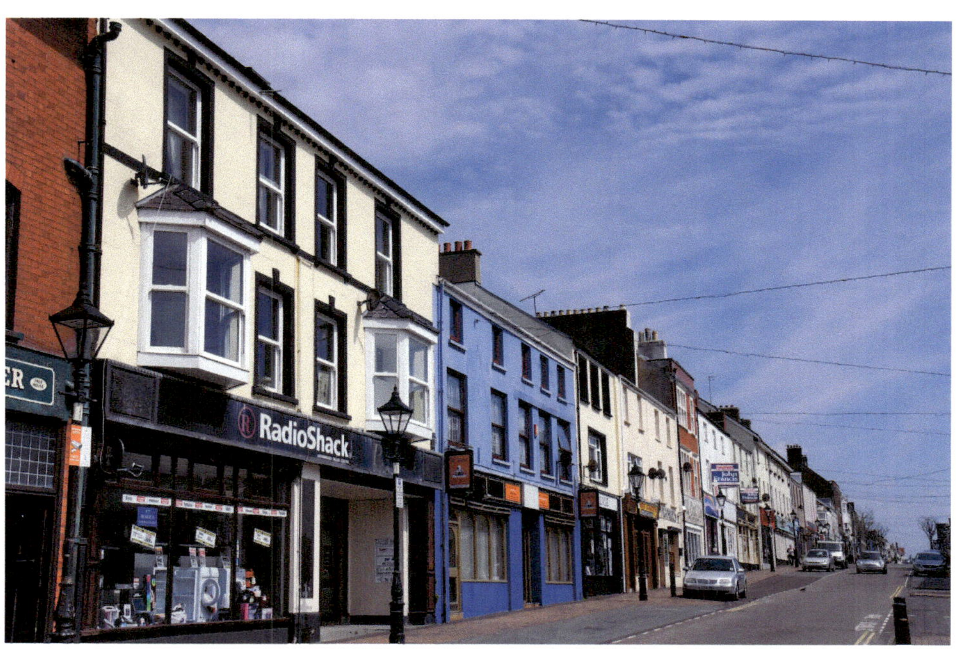

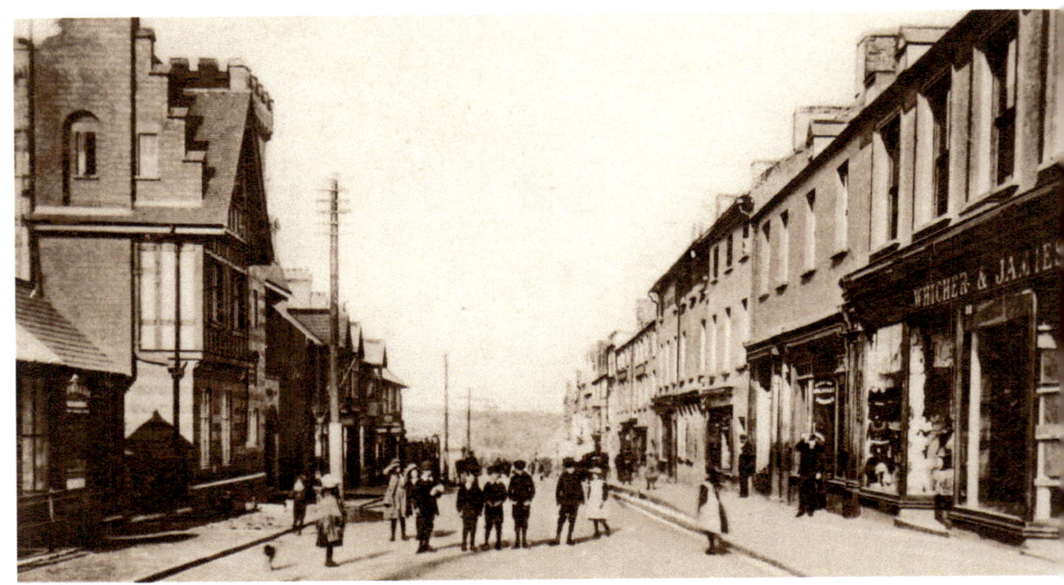

Charles Street

The traditional shopfront of Whicher & Jamieson at Nos 55–57 Charles Street, on the corner of Priory Street, was replaced by a modern concrete supermarket at the end of the 1960s. The impressive red-brick building with a tower on the left of the picture is the Bethel Seamen's Mission. Run by the British & Foreign Sailors Society, it opened in 1908 and was paid for by John Cory, a Cardiff shipping magnate, as an acknowledgement of the contribution to the maritime industry made by sailors. It provided opportunity for leisure and food, and a place of rest for visiting sailors. The Bethel was demolished and replaced by a retail store. The road surface has been replaced by blocks reflecting pedestrian precedence, and regulated car parking bays have been installed.

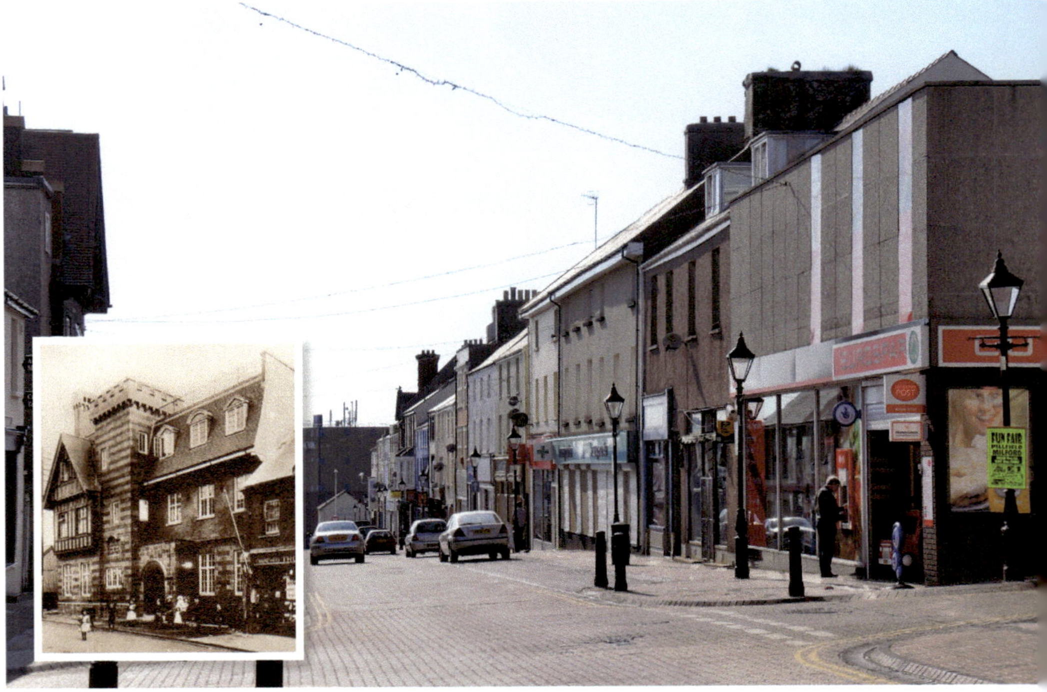

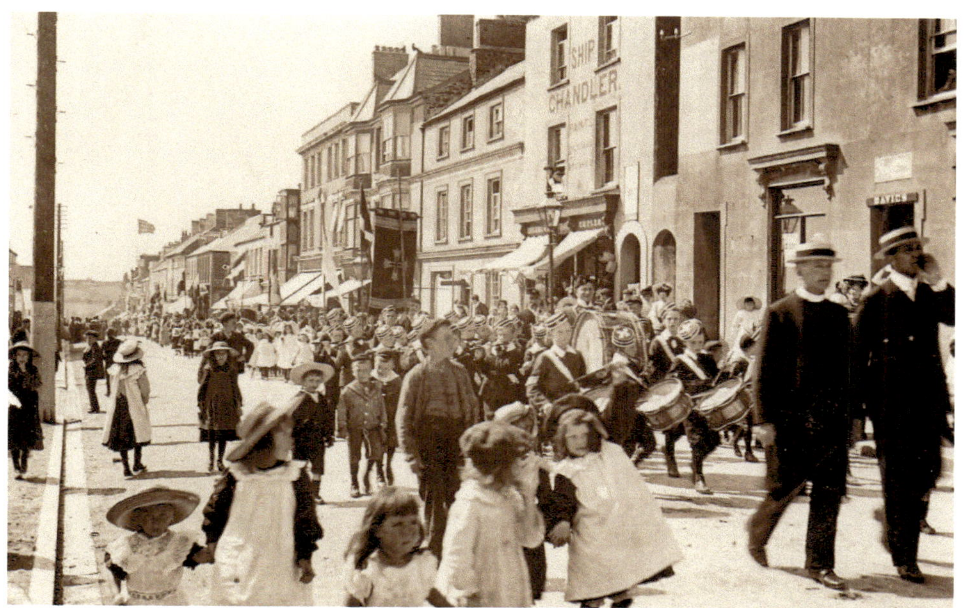

Charles Street

Dating from the early 1920s, this photograph shows a long parade of St Katharine's Sunday school pupils, headed by the children's fife and drum band, on their way to a picnic. The Ship Chandlery was run by John Francis, and his shopfront indicates that he was also a cutler and ironmonger. Next door was Miss Emily Gertrude Davies' confectionery shop. Charles Street, which until recently was the traditional shopping centre of the town, is now experiencing the problems common to most High Streets. At the end of the street is the Torch Theatre, which opened in 1977. The Amoco Corporation donated £22,000 to the Milford Haven Further Education and Community Centre to help finance the theatre, and the torch on their logo gave the theatre its name.

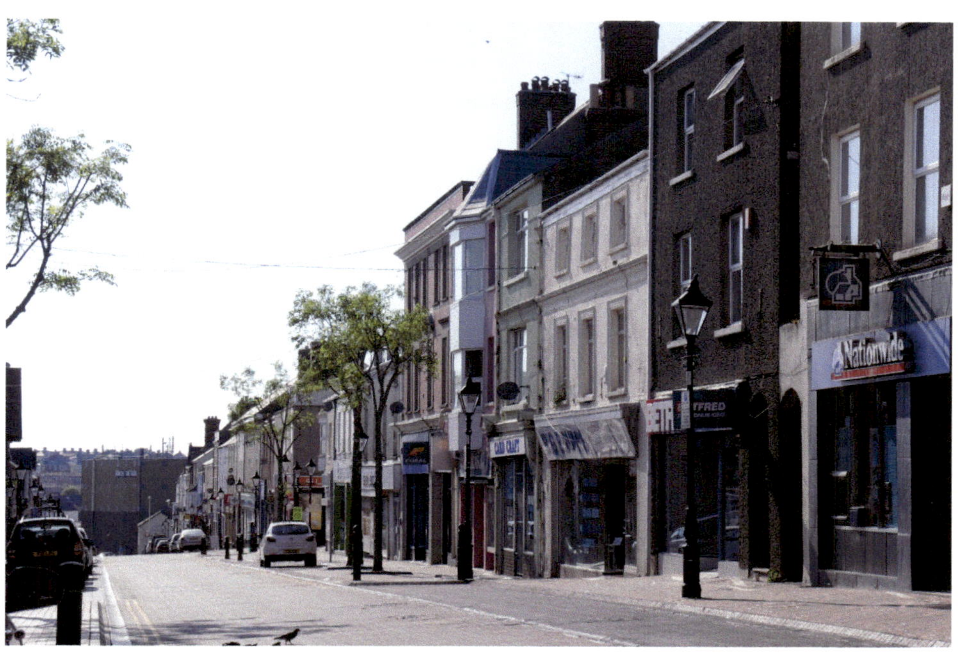

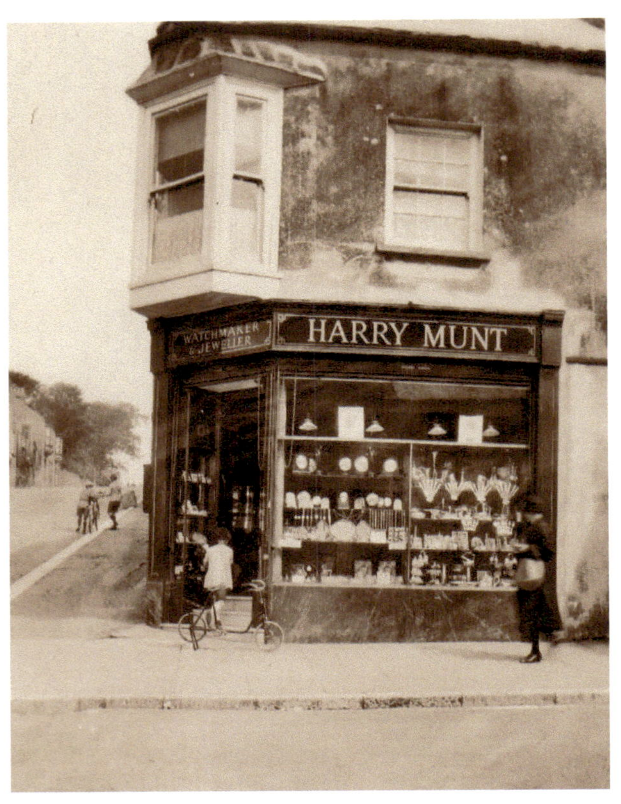

Charles Street, Munt

The 1911 census shows that Bisley Henry Munt was keeping this shop on the corner of Priory Street. The Munt family had run a watchmaker's and jeweller's shop in Haverfordwest since 1796, and Bisley's son, Harry, then took over running the shop. It has remained a jeweller's shop, being run 'for over half a century' by Jeffreys, who also had a shop in the county town. Munt's was one of two watchmakers in Charles Street in 1911. In addition, there were two photographers, five boot and shoemakers, three confectioners, five butchers, an artificial teeth maker, seven grocers, a green grocer, three ironmongers, three tailors, two tobacconists, two fancy goods shops, a fried fish shop, two chemists, two drapers, an outfitter, milliner, stationer, hairdresser and coffee rooms.

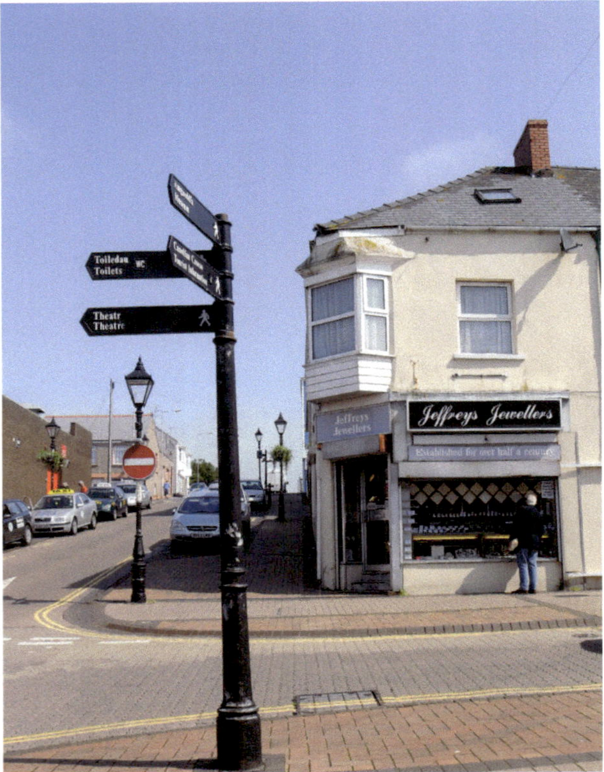

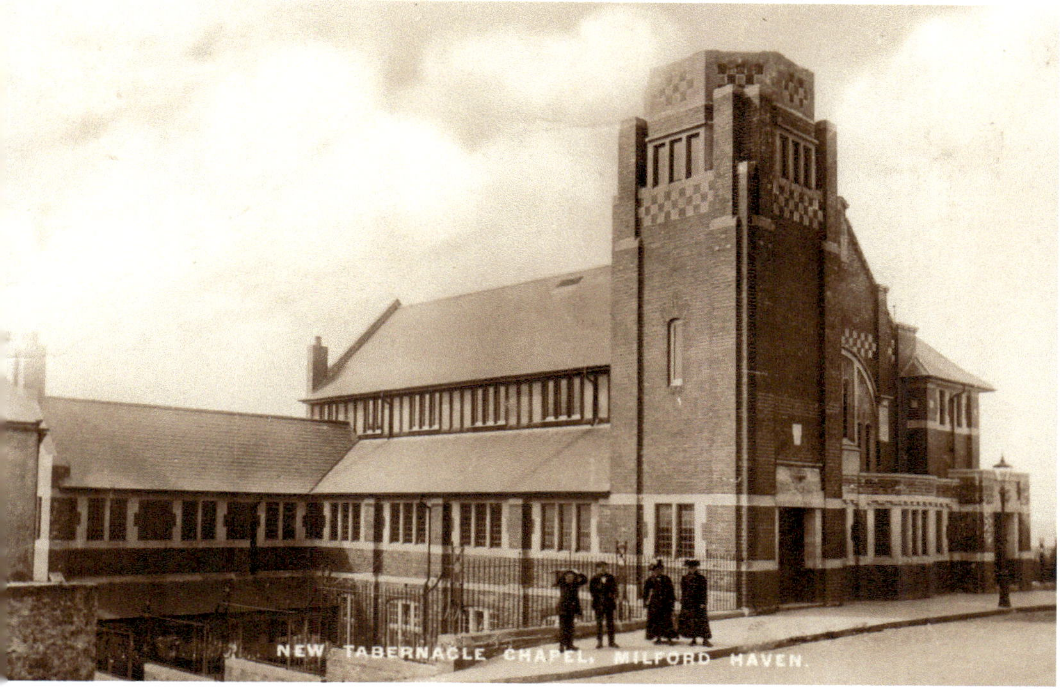

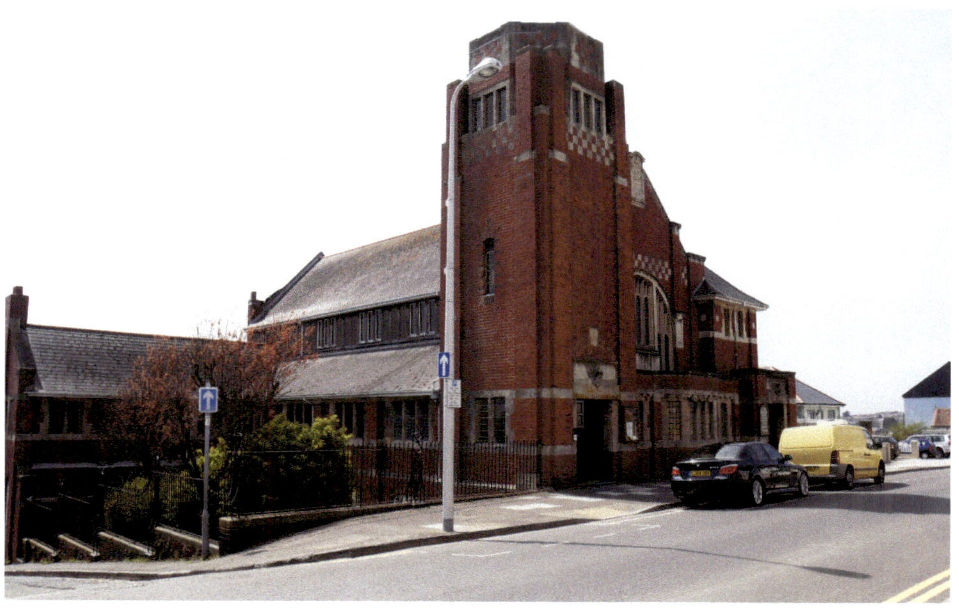

Charles Street Tabernacle Chapel

This was the second chapel on the site. The foundation stone of the first was laid in 1807 when the chapel was named after the Tabernacle chapel in Haverfordwest. The architect of this impressive red-brick and Bath-stone building was Owain Thomas. Opened in 1910, it is very large with extra accommodation below, a chapel house at the south-west, a tower, and gardens within wrought-iron railings. Tabernacle United Reform Church closed in late 2011 when the congregation merged with the Wesleyan chapel in Priory Road. It is now the Shah Jalal Jamia Mosque.

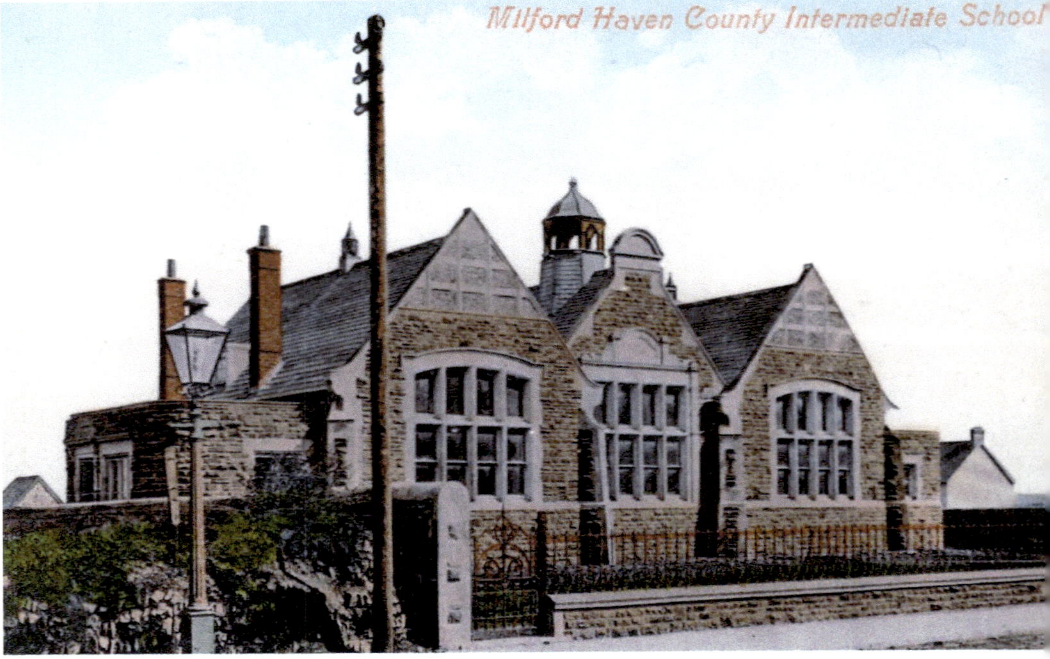

Milford Haven County Intermediate School in North Road

The town's Intermediate School began in a small building in Marine Terrace in 1896. It moved to this building on the corner of Yorke Street in 1901 and was enlarged in 1937. The Grammar School vacated this building in 1964, moving to a new site on the Steynton Road. For some years, the building was occupied by the Lower Central School, but in 1988, with the creation of the Milford Haven Comprehensive School, its life in education finished. It was transformed into the Elizabeth Venmore Court retirement apartments, which opened in 2001/02.

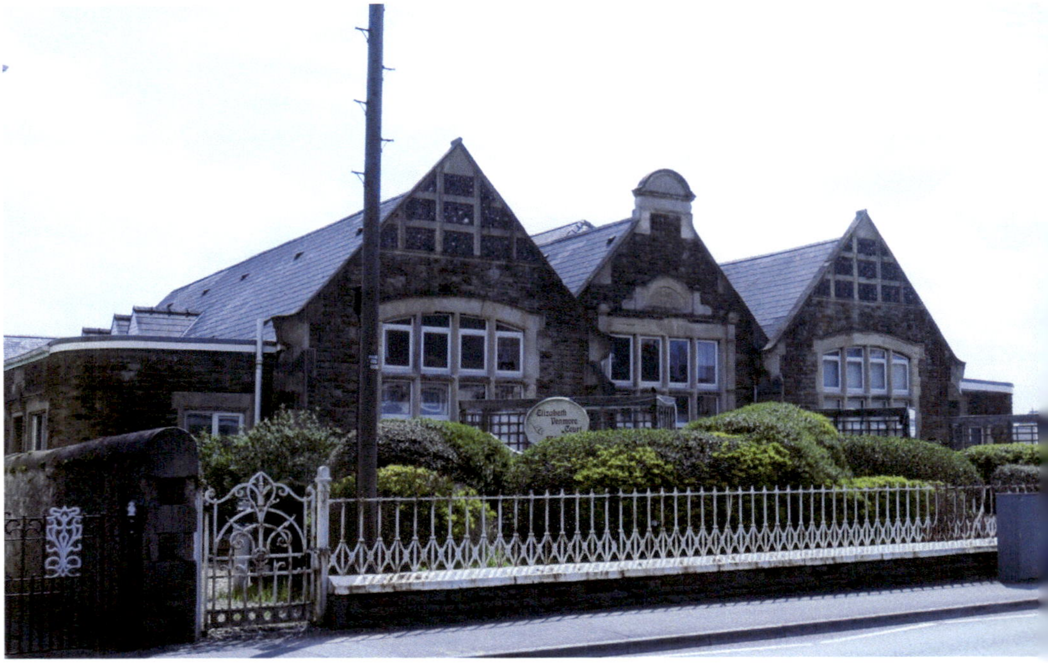

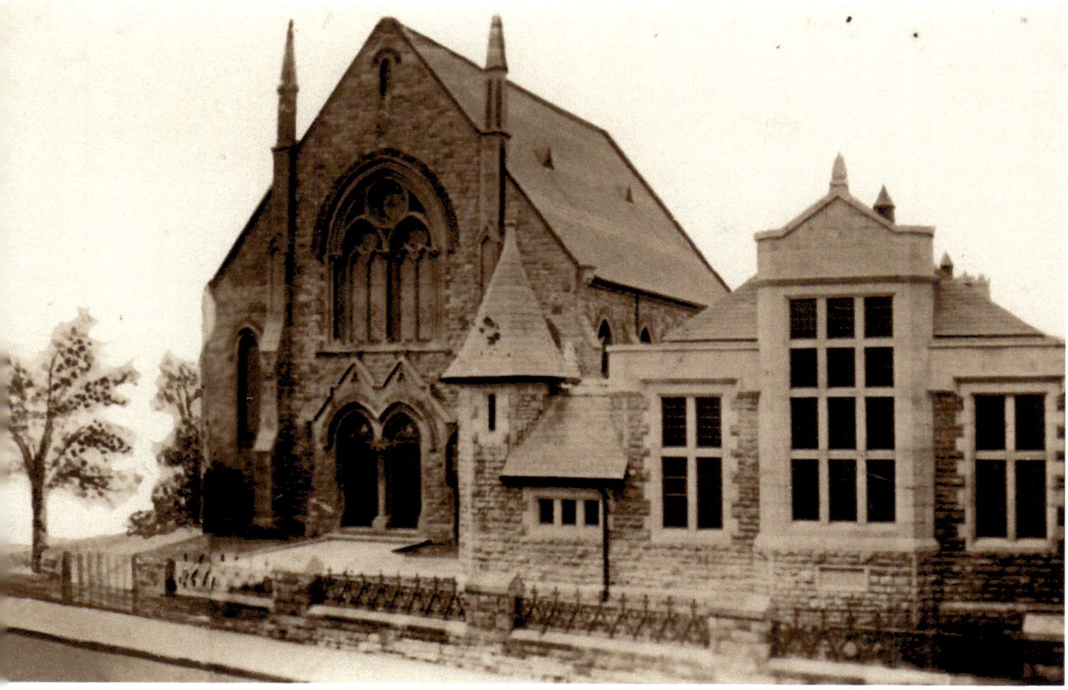

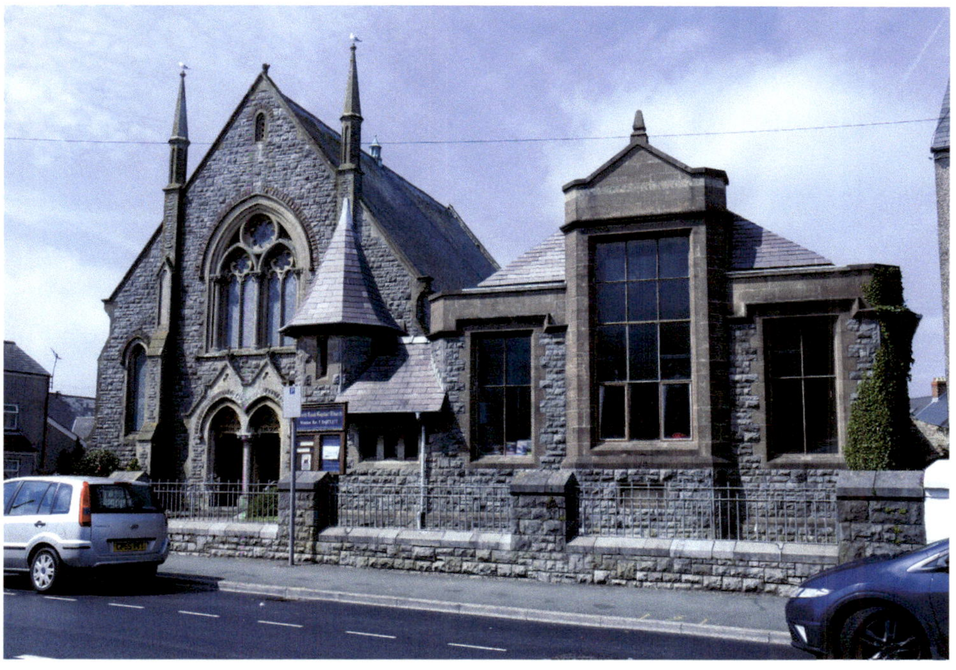

North Road, Baptist Chapel

Little has changed since this photograph was taken in 1927. Designed by George Morgan of Carmarthen, the chapel, with its striking flying buttresses, is considered one of the finest Gothic Revival chapels in South Wales. Built in 1878, it accommodates 650. It replaced the smaller Short Lane Baptist chapel. The Memorial Schoolroom was opened in 1927 and is in memory of those members of the congregation who died in the First World War.

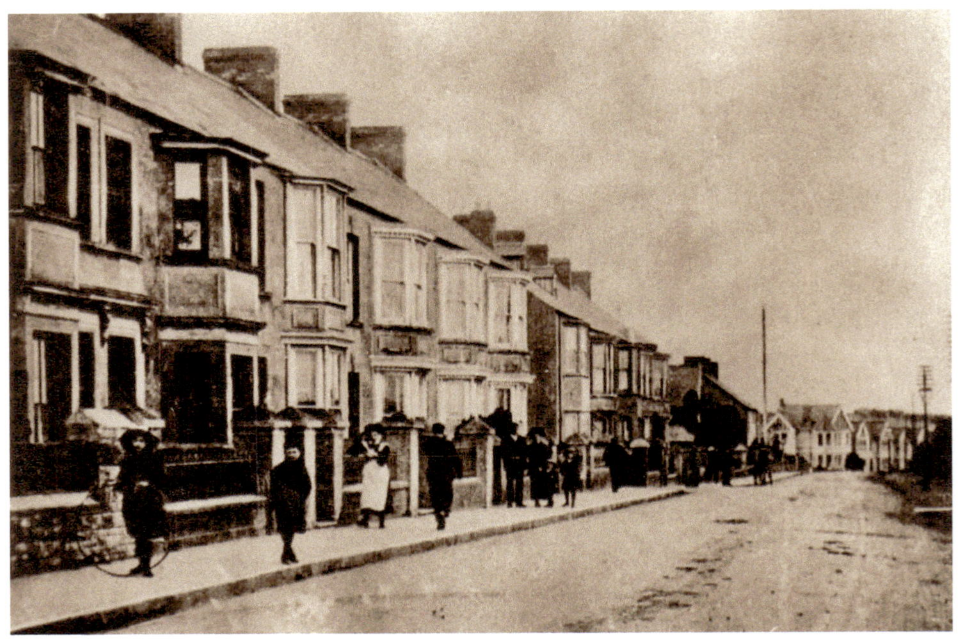

Great North Road

Great North Road linked with the Steynton Road on the journey to Haverfordwest. In the 1891 census it was named North Road, the name it is more usually known as today. It was lined by terraced houses graced with bay windows. Most of the inhabitants in 1901 were involved in the maritime trades as fish merchants, shipwrights, or clerks. Since then, many of the houses have been demolished to make way for the garage, now a fuel station. Just out of sight is the location of the North Road Boys School, now occupied by a Lidl supermarket.

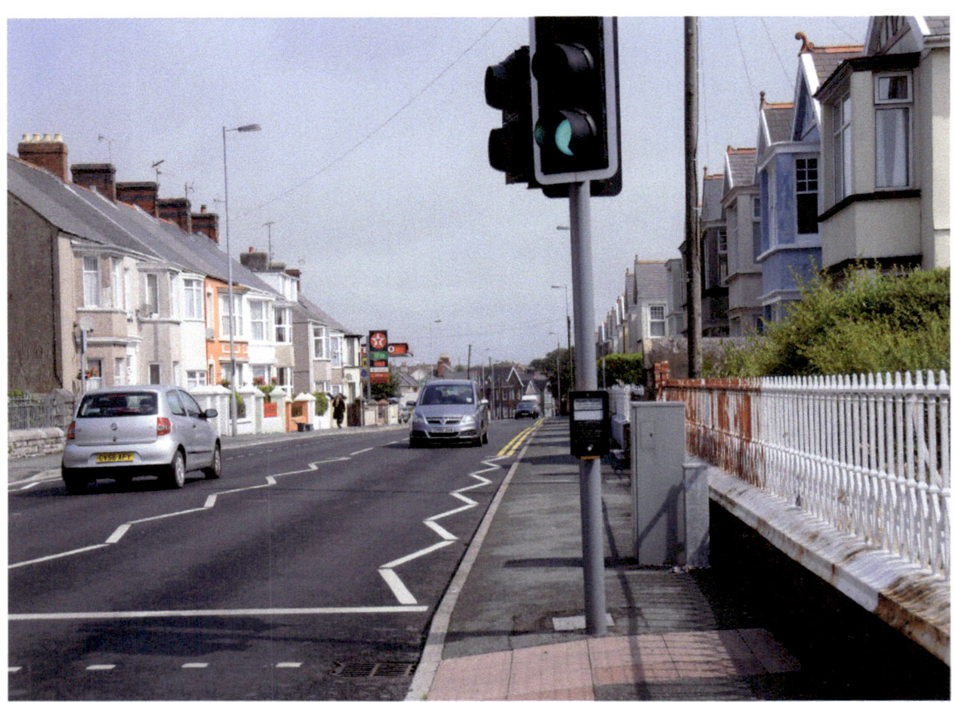

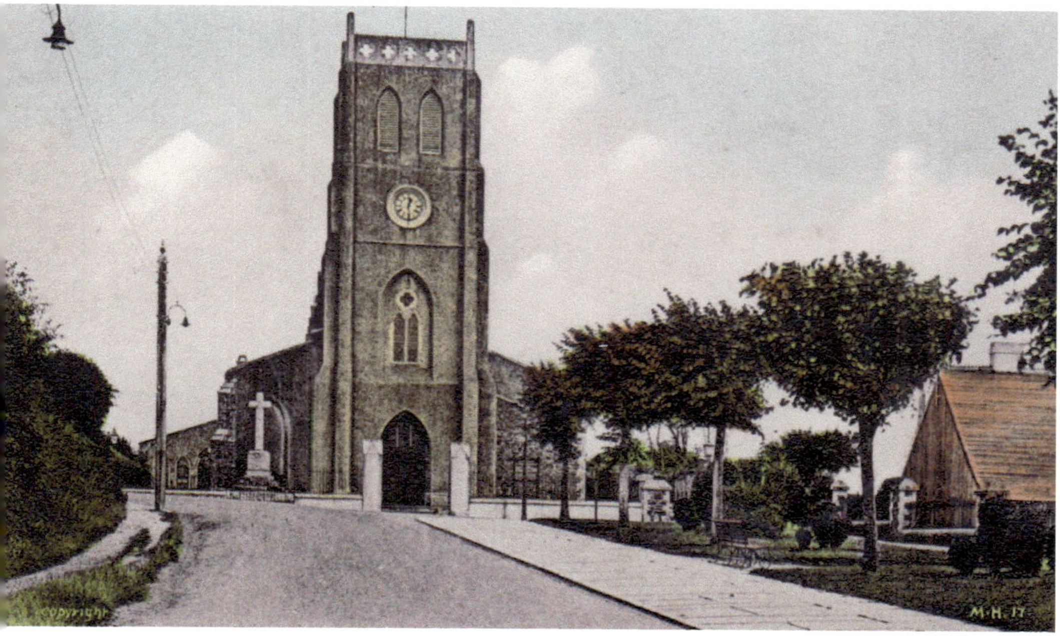

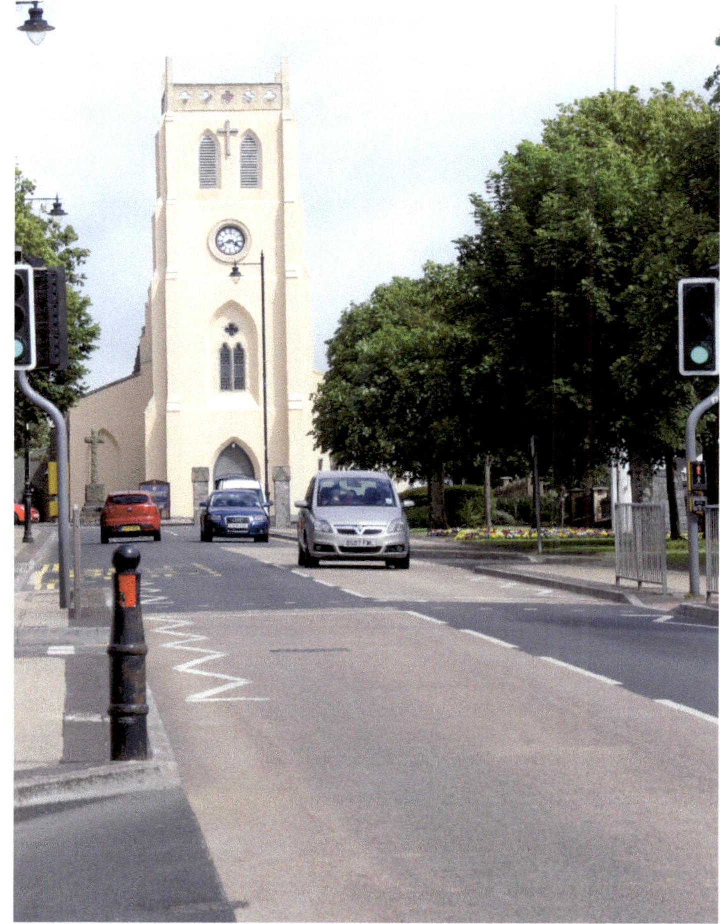

St Katharine's Church

The church of St Katharine of Alexandria was consecrated in 1808, some six years after the foundation stone was laid. Charles Greville intended it to be the central focus of his new town but it did not gain the status of a parish church until 1891. In 1907, the poor state of the church and the need to accommodate the increasing population of the town led to its expansion. To the left of the church door is the First World War memorial cross. The later photograph shows the new smooth sandstone rendering, which recently replaced the dark grey cement roughcast, so the church now dominates the skyline, a landmark to seafarers coming up the harbour.

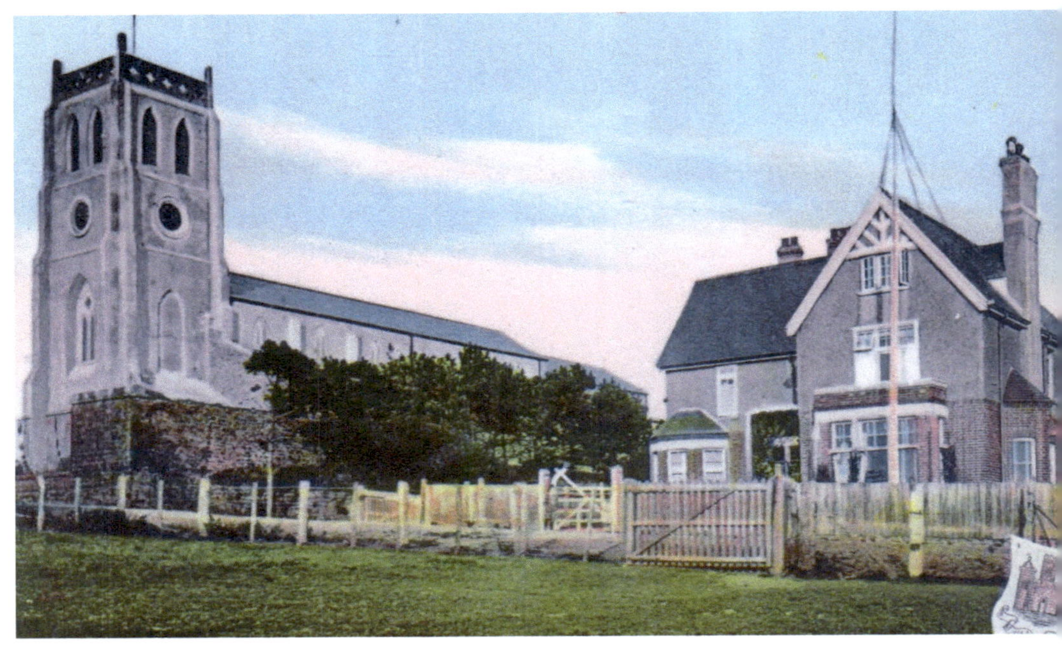

St Katharine's Church and Vicarage

The year 1808 was significant in the history of religion in the town. It saw the consecration of St Katharine's, the opening of the first Tabernacle chapel and the Hakin Point Wesleyan church. Following a devastating fire in 1994, which destroyed the church of St Peter in St David's Road, this church is now dedicated to St Katharine and St Peter. The vicarage was built in Sandhurst Road in 1899/1900, but in 2012 was relocated. The bell tower houses a peal of tubular bells, installed in 1905.

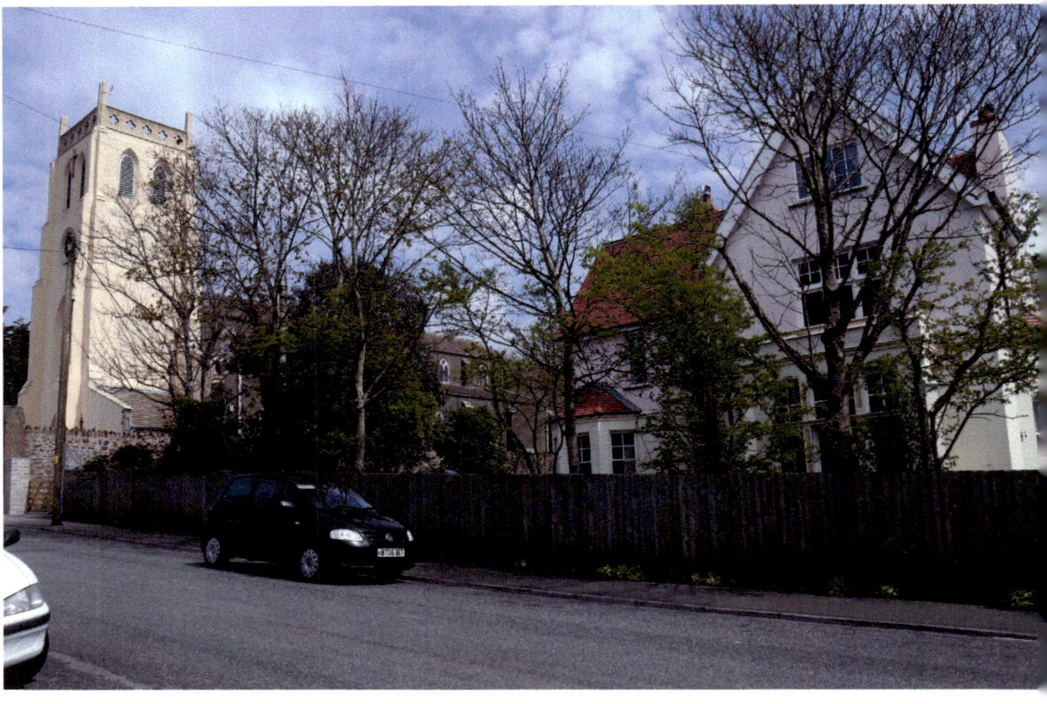

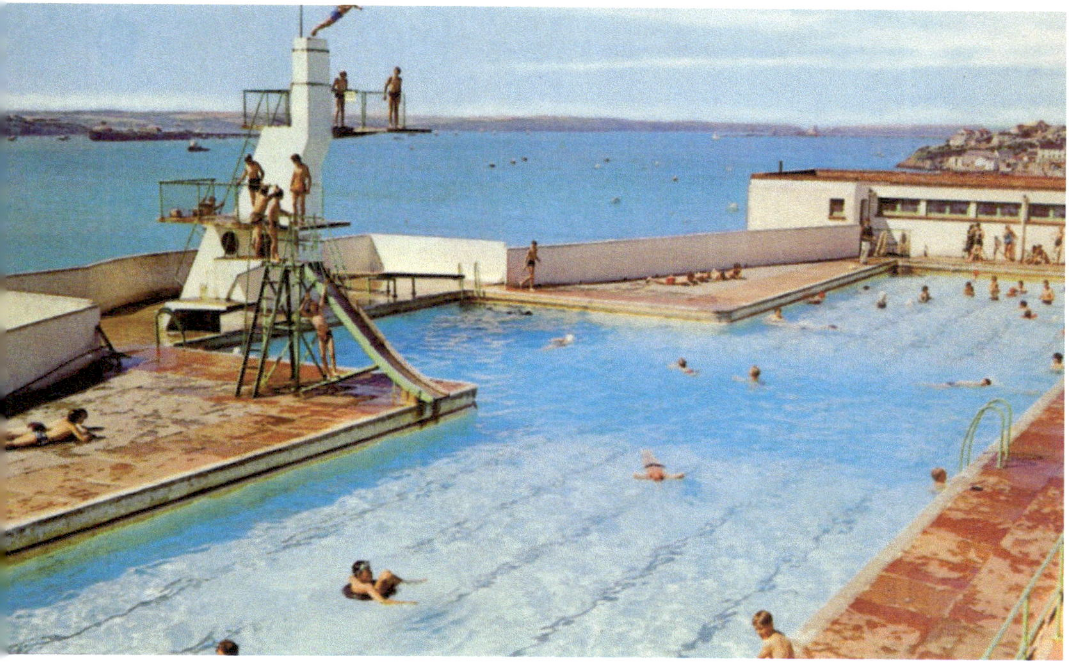

The Rath, Swimming Pool

The open-air swimming pool, opened in 1940, was part of the major town improvements carried out by the Milford Haven Urban District Council. It was 45 metres long and 9 metres wide. Alongside was a children's paddling pool. This major pre-war leisure development attracted a large grant from the National Fitness Council and became a major attraction, drawing swimmers and sunbathers from many parts of the county. It was advertised as 'the only open-air sea water bathing pool in West Wales'. The picture shows the diving boards and a water chute. The changing rooms on the right of the picture now form part of a Chinese restaurant.

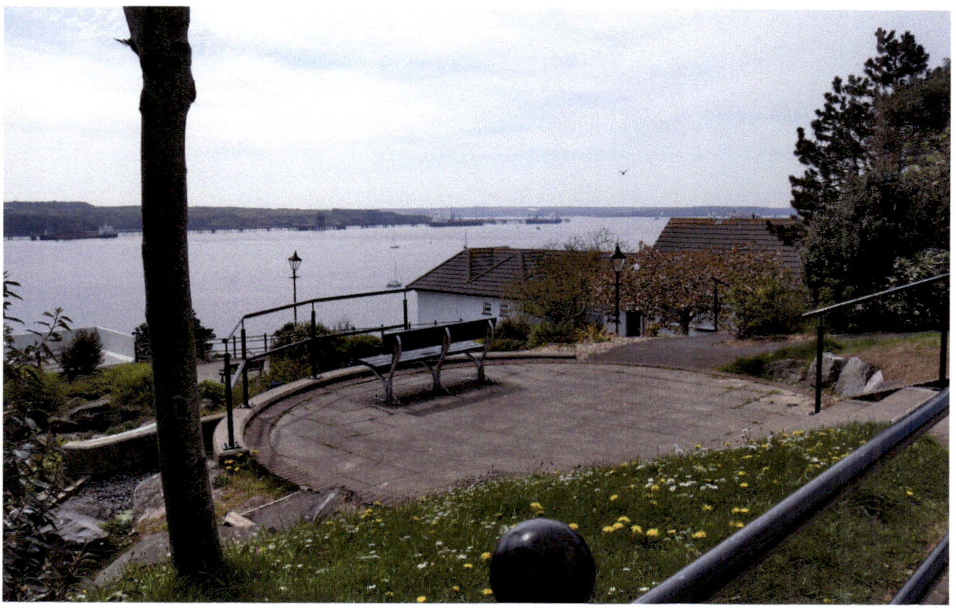

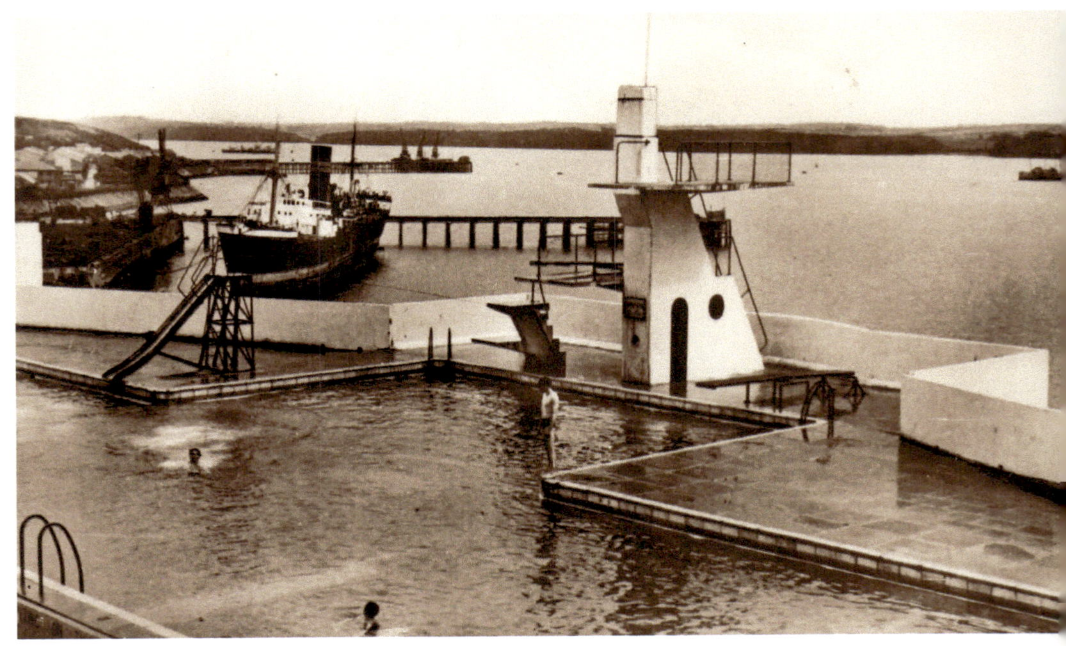

The Rath, Swimming Pool

The provision of an indoor pool at the new Meads Sports centre swimming pool led to a decrease in those attending this pool and it was closed in 1987. It was replaced by a terraced water garden, which was opened by the Prime Minister, Margaret Thatcher, in September 1990. She described it as 'a beautiful advantage to the town'. All that now remains of the pool is the curved wall that stood behind the high diving board. Nothing remains of Wards Yard, where a ship was waiting to be broken up. In today's picture, there are a couple of tankers at the Valero jetty and refinery across the water.

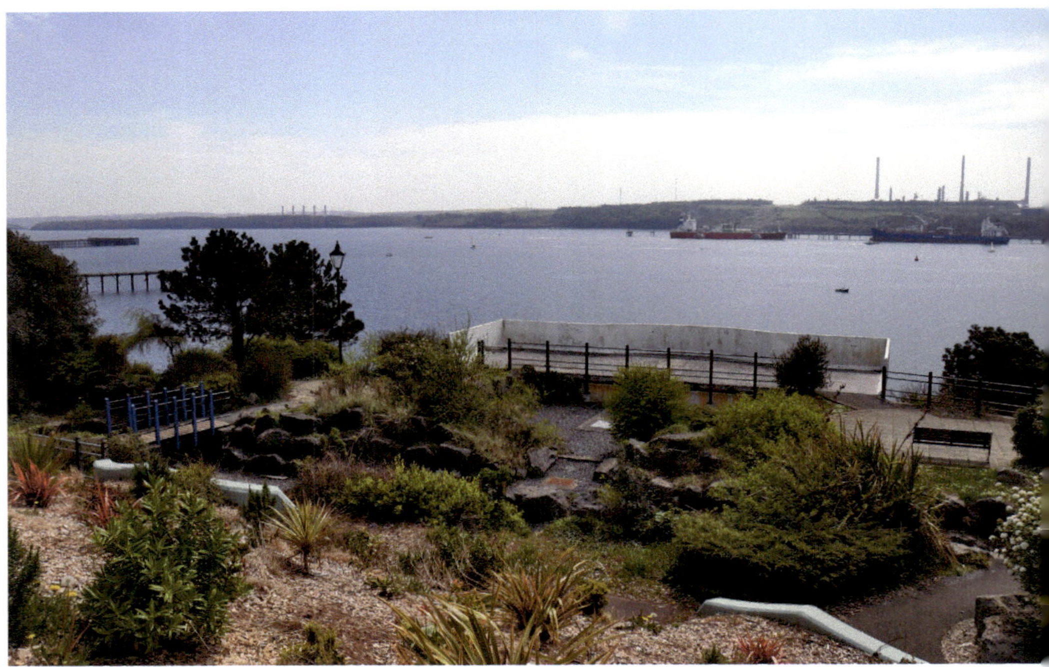

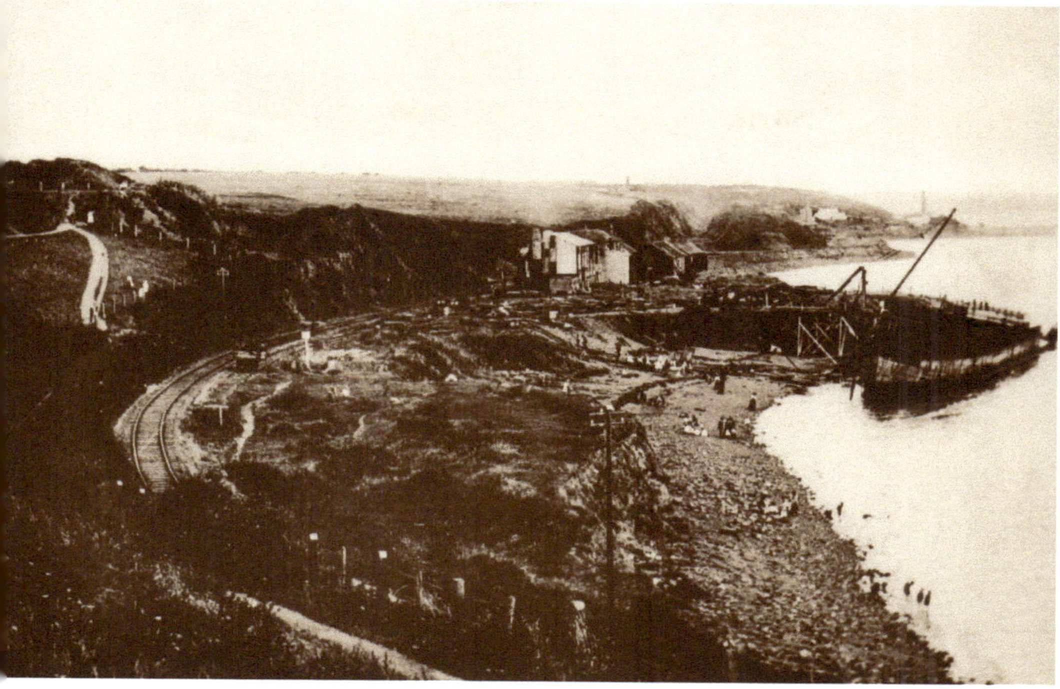

Scotch Bay

In the earlier picture, a few families are enjoying the sand and shingle beach, a popular bathing spot before the swimming pool was built. Alongside is the industrial scene of the shipbuilding and repair yard. In the later photograph, the railway line that linked Milford to Newton Noyes pier has gone and the vacated Mine Depot buildings can be seen in the distance. There is now a large tank at Waterston, on the skyline, and a housing development.

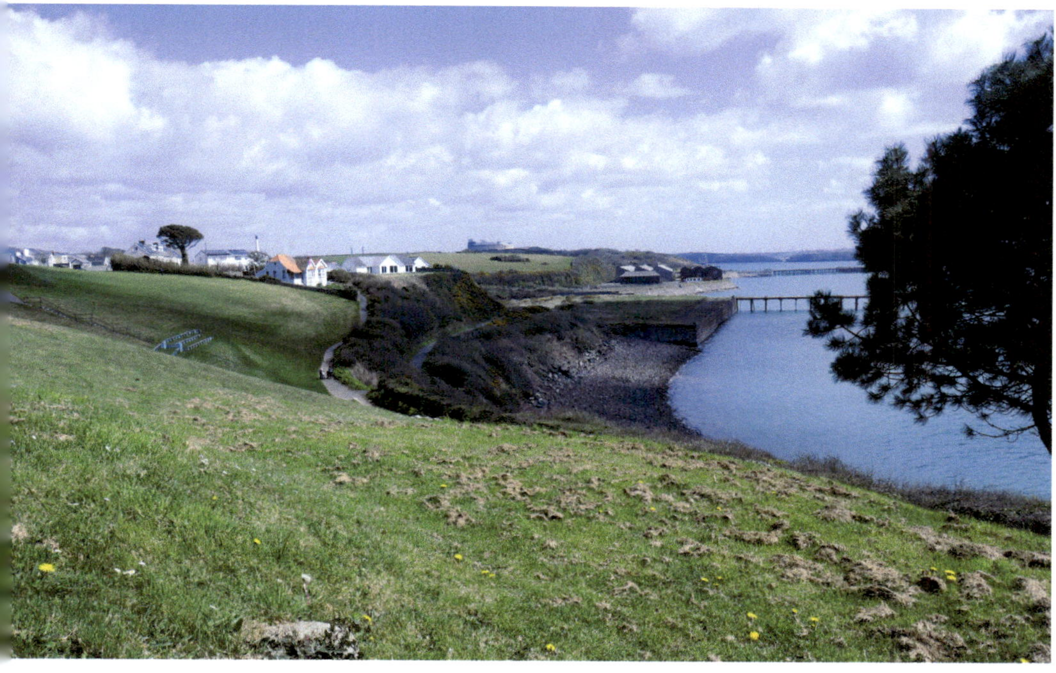

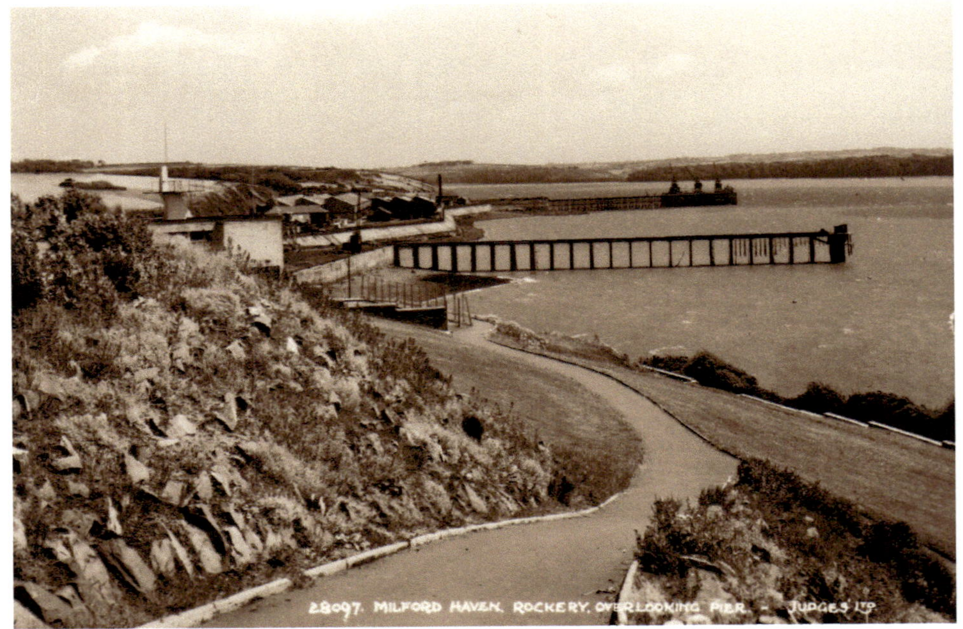

Rockery Overlooking Pier

Beyond the back wall and the high diving board of the swimming pool can be seen the Newton Noyes pier and railway. These were opened in 1882 and sold after the First World War to T. W. Ward, who established a ship-breaking yard and pier at Castle Pill. In 1934, the Newton Noyes pier and the very large residence of Castle Hall were sold to the Admiralty for the creation of the Royal Naval Armament Depot, known locally as the Mine Depot, a significant source of employment until its closure in 1991. Wards continued their ship-breaking business on the west side of Castle Pill for many years. The cranes on the end of the Newton Noyes pier have gone, but the five chimneys of the new Pembroke Power Station can be seen on the other side of the Haven.

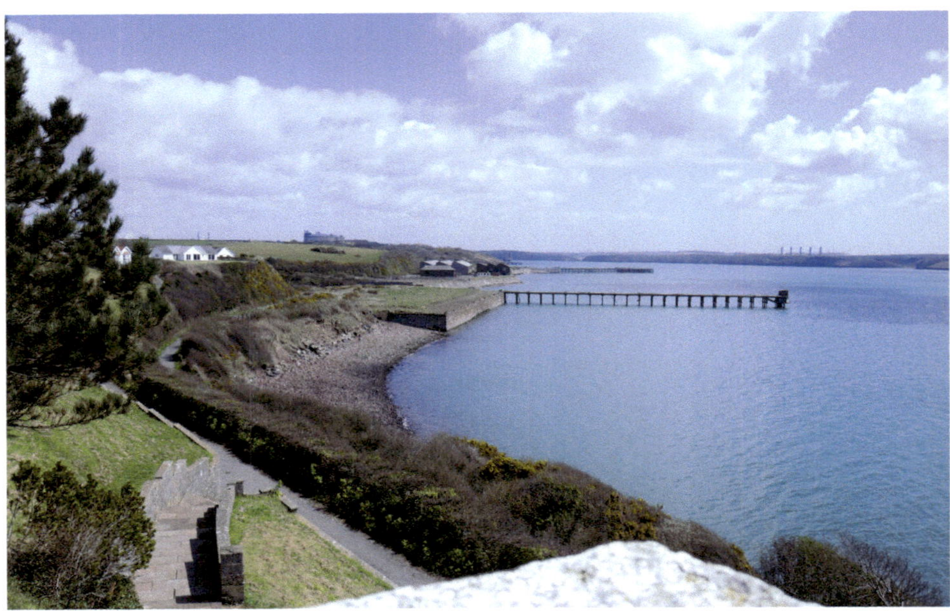

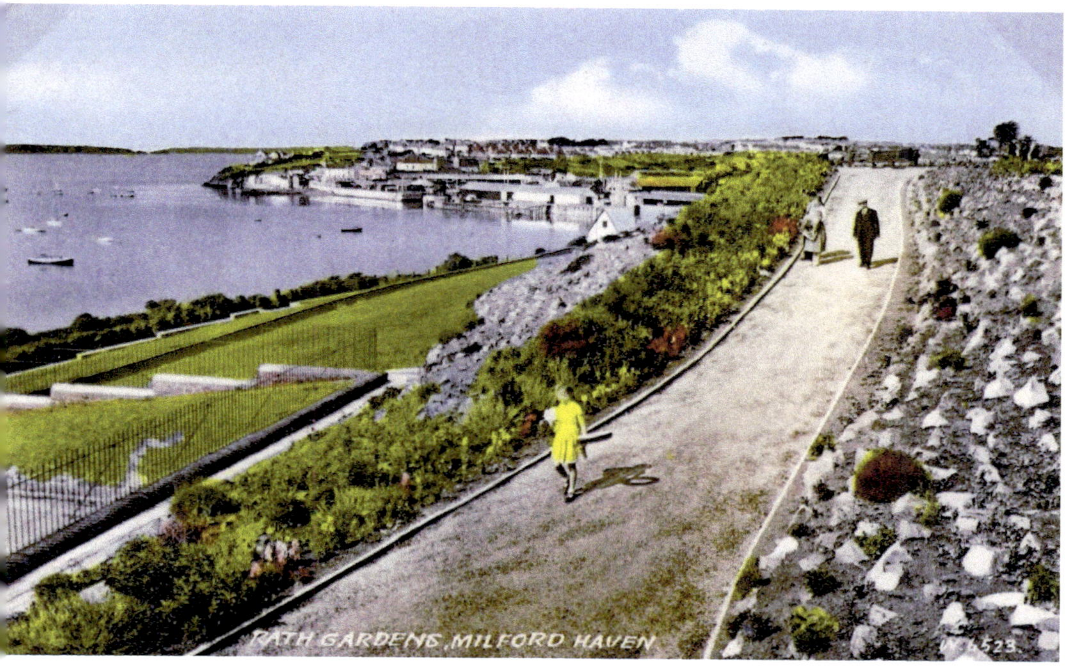

Rath Gardens

As late as the 1920s, the Rath was just a hill overlooking the Haven. In the nineteenth century it had been the location of a defensive gun battery. In the 1930s, the hill was banked, terraced, landscaped and transformed into a popular walk providing a panoramic view of the Haven. Soon afterwards, many exclusive houses were built along the Rath by men engaged in the lucrative fishing industry. Just to the left of the 1950s photograph is the wall of the paddling pool. This is now empty but a new landmark, in the style of a bandstand, is visible.

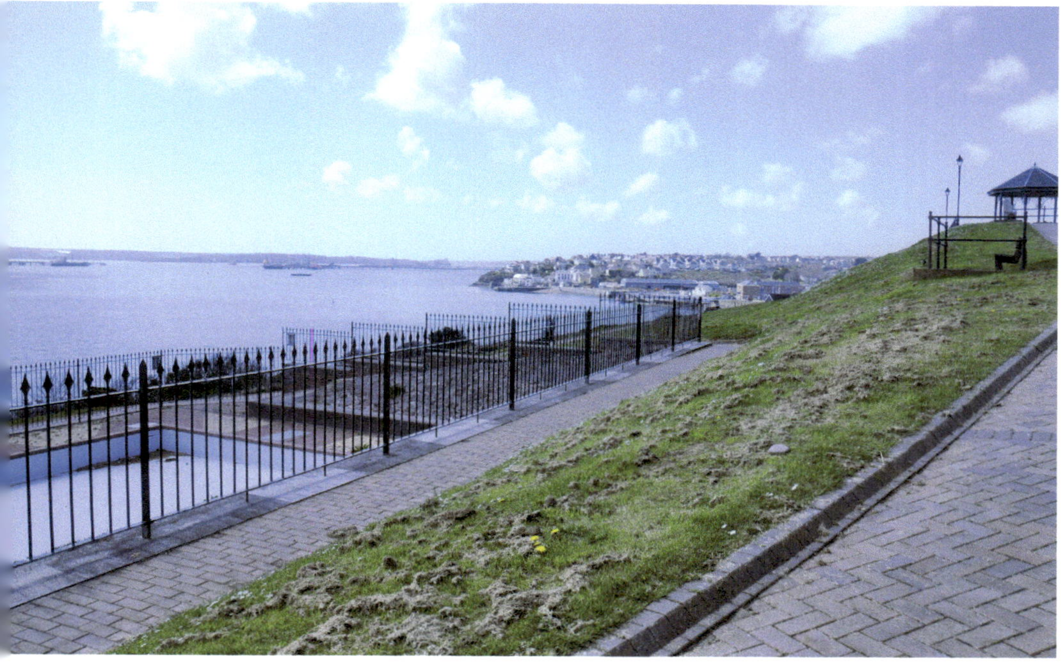

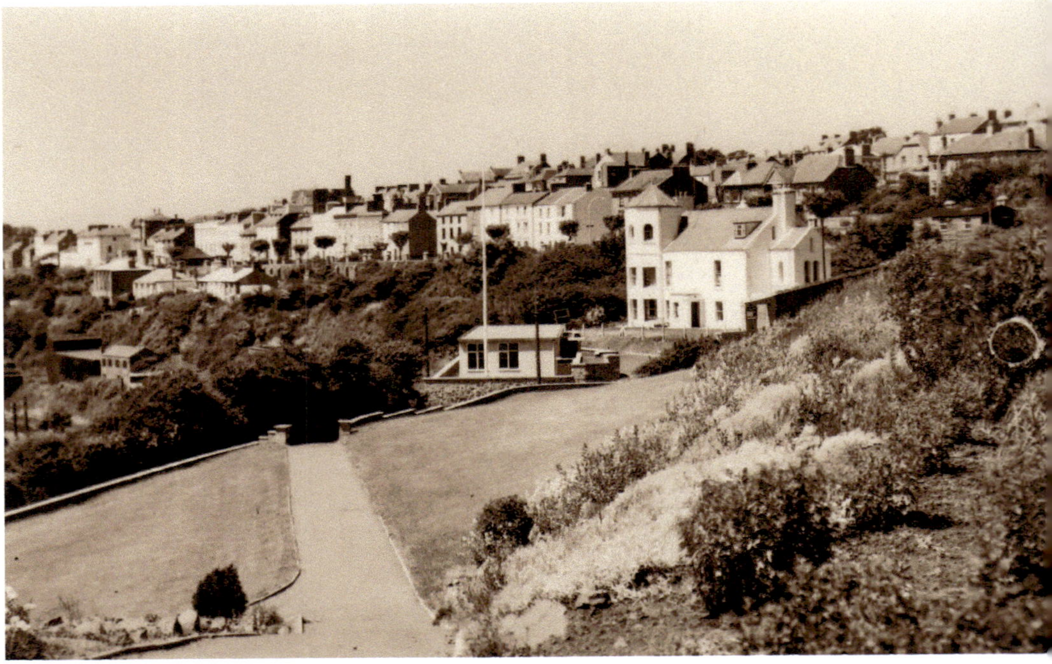

Milford Haven from the Rockery

In the earlier photograph, the tall three-storey building with a tower was Marine Villa. In 1891, the occupier was Frederick Sellick, ship owner. From 1896 to 1901, it was rented from the owners, Milford Haven Estate Company, to accommodate the town's newly founded Intermediate School. Later, it was demolished and replaced by the premises of the British Legion Club, which has been operating in the town since 1921, but which in the later photograph is obscured by trees.

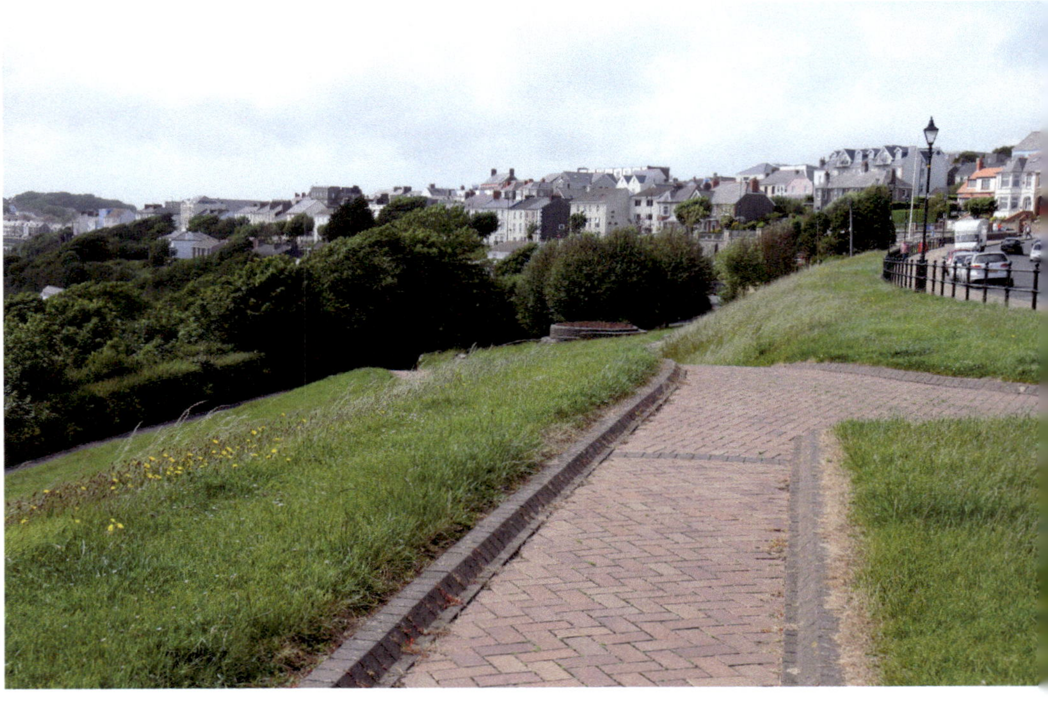

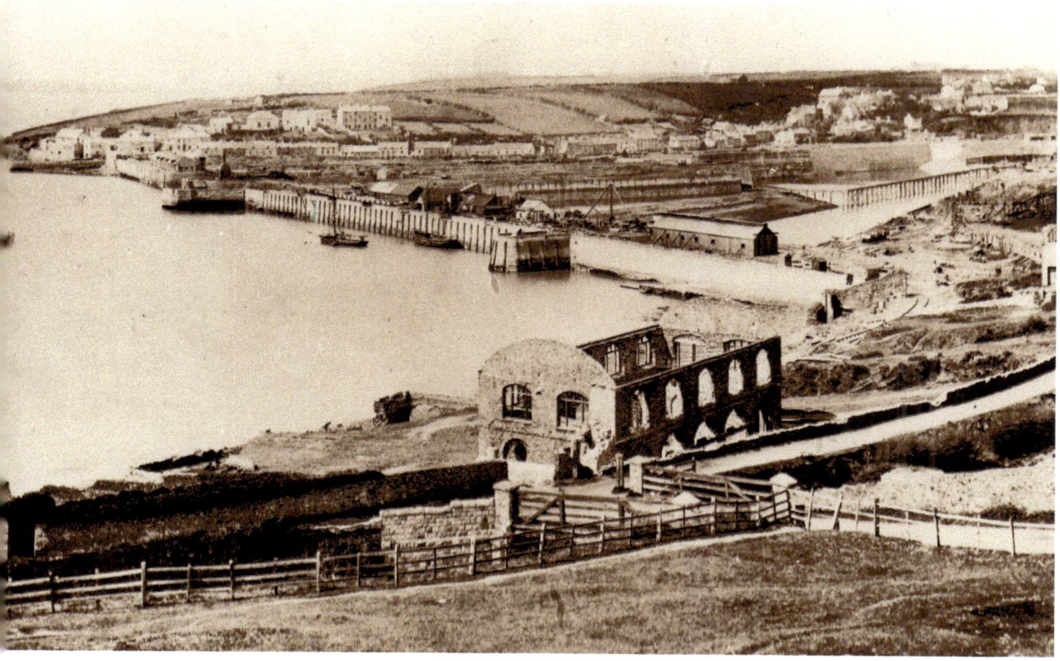

View of Hakin from the Rath

One of the earliest views of the docks and Hakin from the Rath, this photograph dates from the 1880s when the new docks were, at last, close to completion. The ruined building in the foreground was part of the town's shipbuilding industry. Situated prominently on Hakin Point and overlooking the dock's entrance in both pictures is the Kings Arms. Over the 130 years between the pictures, the population of Hakin increased dramatically and the fields of the headland are now full of housing.

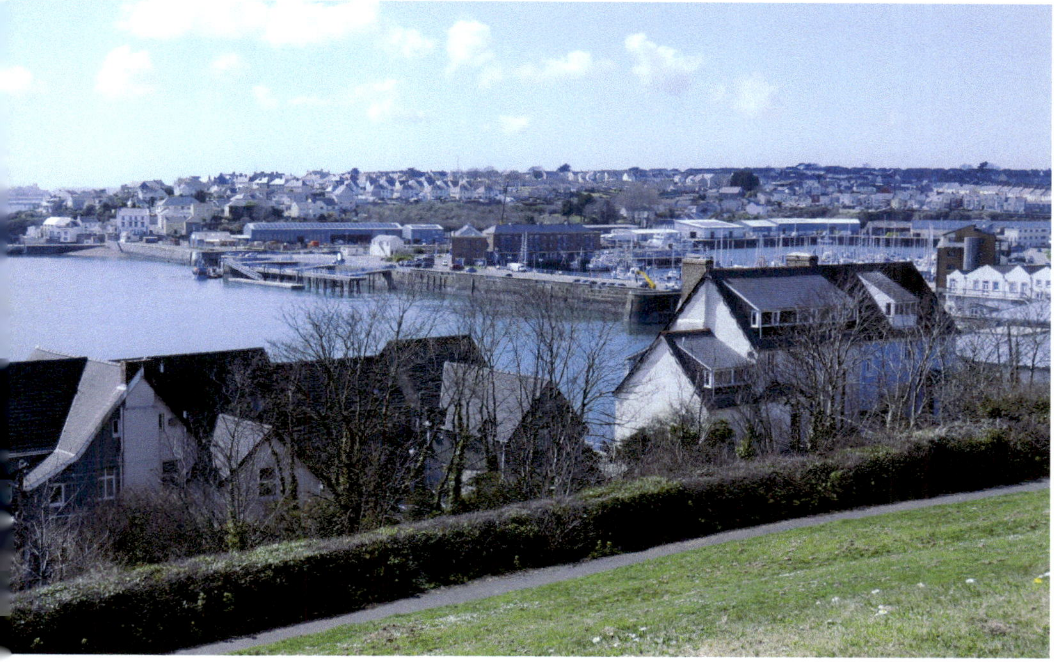

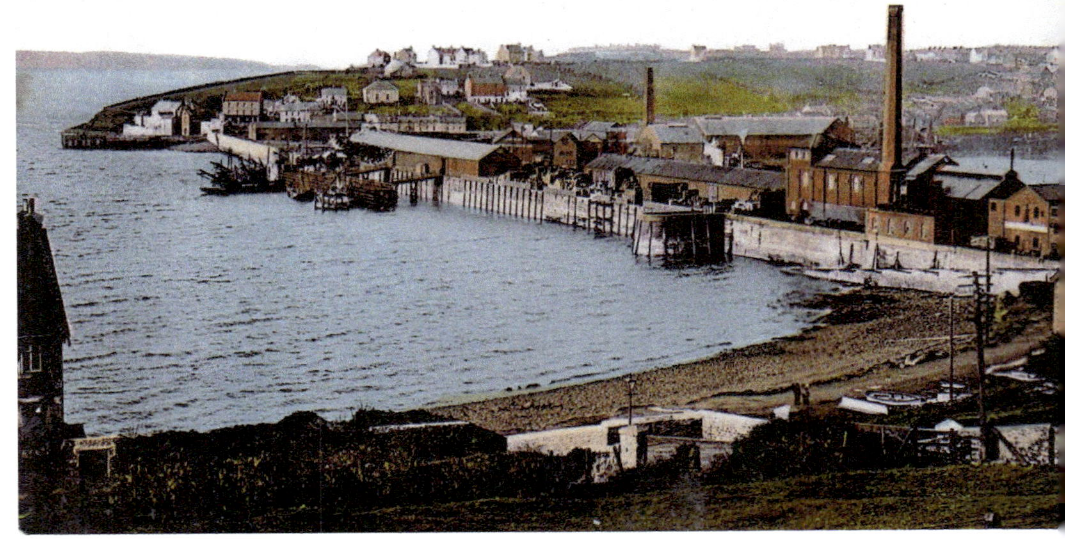

Sea Front of Docks

This postcard was posted in 1910, by which time the docks had been significantly developed but there were few houses on the Hakin headland. The mackerel stage and the stack of the Milford Haven Ice Company factory are in place. By the early 1900s, the two ice factories produced over 700 tons of ice each week for use on ships and on the market.

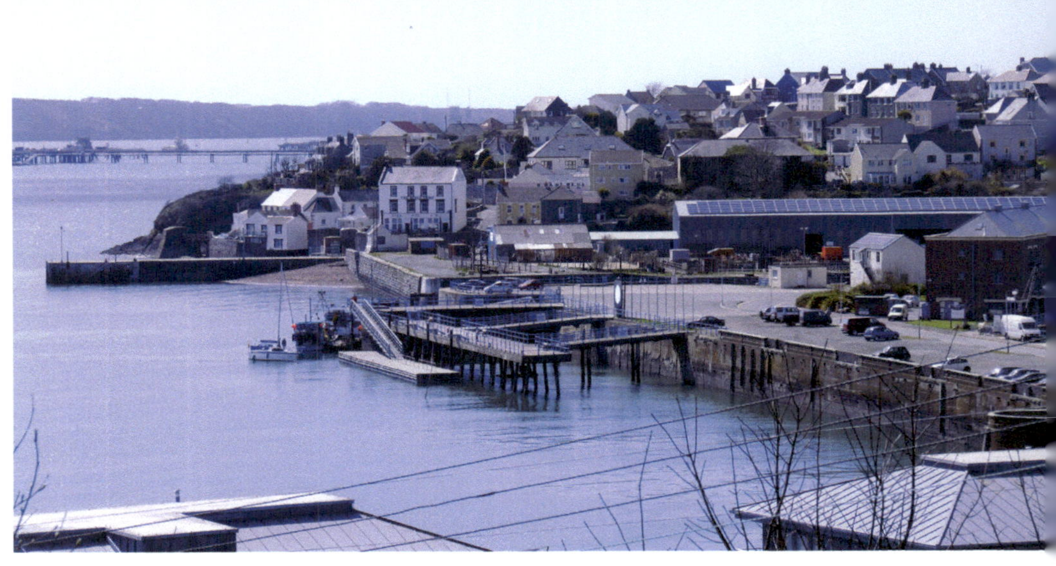

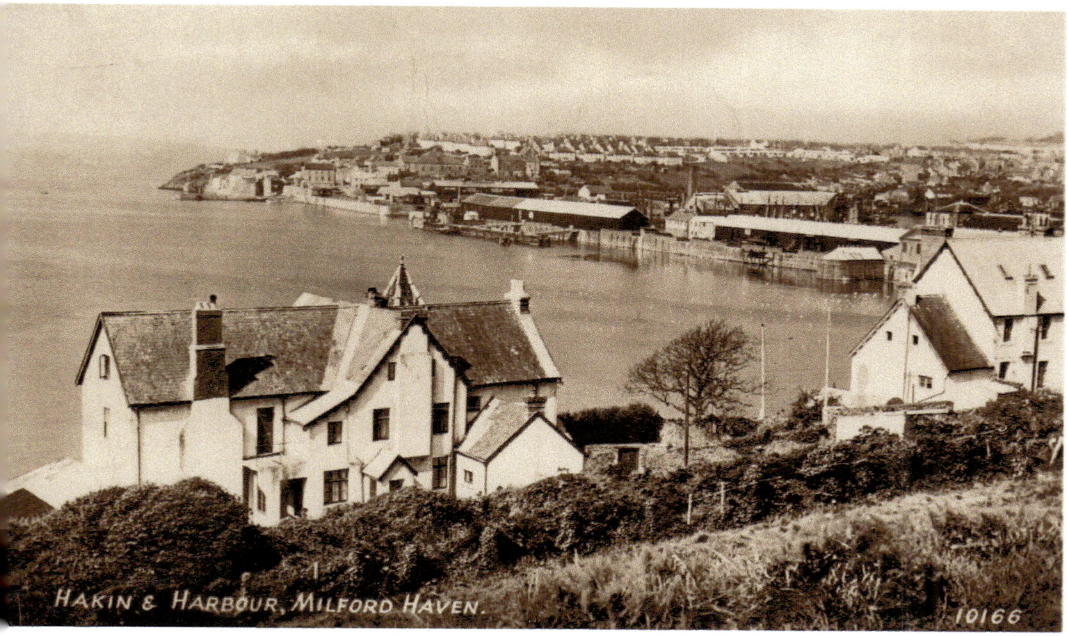

Hakin and Harbour

Car parking for those visiting the marina has replaced many of the working sheds, but the mackerel stage, built outside the docks to allow access for swift unloading by the mackerel drifters at all times, has survived. Seats have been provided so that the exceptional views can be enjoyed. Beyond Hakin Point, one of the several jetties designed for oil and gas tankers protrudes into the Haven. The new grey shed on the west side of the dock has been fitted with large solar panels.

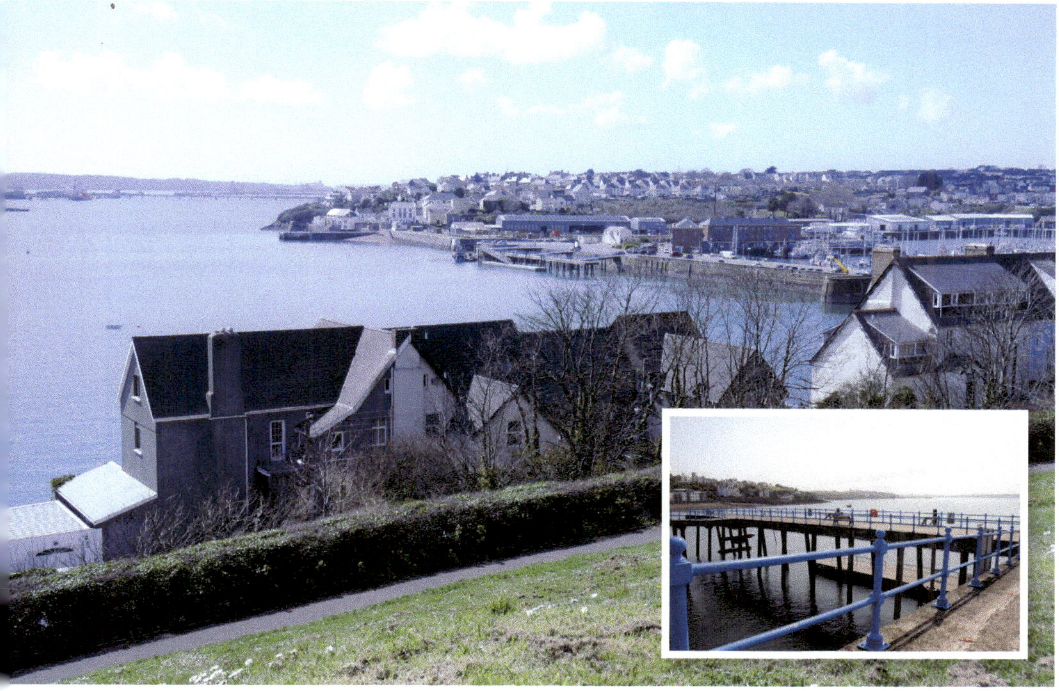

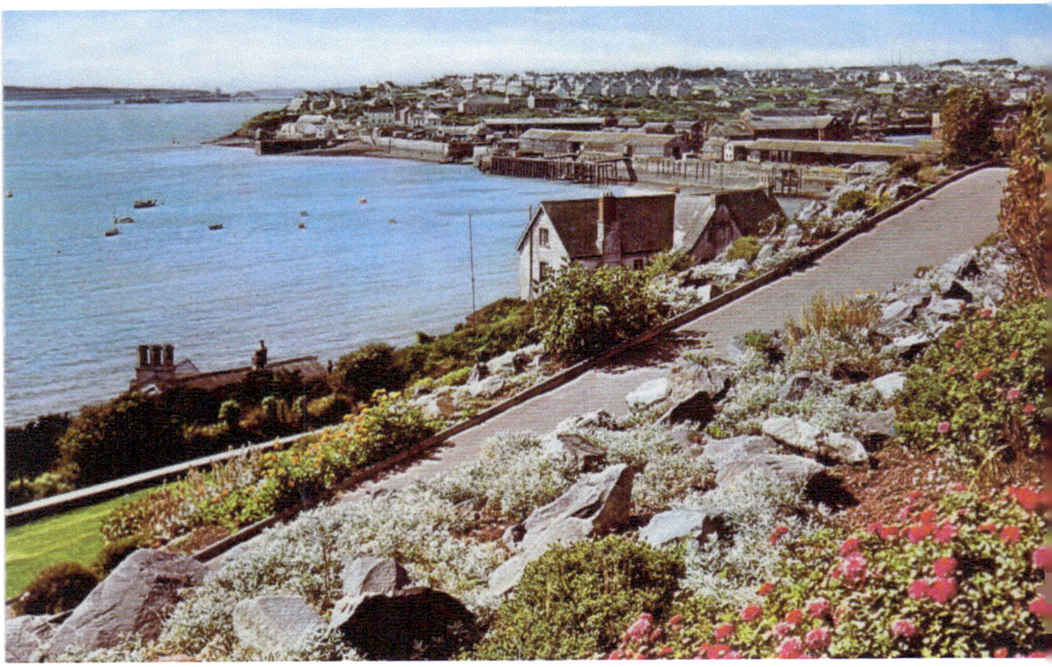

From the Rath

Taken after the Rath had been laid out as a rockery and gardens, this colour postcard highlights the spectacular panoramic view of the Haven. In 1992, local sculptor Bryan Hackett created a large bronze statue of a fisherman, clad in oilskins and looking out to sea, as a tribute to all those who made Milford one of the country's leading fishing ports. The fishing community has suffered many tragedies over the years. The statue's plinth was formed from five stones from the Milford Dock given by the Docks Company.

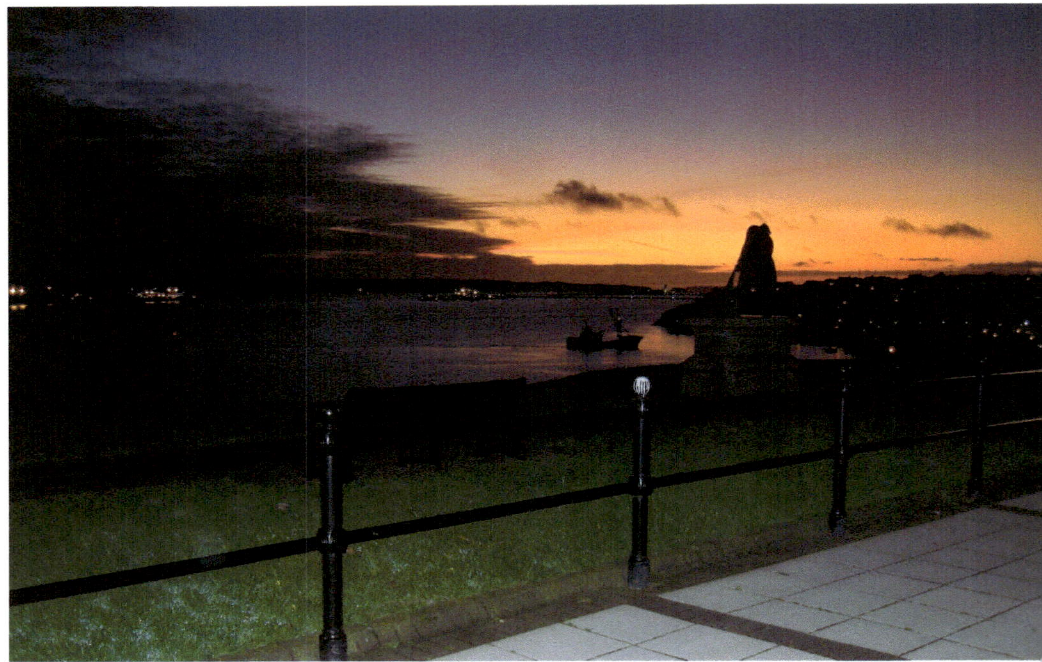

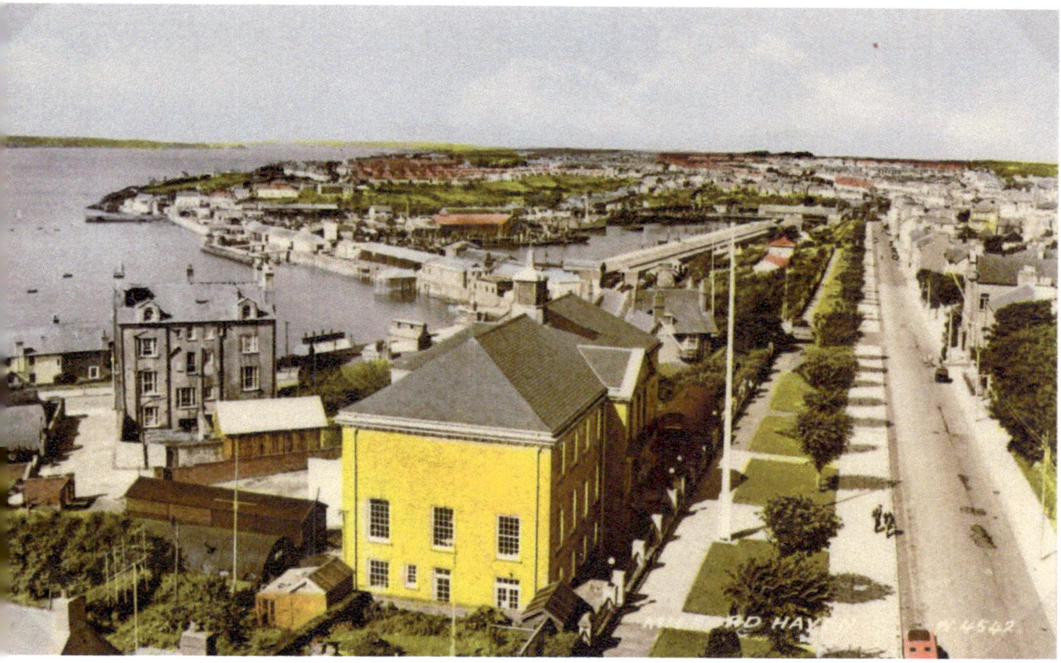

Hamilton Terrace from St Katharine's Church Tower

Thanks to the vicar of Milford and his church warden, I was able to ascend the tower of St Katharine's church to provide a comparison with the earlier photograph, which was probably taken in the 1950s, certainly before the library was built next to the Town Hall. The absence of traffic is striking and the docks have been transformed into a leisure marina. The tower affords magnificent views of the Haven and the area north of Milford. Just to the left of the Town Hall is Murray Crescent House, which has been rebuilt recently.

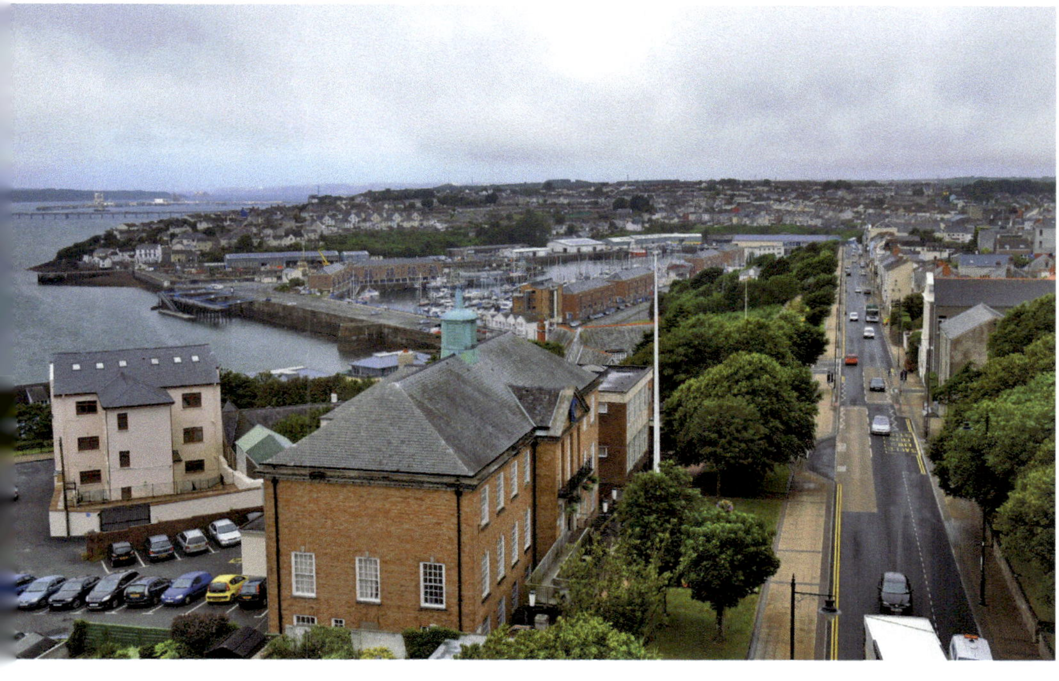

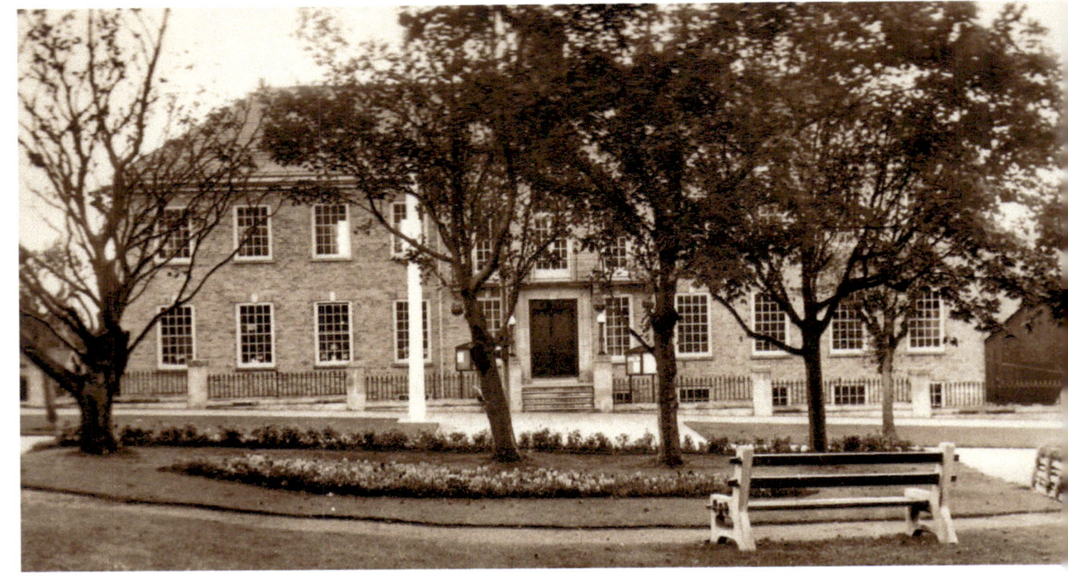

Town Hall

Milford Haven Urban District Council demonstrated their forward-looking policies by commissioning a modern Town Hall to replace the previous offices, which were located in Charles Street. The foundation stone was laid in 1938, and construction was completed in 1939. The building was designed not just for council meetings and administration, but also had an integral fire station. The Murray Suite was designed for exhibitions and recitals, which were a large part of Milford's cultural life. Later, a library was added alongside. The Council Chamber doubled as the Magistrates' Court until the early 1990s, when all court business was transferred to Haverfordwest. Now, in front of the building is a drinking fountain, which used to be on the Market Square. The Memorial Gardens opposite the Town Hall were created in 1950 in recognition of those who died in the Second World War.

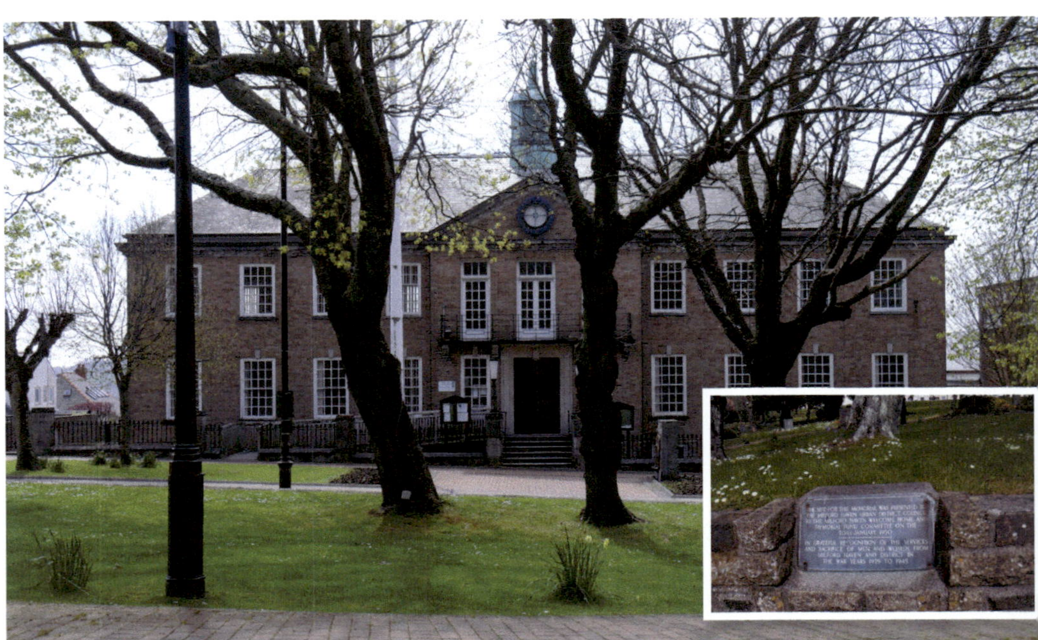

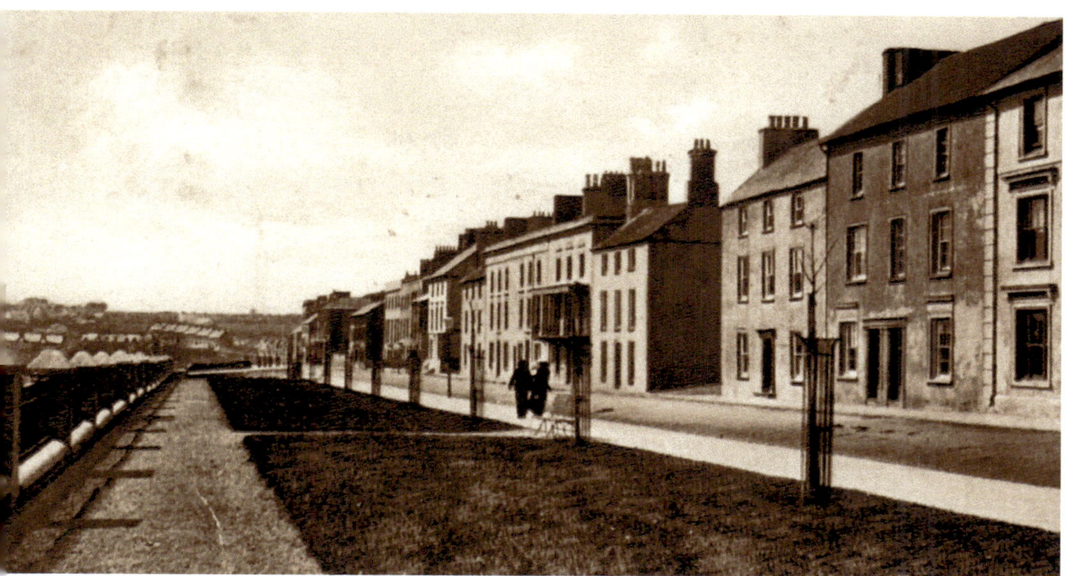

Lower Parade

Hamilton Terrace, originally named Front Street, is spacious and broad with grass lawns and a promenade on the sea side. Overlooking the waterway, it is lined with three-storey early nineteenth-century town houses, showing the American Quaker influence. The house with the ornate iron balcony, built around 1800, was the site of the Milford Haven Bank, founded by Starbuck, Rotch & Phillips. Its style is reminiscent of Nantucket architecture. The balcony was reinstated in 1991, having been removed for safety reasons some forty years before. With the exception of the war memorial, yellow lines and controlled car parking spaces, little has changed in the general view over the century that elapsed between these photographs. As most of the buildings are now listed, this should remain the case.

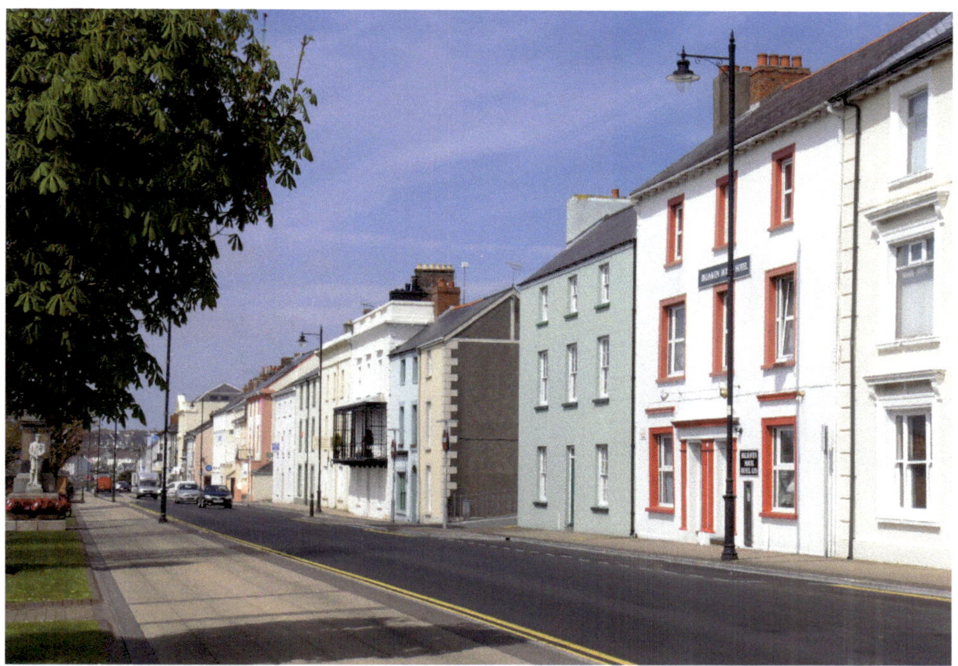

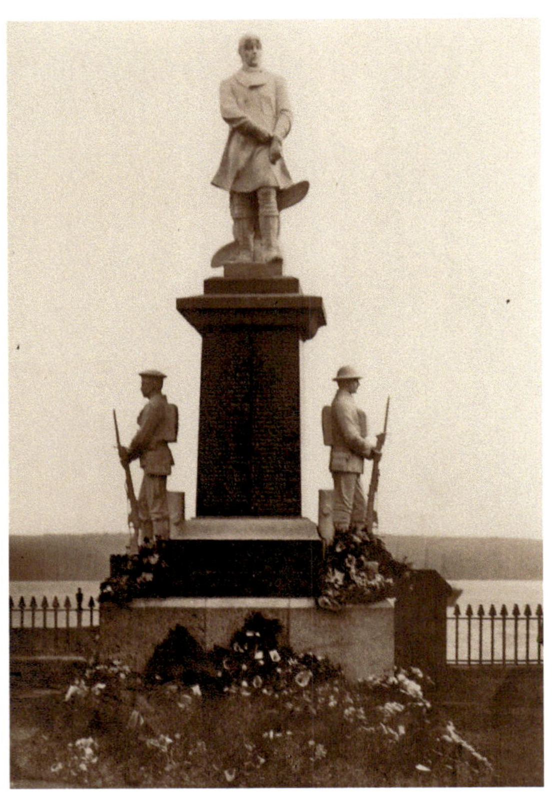

War Memorial

The war memorial was erected in 1924 to honour those who lost their lives in the First World War. On the top of the polished granite plinth, an airman faces the town. A sailor (naval rating) is on the east side and a soldier faces west. As well as listing the local men killed, the memorial also includes the names of ninety-one officers and men of the naval base in the town. The names of those killed in the Second World War are on a plaque added to the base. The guns of the soldier and sailor originally had fixed bayonets, but these were removed at some stage. New marble bayonets were made in 2004 but they are only mounted on the guns for Remembrance Day services.

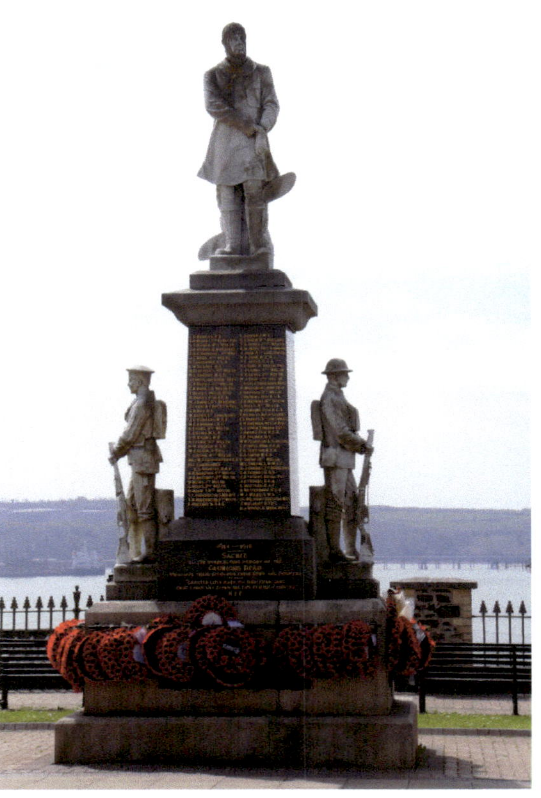

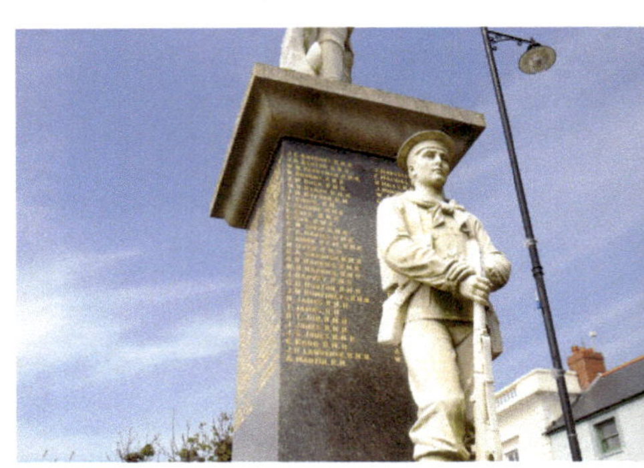

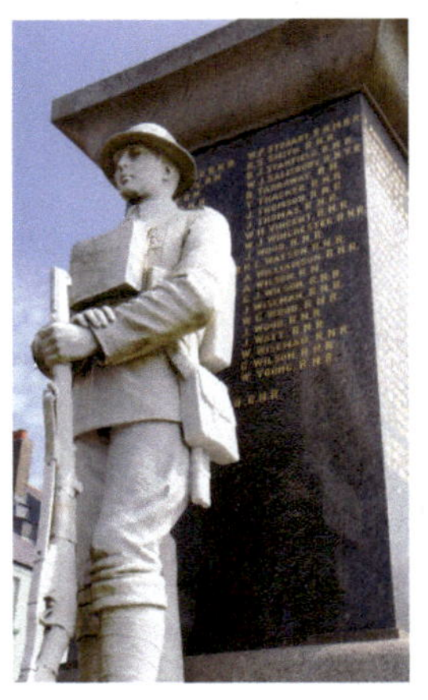

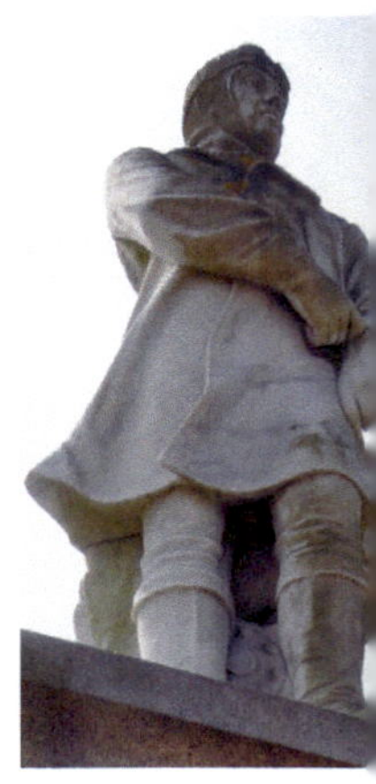

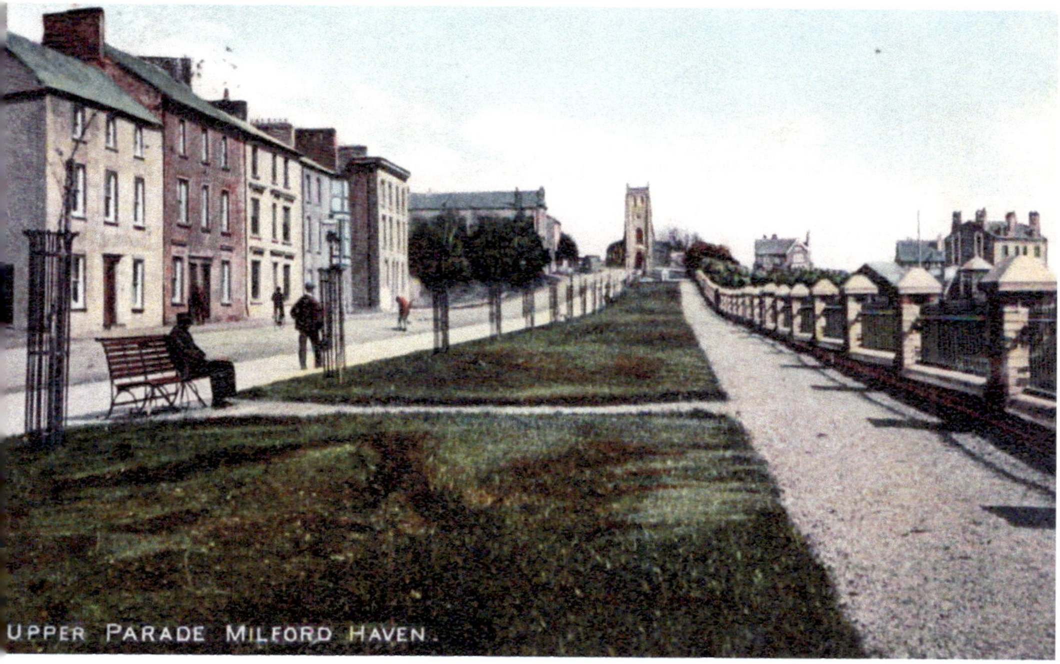

Upper Parade

Looking east along Hamilton Terrace towards St Katharine's church, the view of Murray Crescent House and the Vicarage is now obscured by trees and the memorial. Carefully manicured floral gardens are now an annual feature of Hamilton Terrace and other areas of the town. The prominent tall building just obscured by trees in the earlier picture is the Masonic Hall, which was opened in 1882 and enlarged in 1906 and 1925. The public function room there has long served the town as a dance hall, a banqueting hall and a venue for other events.

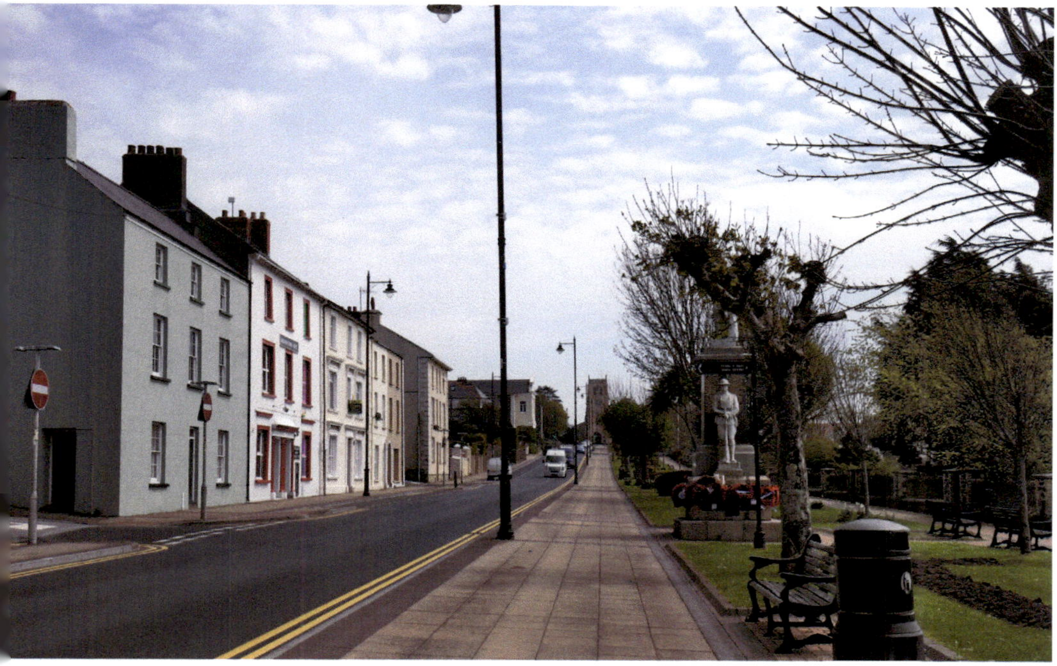

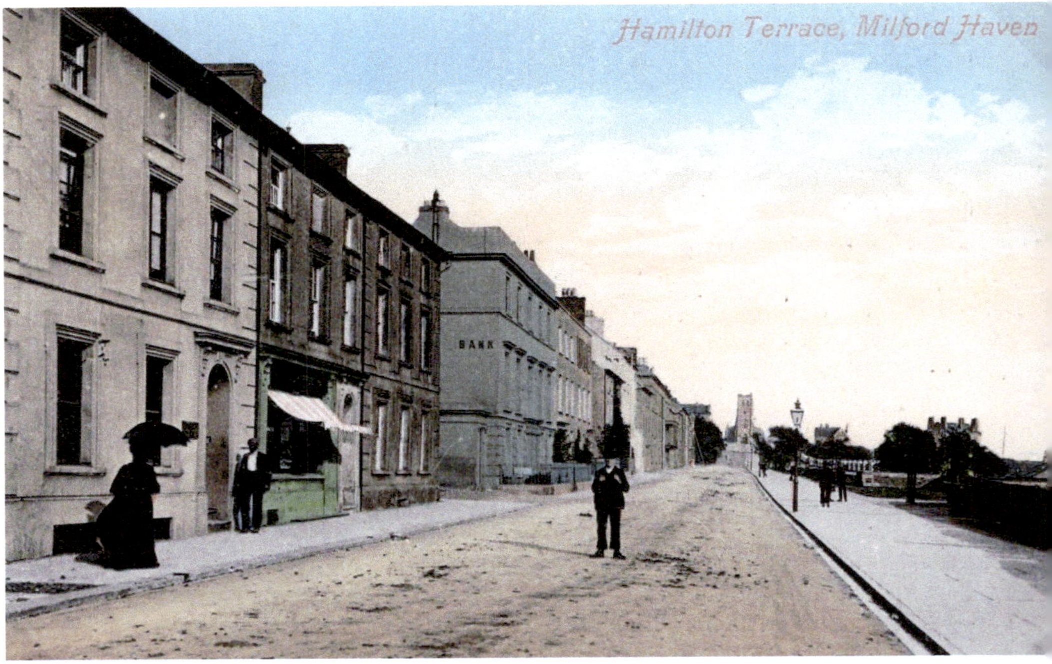

Hamilton Terrace

Taken in the early years of the twentieth century, this view includes evidence of the house that was demolished in around 1920, to be replaced by a new building for the London City & Midland Bank. Next door, the shop with an awning was for many years the popular hardware shop of Tom Newing. Barclays bank still occupies the large premises on the corner of Priory Street. A total lack of traffic allowed a local character to feature on this colourful postcard.

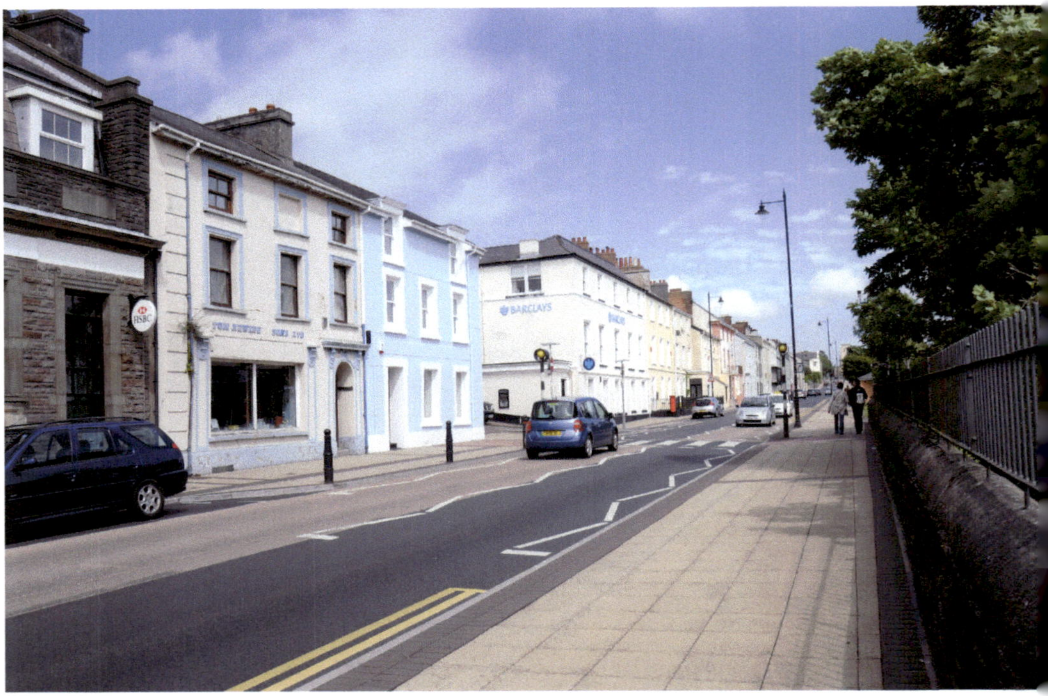

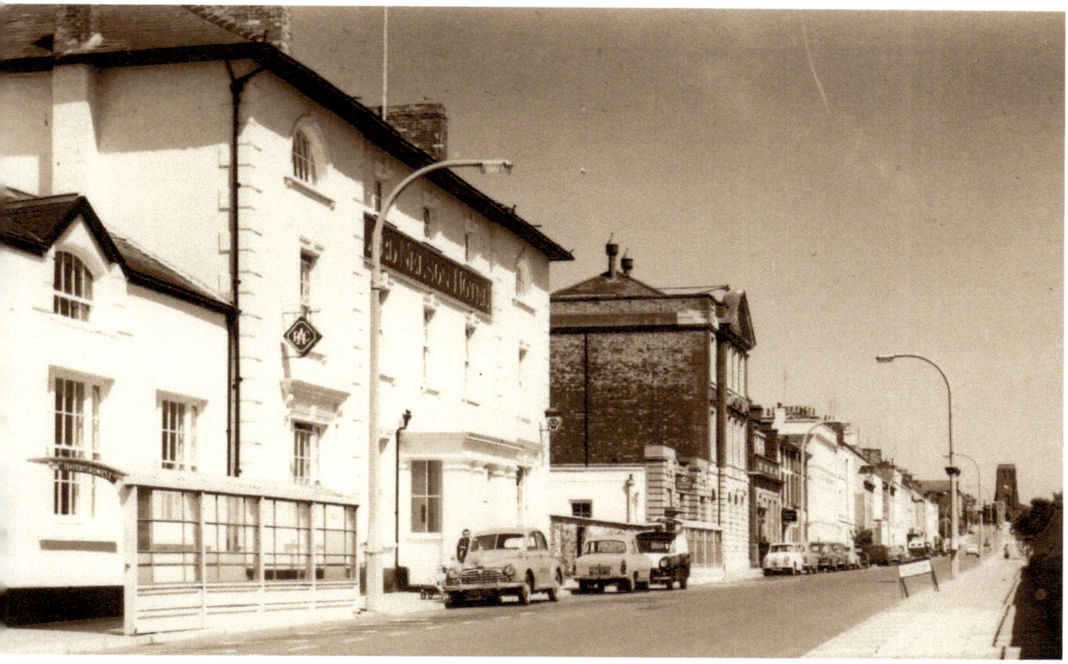

Lord Nelson Hotel

When the New Inn opened in 1800, it was one of the first buildings on Front Street. An early account described it as being in the Georgian style, having a dignified entrance and front, and a fine ballroom looking onto a garden at the side. It was renamed to commemorate Lord Nelson's visit to the town in 1802, when he was a principal guest at a banquet held there. The mail coach ran from here to London, a forty-eight-hour journey. The bus stop has been relocated from its earlier position outside the ex-stable block to outside Lloyds Bank. Alongside the bank is the impressive premises built as a post office in 1908.

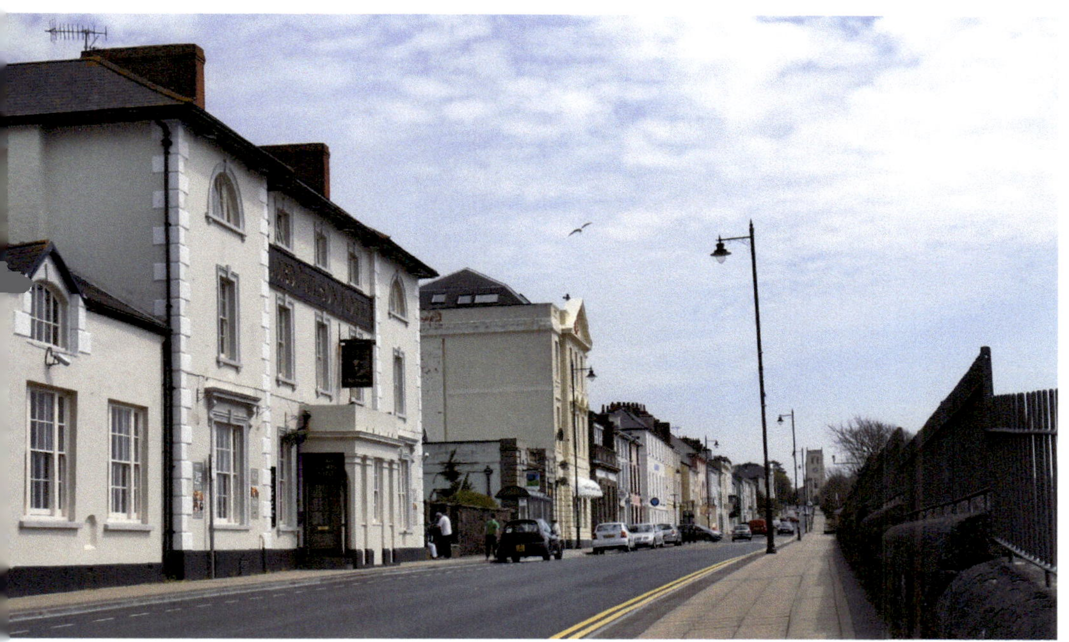

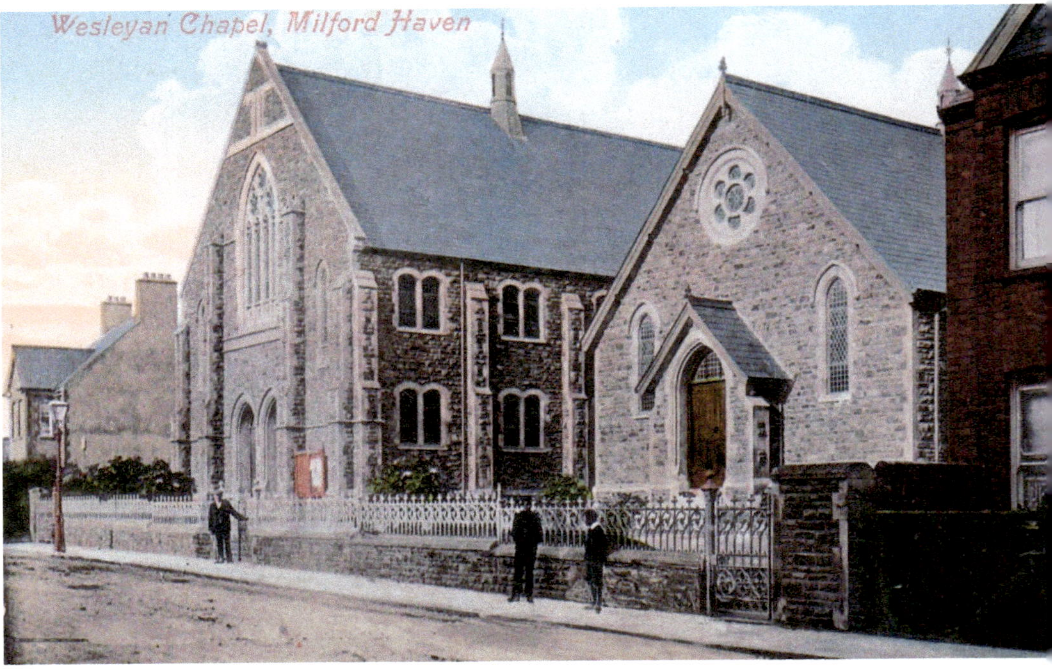

Priory Road, Wesleyan Chapel

The chapel opened in Priory Road in 1902, replacing a Wesleyan Methodist chapel located in Robert Street. This place of worship has recently been renamed Christ Church to reflect the new congregation formed when the members were joined by those from the Tabernacle chapel following the closure of their church. The chapel is noted for the impressive organ built in 1919 at a cost of over £1,000.

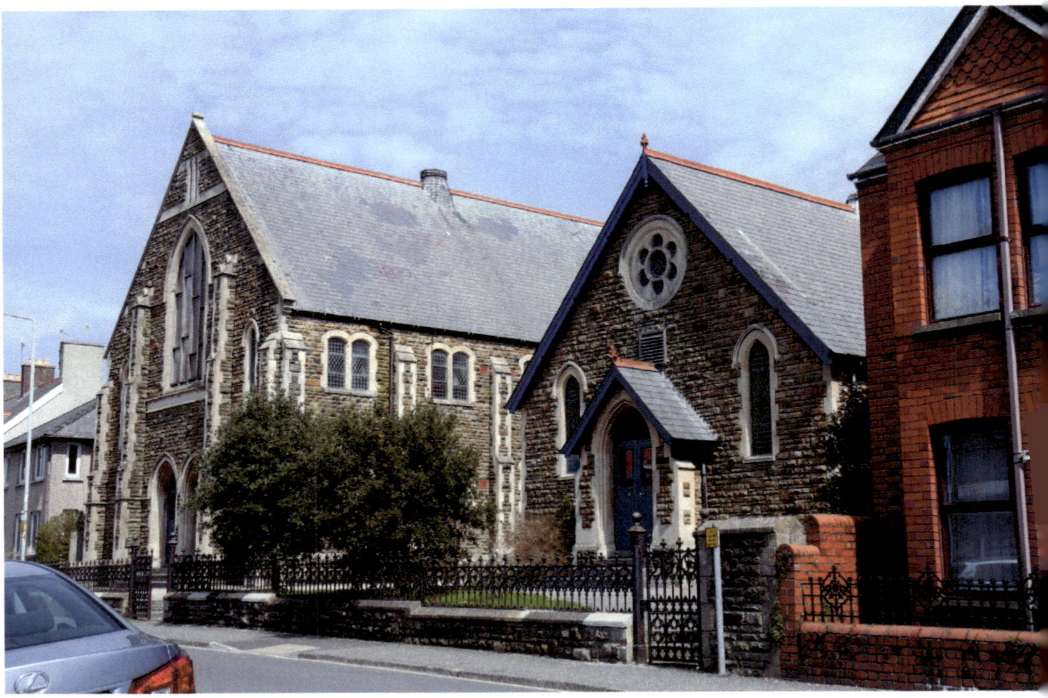

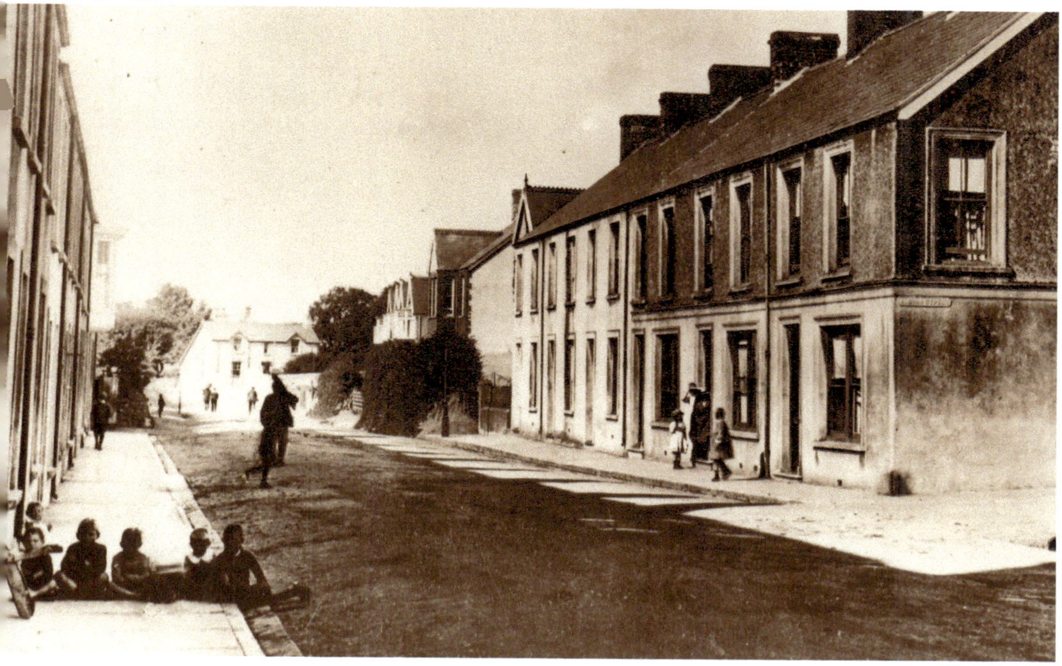

Priory Road

Priory Road was one of several streets of terraced houses constructed in the later nineteenth century to accommodate the growing population of Milford. The 1901 census shows that most of the inhabitants were involved in the fishing industry as fishermen, marine engineers or fish packers. There was also a sailmaker and a brass moulder.

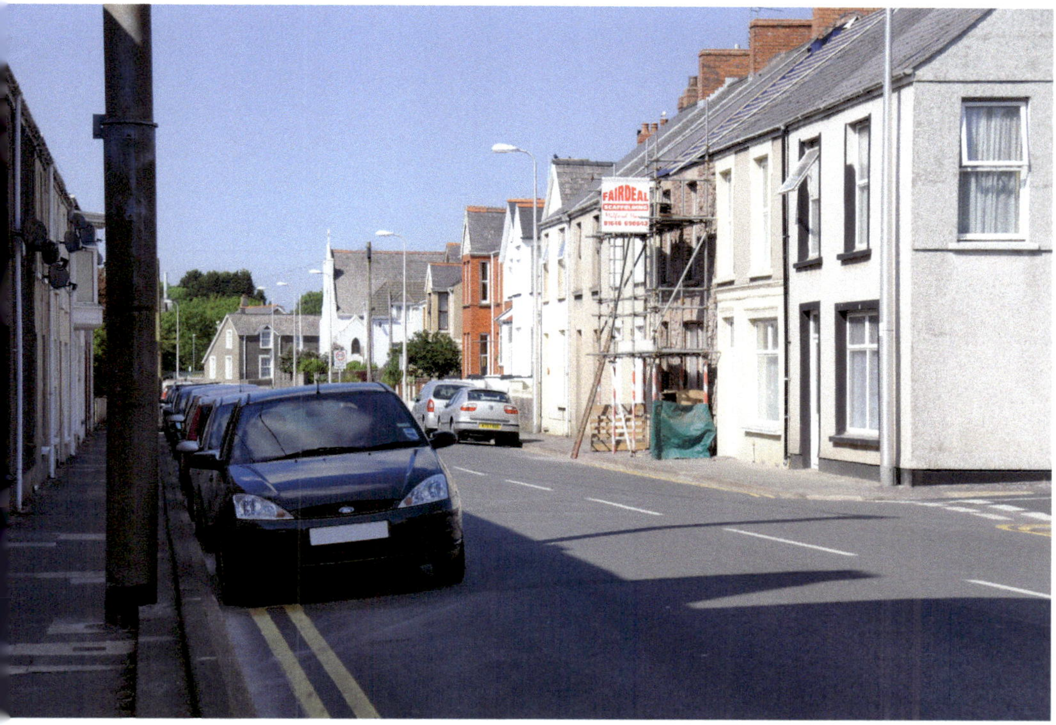

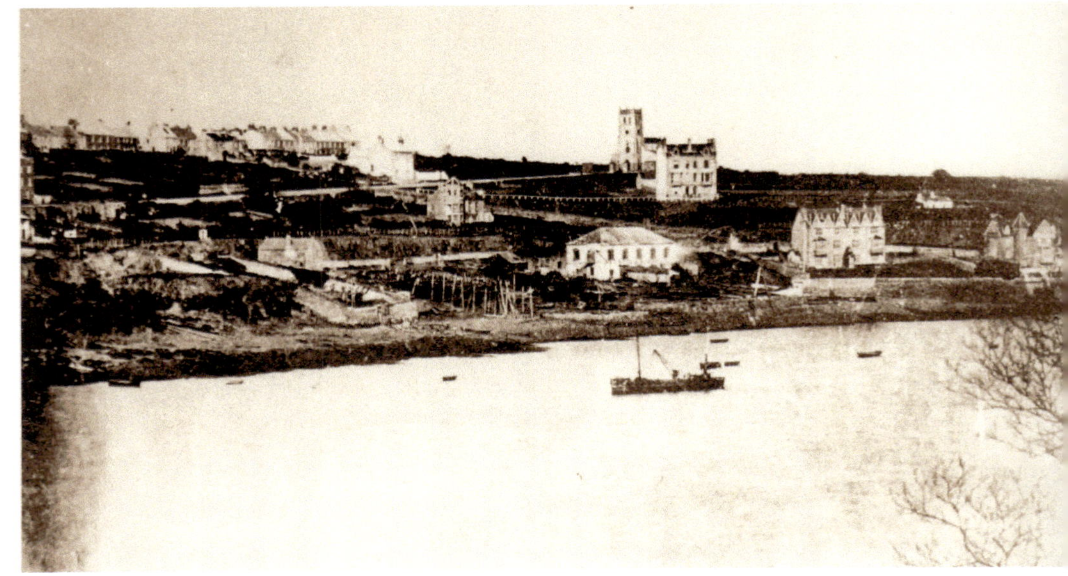

Milford

This very early photograph includes the Murray Crescent House, which was the Royal Navy HQ at Milford in the First World War. Later, it was occupied by a shipping agent and Milford Travel Agency. The house was named after Lady Caroline Murray, the half-sister of Robert Fulke Greville. Although she did not live in the town, in 1862 she donated £300 towards the rebuilding of St David's church, Hubberston. Murray Crescent House has recently been rebuilt. In the old photograph, the Rath is bare, and Hamilton House at the east side of Hamilton Terrace can be seen. The original plan was that Hamilton Terrace should continue to the east of St Katharine's church and that the houses planned on the Rath should be known as Murray Crescent, neither of which was realised.

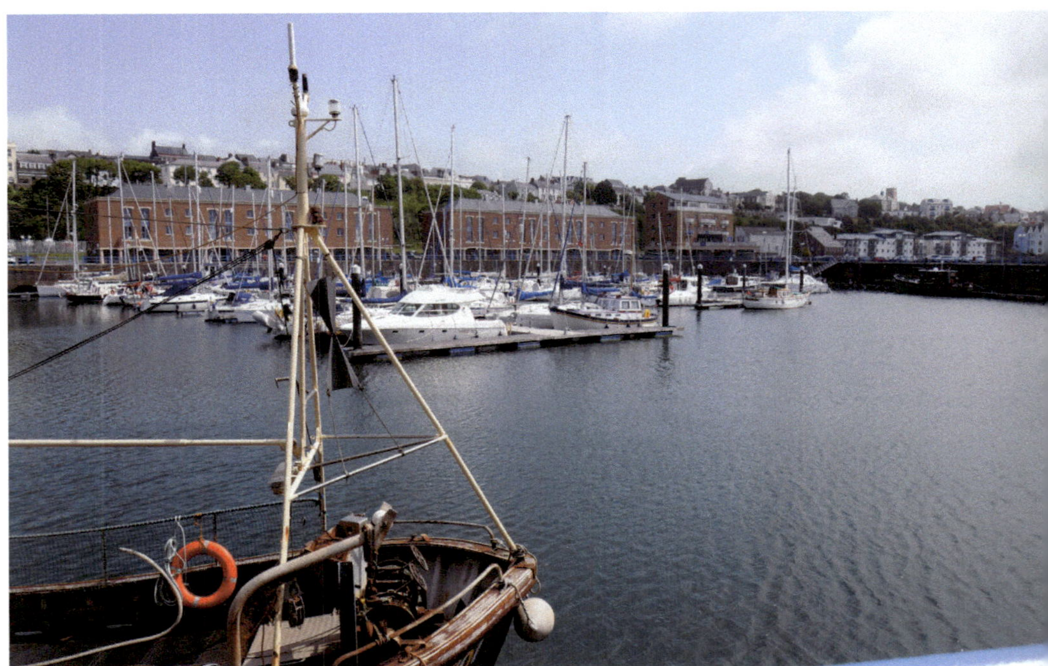

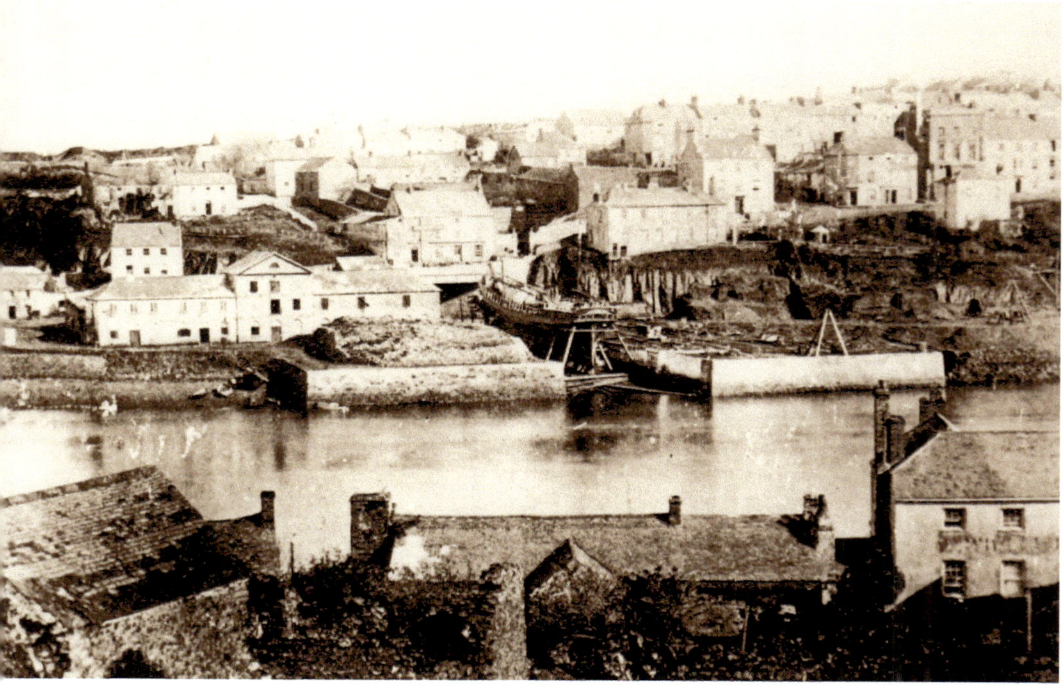

Milford from Hakin

This early photograph shows the shipbuilding and repair industry of the town prior to the building of the dock. One of the town's earliest buildings, the customs house, dating from around 1860 (opened as the town's Heritage and Maritime Museum in 1989), dominates the front and a ship is under construction in Hogan's yard. At the time of the picture, some 130 sailing vessels used Milford as their base. The later photograph dates from around 1990 and demonstrates the development of the area following the construction of the dock. This particular view has now been obscured by the modern marina buildings.

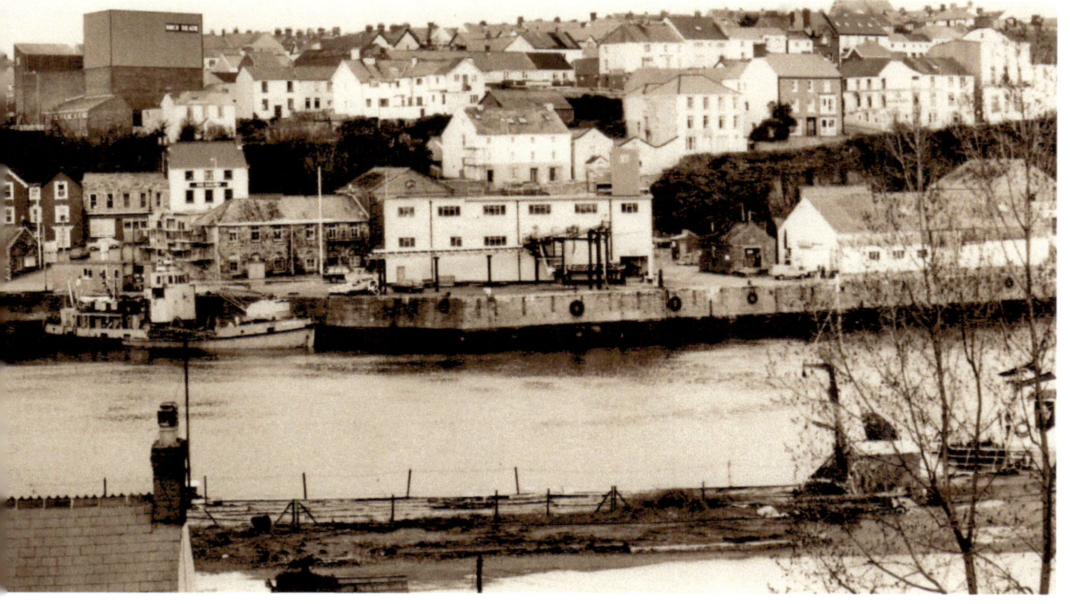

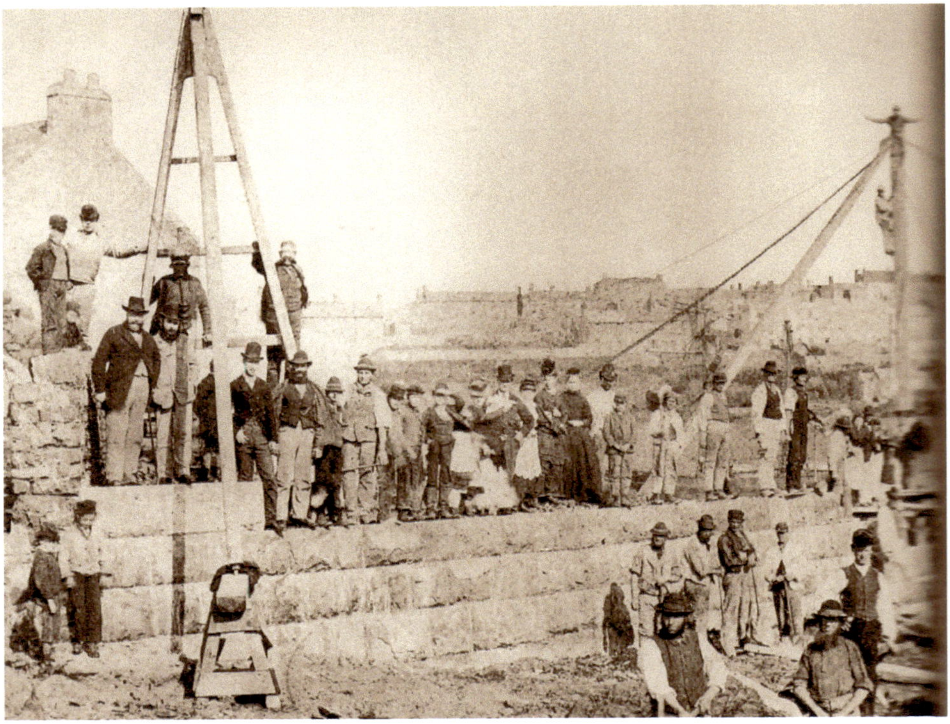

Docks Foundation Stone

The foundation stone of the new dock was laid in 1874 by E. J. Reed CB MP. Previously Chief Constructor of the Navy, he was chairman of the Milford Docks Company and represented the Pembroke Boroughs at Westminster until 1880. Many of the workers in the photograph would previously have been employed in the local shipyards, many of which closed down in order to build the dock. The foundation stone is still visible close to the Hakin Jetty. Following years of delay, the dock was eventually completed and opened in 1888.

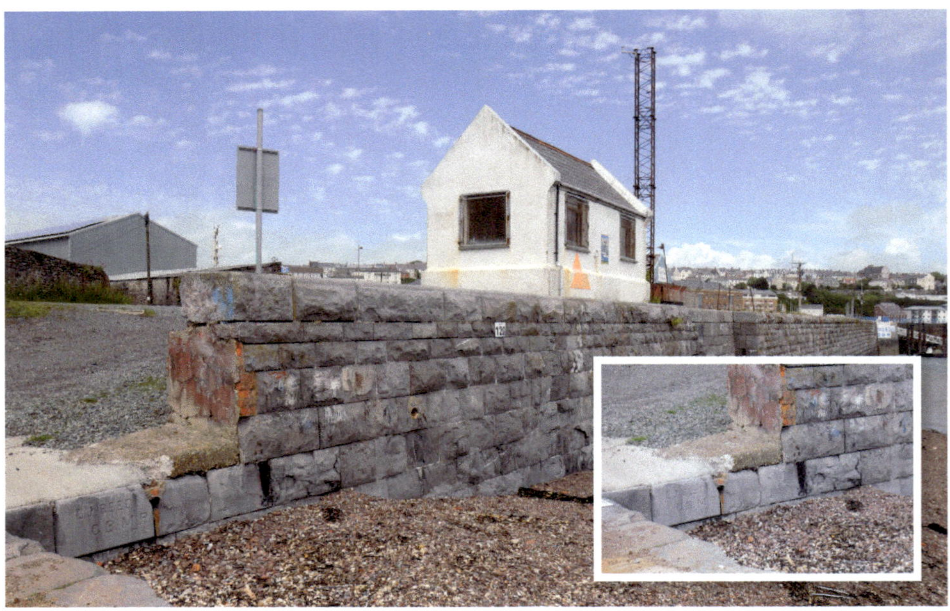

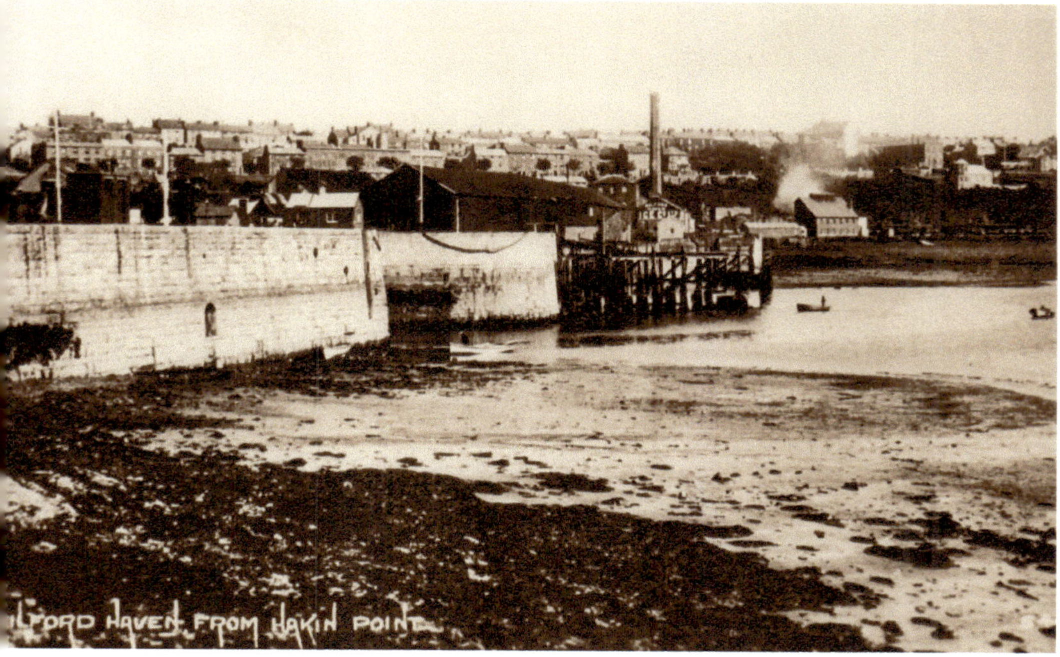

Docks from Hakin Point

Just beyond the entrance to the dock is the 400-foot-long mackerel stage constructed in 1902. Within three years, seventy drifters were using the wharf. The timber construction was upgraded to concrete just after the Second World War. It is now a landing stage for pleasure boats and cruise ship tenders. The tall chimney belonging to the Milford Haven Ice Co. was damaged in July 1942 when an RAF Wellington bomber crashed into the docks. A memorial to the six crewmen who died has been placed above Marine Gardens.

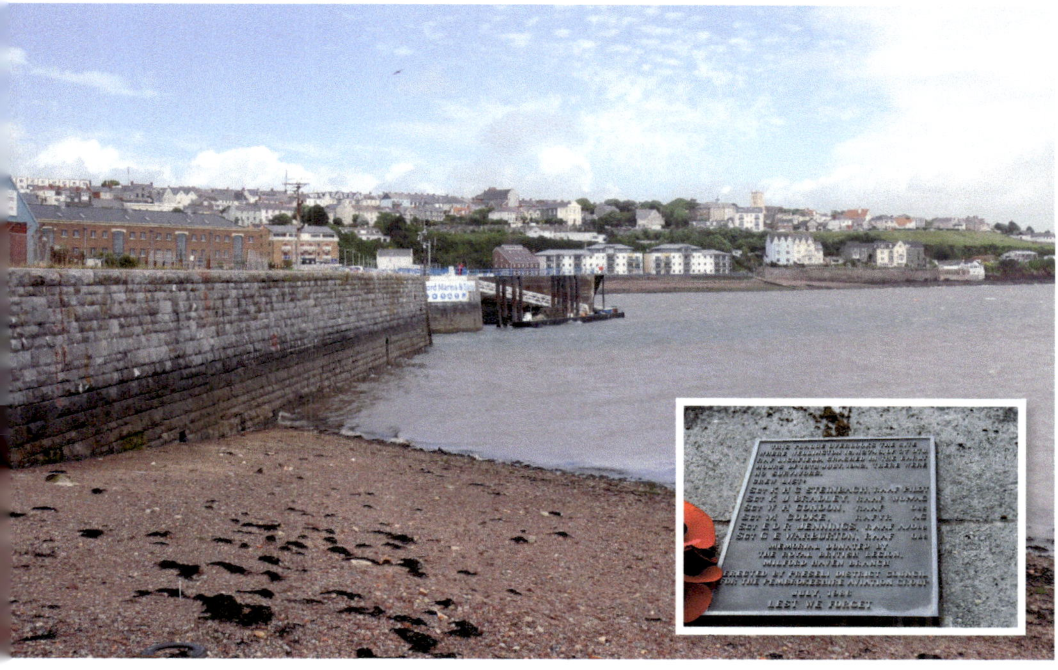

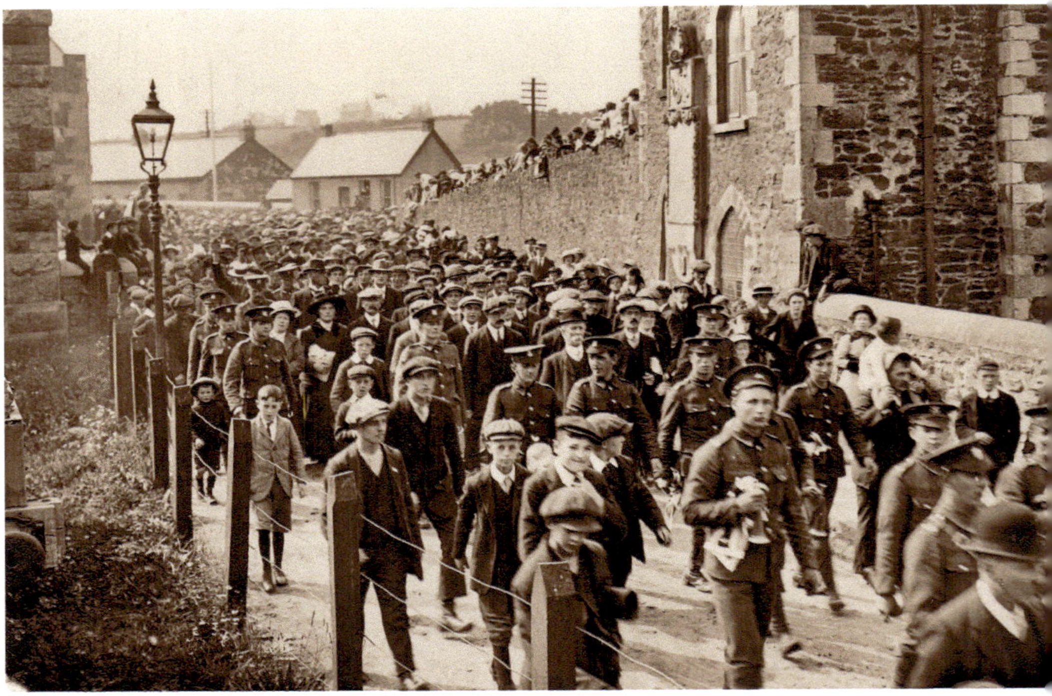

Victoria Bridge Toll Gate

This photograph was taken in 1914 as a group of volunteers walked towards the station to make the journey to their training depot. The toll gate had become redundant when the charge for crossing Victoria Bridge was removed in 1909. The new vehicular entrance into the docks was created in the 1990s.

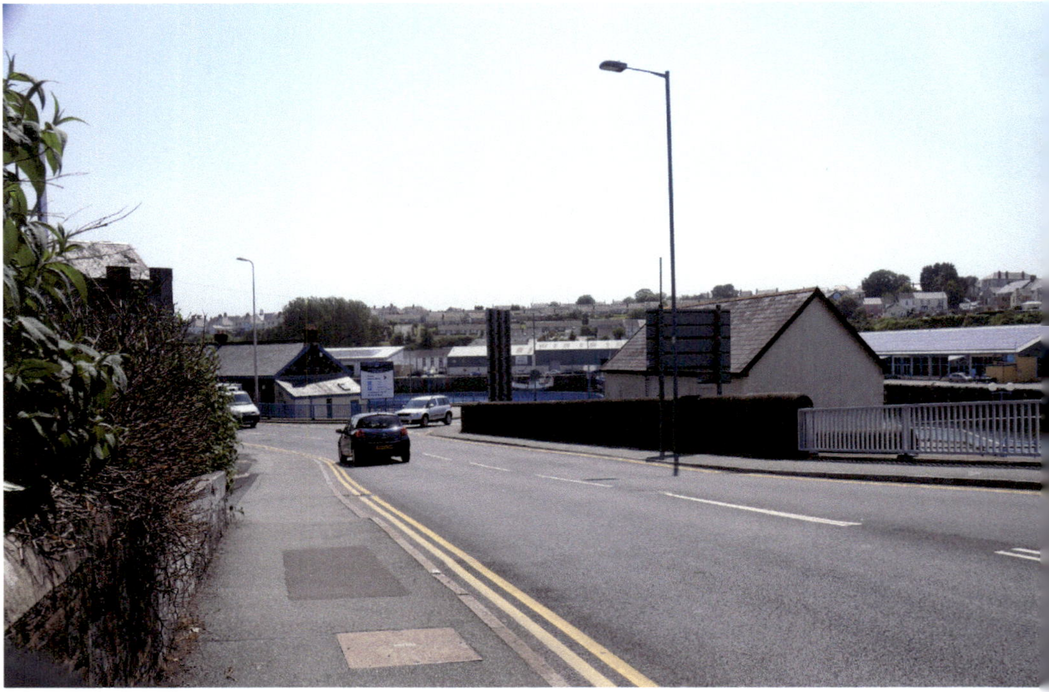

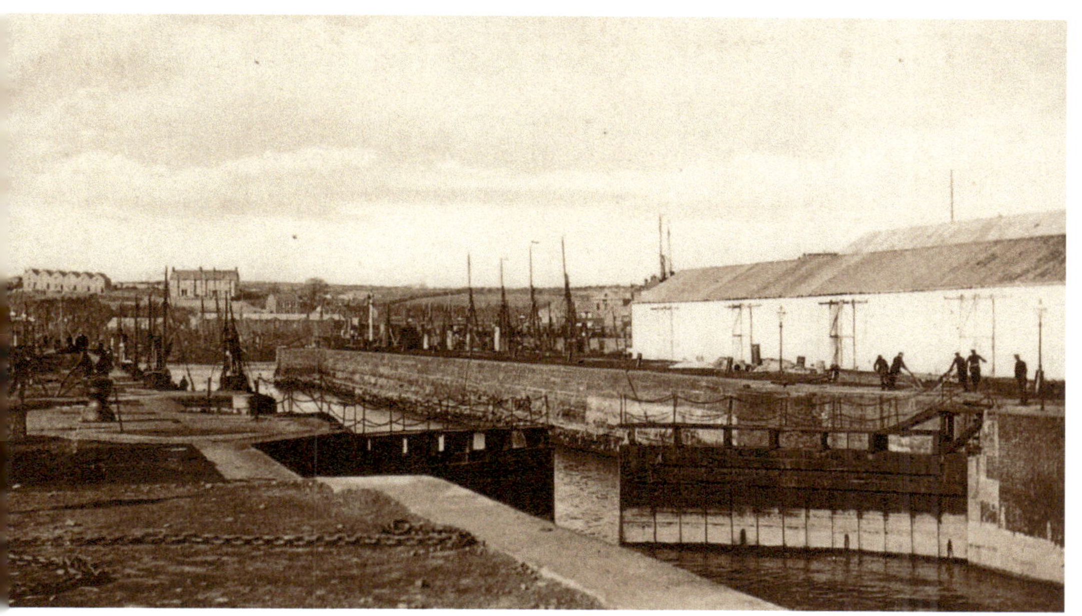

Opening the Dock Gates

Four men were needed to open the manually operated gates. New dock gates were installed in 1996. It used to be possible to walk from Hakin to the Milford side of the docks across the lock pits when the gates were closed. Many of the original bollards in this area of the dock have survived. In the contemporary photograph, one of the wind turbines springing up in the area can just be seen on the horizon.

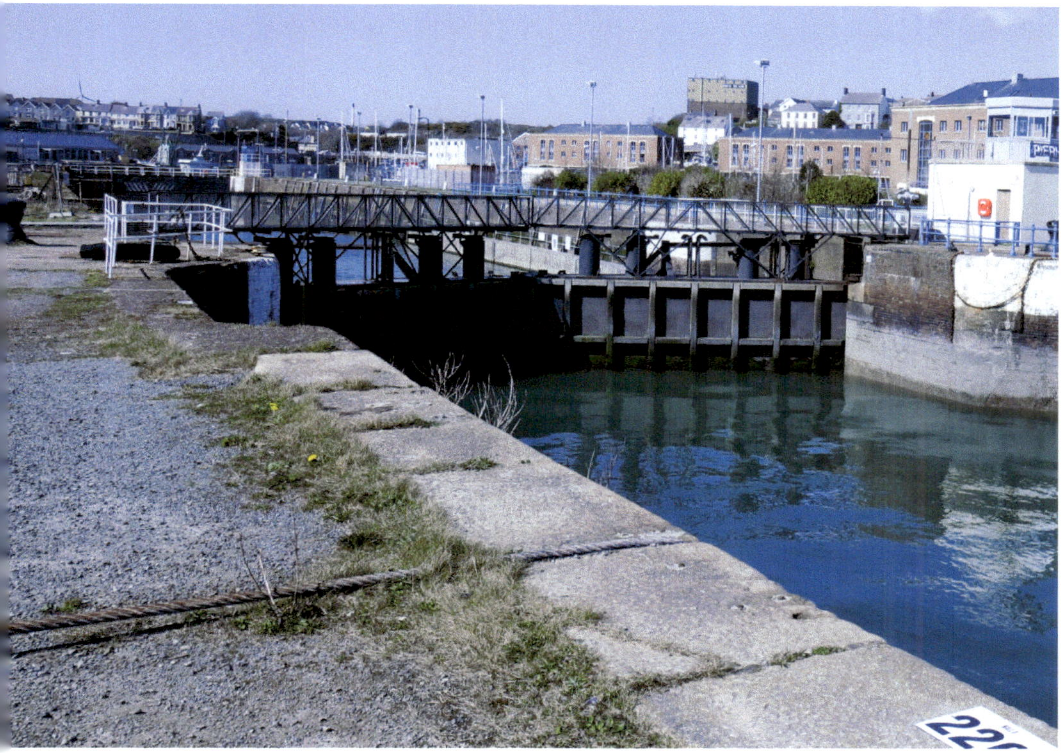

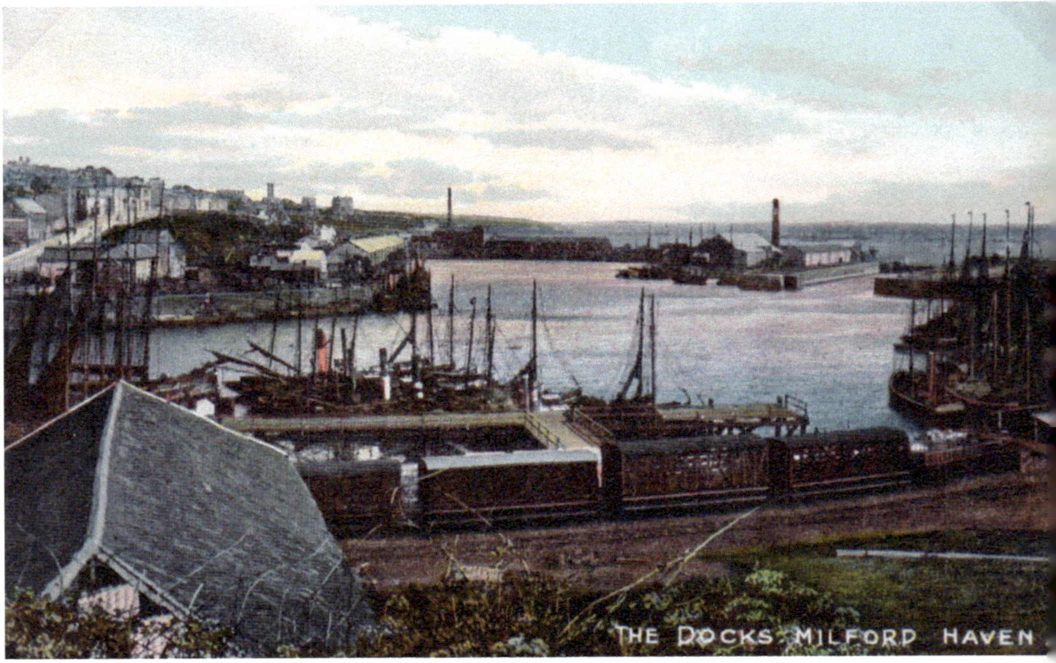

The Docks

The view from St Anne's Road shows a number of trawlers tied up at the Hakin wharf, alongside railway lines and trucks. At one time, there was a railway station on the Hakin side, built to allow disembarking passengers from the SS *City of Rome* to catch the train to London, a journey of six hours. The current view illustrates the dramatic change in the use of the docks as Fish Week, promoted by Pembrokeshire County Council, gets underway. Fresh fish stalls and guest chefs occupy brightly coloured stalls and marquees alongside the Phoenix Bowl, the home of ten-pin bowling in Milford. In the foreground is the circular roof of the Seal Hospital, located in an old oil storage tank.

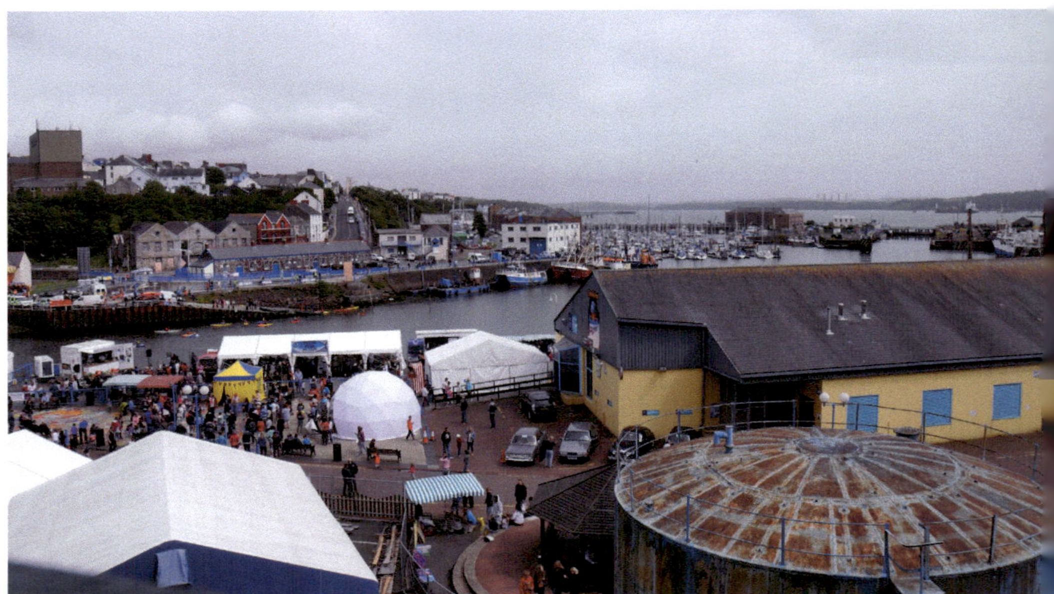

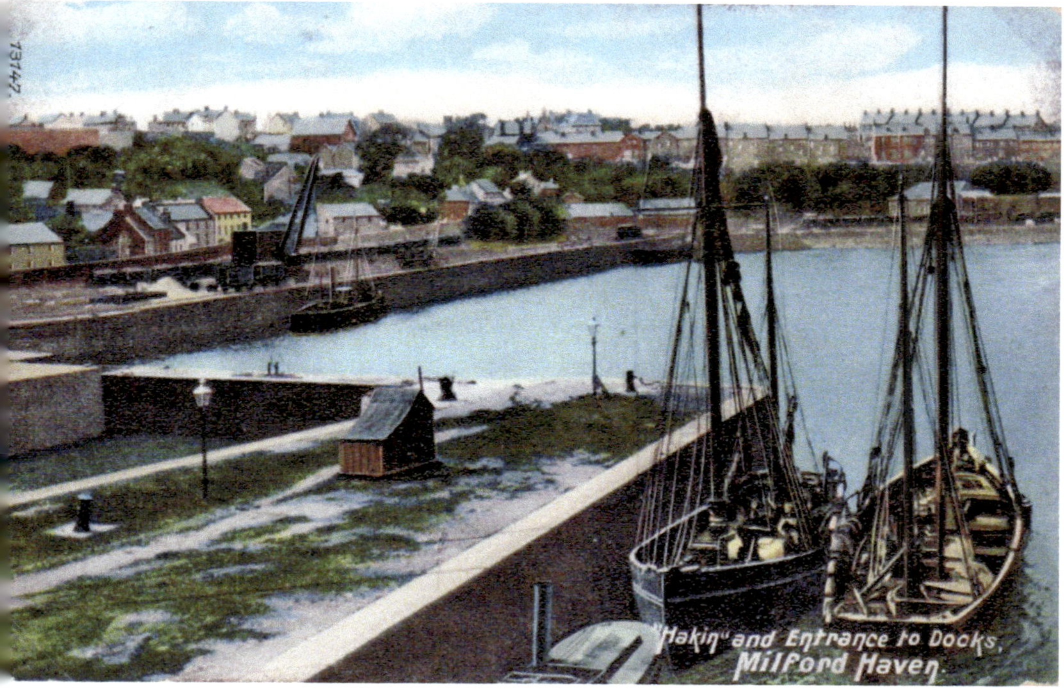

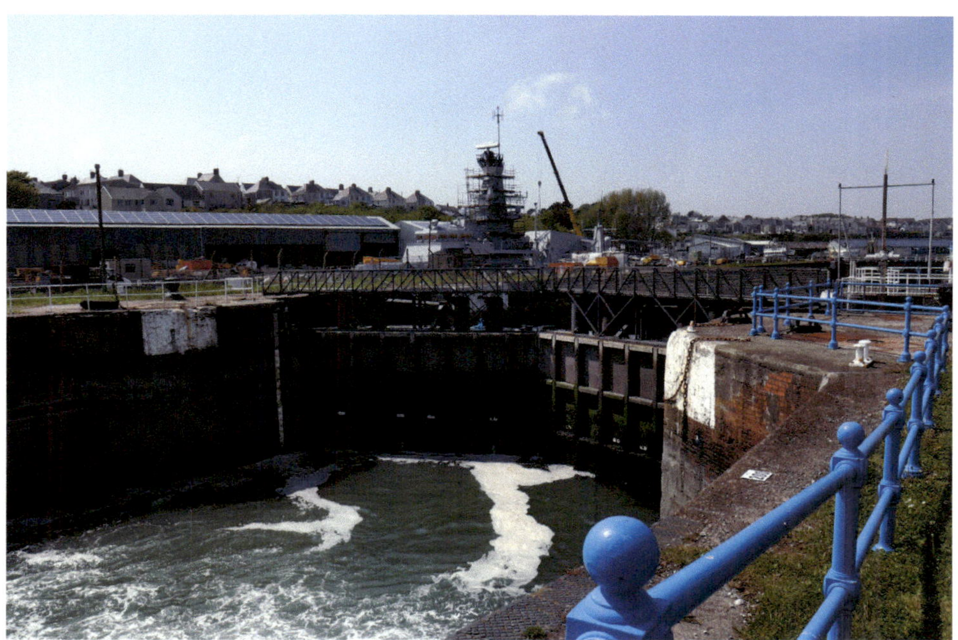

Hakin and Entrance to the Docks

Only a couple of vessels are tied up against the long jetty on the Hakin side, which could accommodate vessels of up to 10,000 tons and was directly in line with the dock entrance. Behind the jetty are the dwellings and inns of the thriving dockside community of Point Street and Lower Hill Street. The timber jetty was replaced after the Second World War by a concrete wharf and two electric travelling cranes. The contemporary photograph shows a vessel undergoing repair in the dry dock.

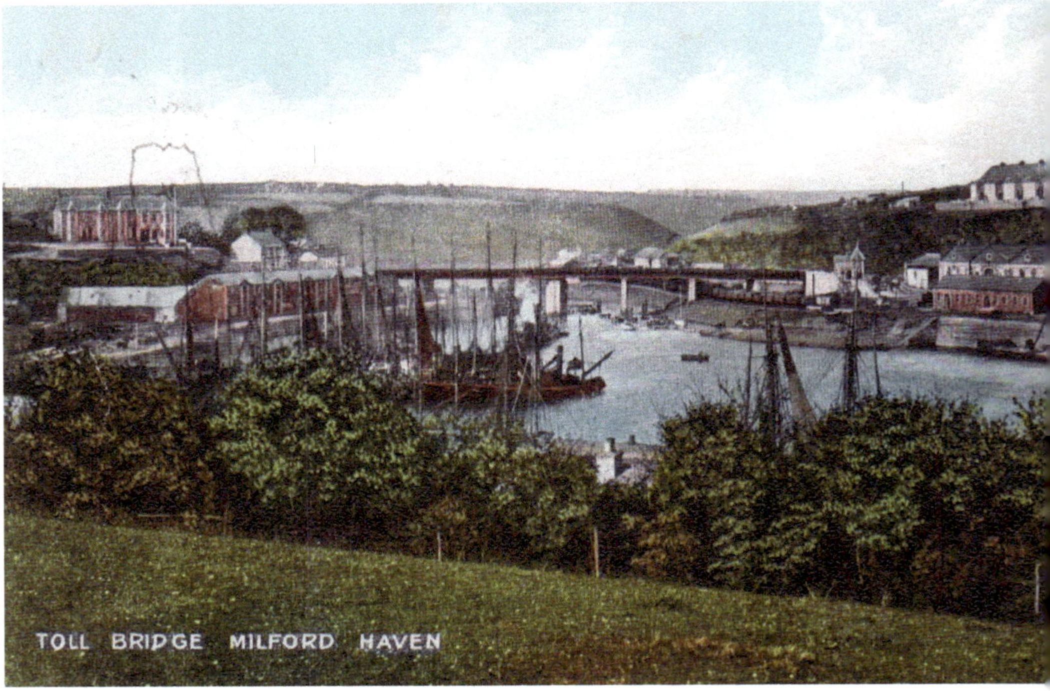

Toll Bridge

This view of the docks from above Point Street shows Victoria Bridge, which linked Milford and Hakin by spanning Hubberston Pill. The old sail loft on the Hakin side is clearly visible. The contemporary photograph shows the roofs of the modern sheds that have replaced the old stone buildings, and the Havens Head retail area beyond the bridge.

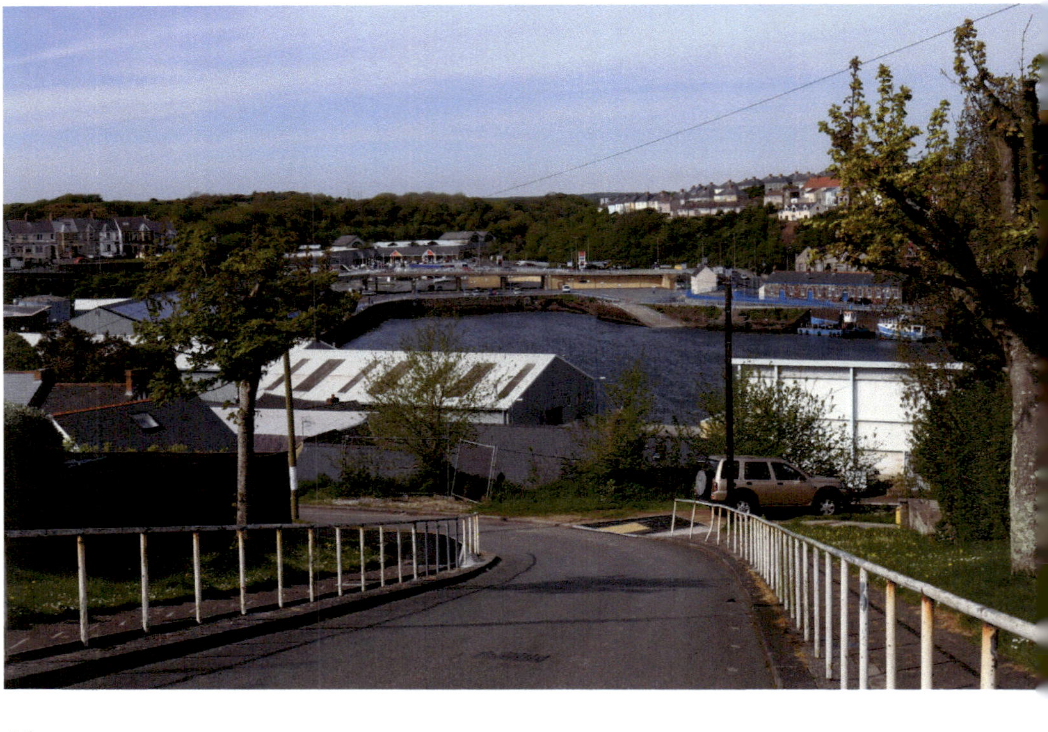

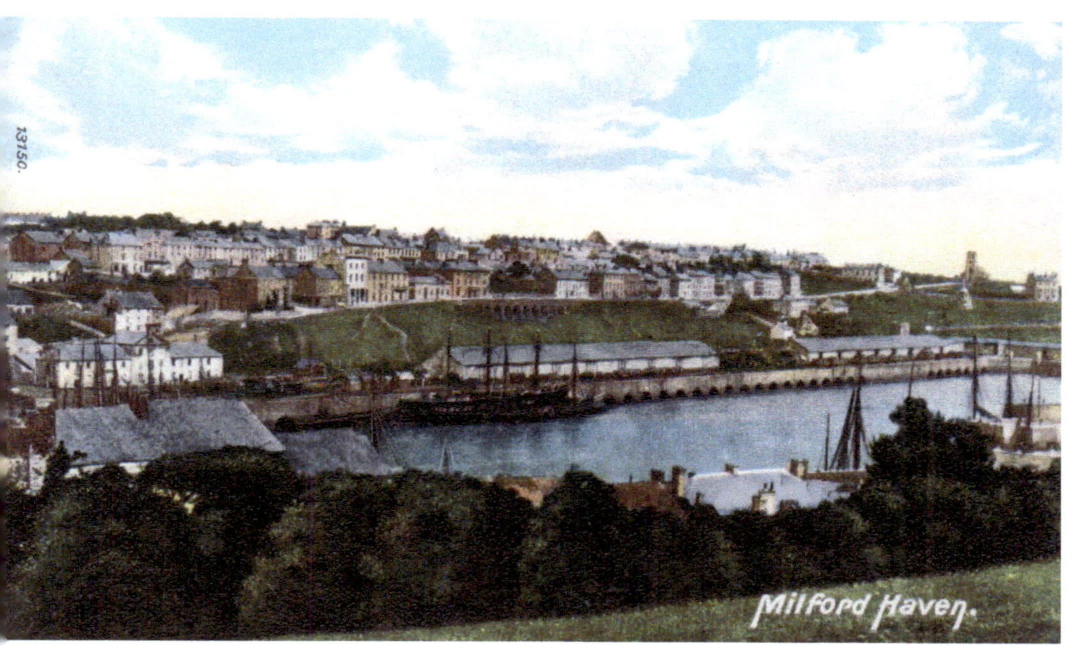

Docks from Hakin

This postcard shows the continued expansion of the docks and the town of Milford. Below the red-brick arches of the embankment retaining Hamilton Terrace, the sheds of the Fish Market stretch along the dockside. Daily morning auctions of the catches led to distribution by rail to the rest of the country. The fish market has been replaced by Nelson Quay, along which are modern red-brick structures named after Nelson's ships: *Victory, Vanguard, Sovereign* and *Agamemnon*. A selection of retail shops, cafés and offices with sheltered walkways occupy these. In the middle is Martha's Vineyard restaurant and the Marina Control Centre. Behind Nelson Quay are the masts of yachts in the large yacht park created in an area previously filled with dock buildings.

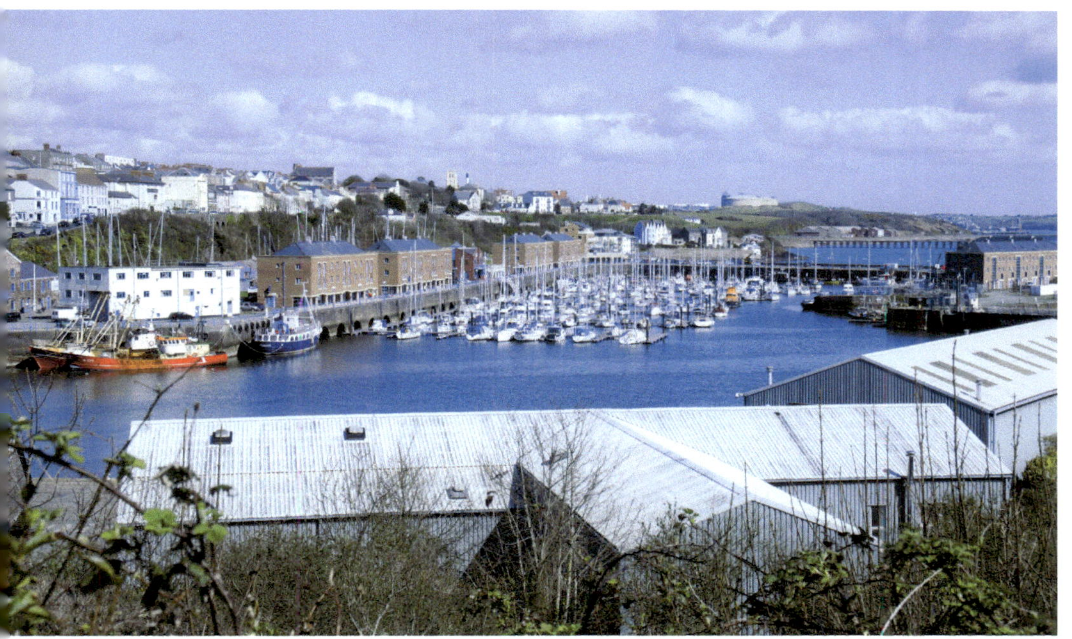

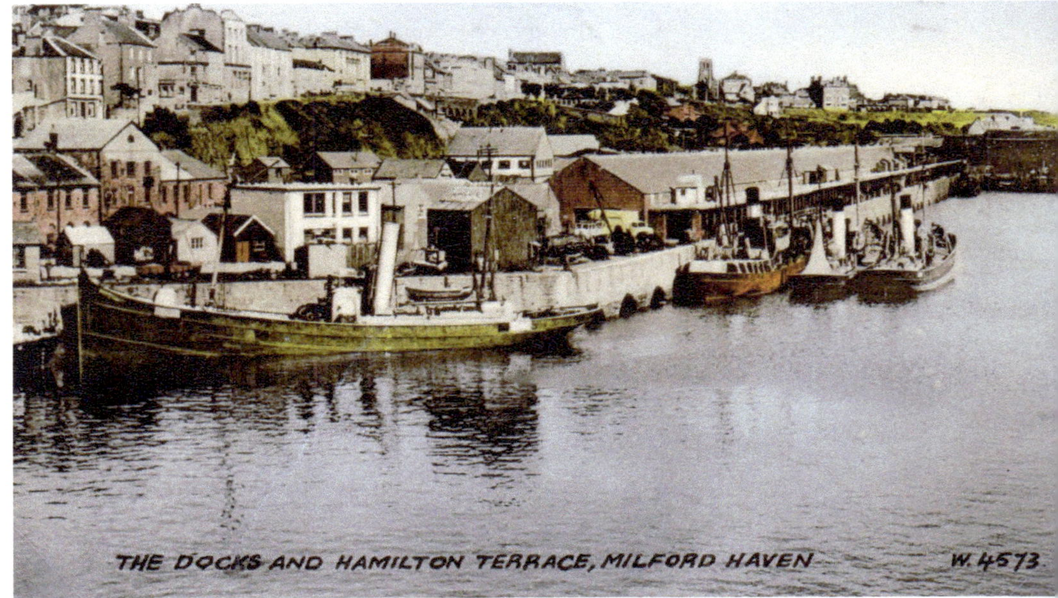

The Docks and Hamilton Terrace

The 1938 *Fish Trades Gazette* described Milford as 'the great fishing port of the west' and summarised the advantages of the port: 'The docks are fully equipped to deal with all the requirements of the fishing industry, having two spacious fish markets, coal skipping appliances which can bunker vessels at the rate of 200 tons an hour, an electrically operated hauling-out slipway and a dry dock 600 feet in length, which can take eight vessels at a time and which are equipped with electrical pumping plant of the most modern type. In addition to a number of kippering houses, there are factories which manufacture ice, fishmeal and fish boxes, also a number of ship repairing works. There are over a hundred merchants waiting to buy the fish.' The contemporary photograph shows a few trawlers tied up alongside the dock wall, but the marina now dominates the docks area. On the horizon are the storage tanks of the Dragon LNG terminal located at Waterston.

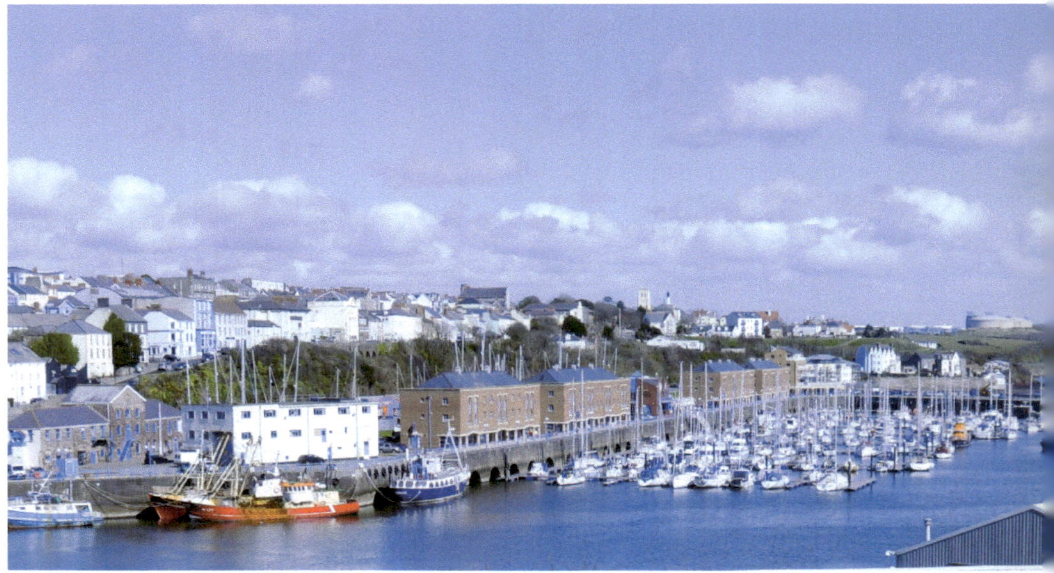

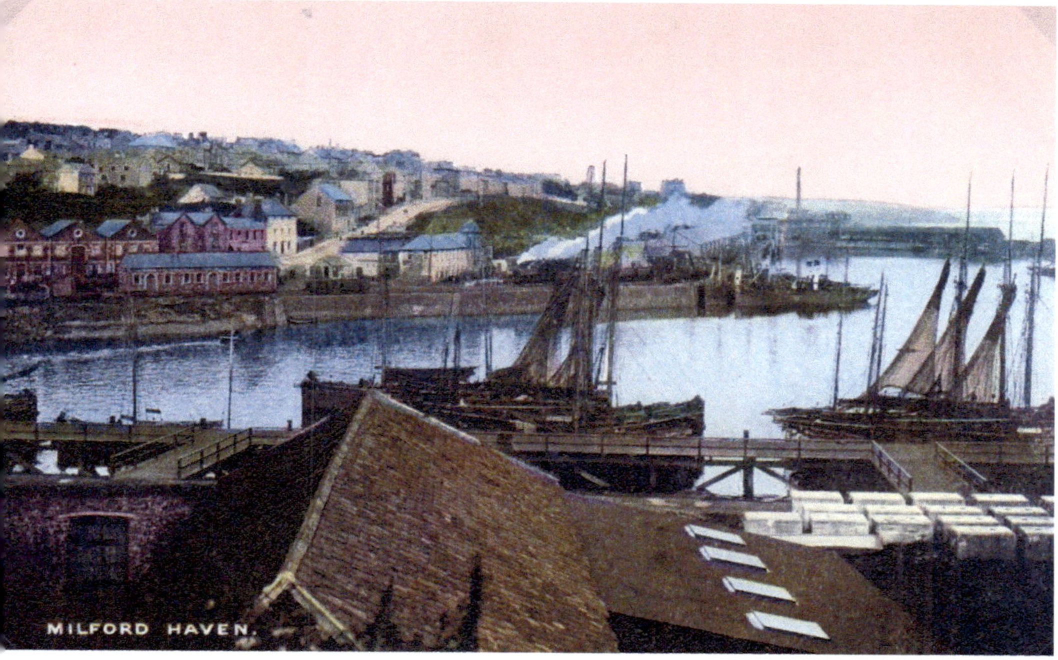

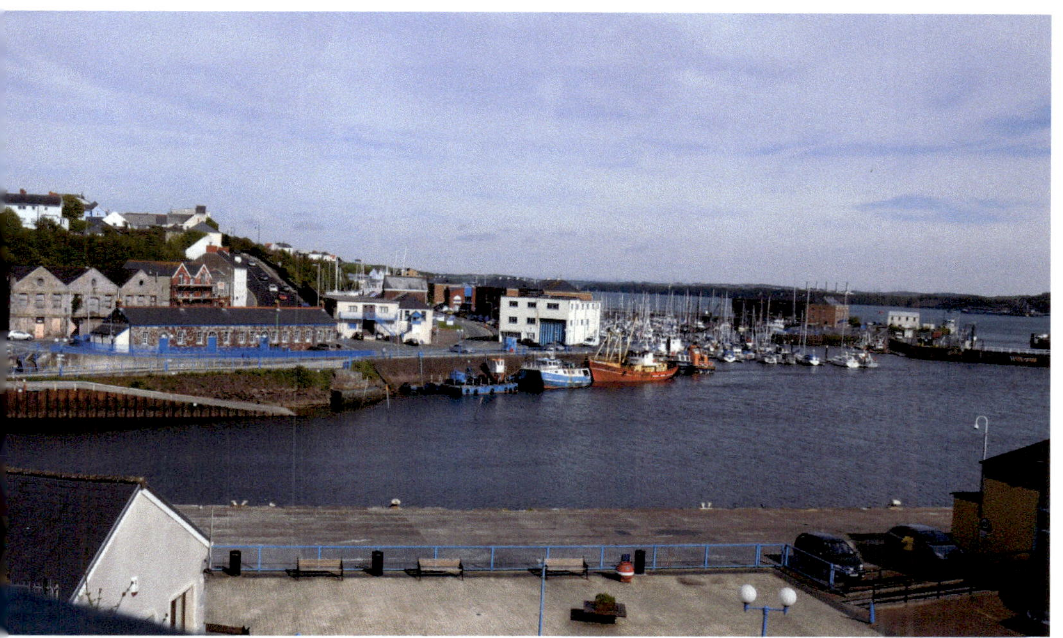

The Docks

The photographer has captured the steam of the railway engines leaving the fish market, their load of packed fish boxes probably destined for London or the Midlands. The buildings on the left have just about survived. On the immediate left is the now derelict red nineteenth-century warehouse on Victoria Road known as the Quay Stores and the Globe Hotel next door. These buildings were opposite the dock gatehouse, which was always manned as security was vital. Close to the entrance, which was realigned in the 1990s, the former Dock Company Office, with its three arched doorways, is now used as a veterinary surgery.

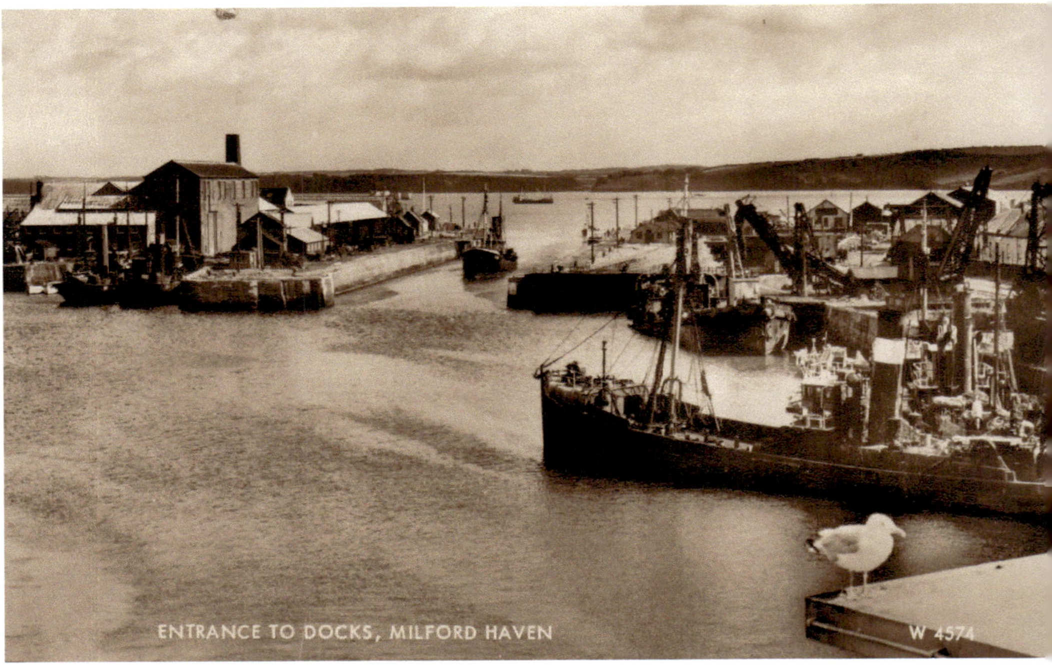

Entrance to the Docks

This card was posted in 1964 before the southern shore of the Haven had been developed. The later picture shows the five massive chimneys of the new Pembroke Power Station, which opened in 2012. It is the largest gas-fired power station in Europe. Also visible are the jetties and tanks of the Valero refinery. A Royal Navy ship lies in the dry dock.

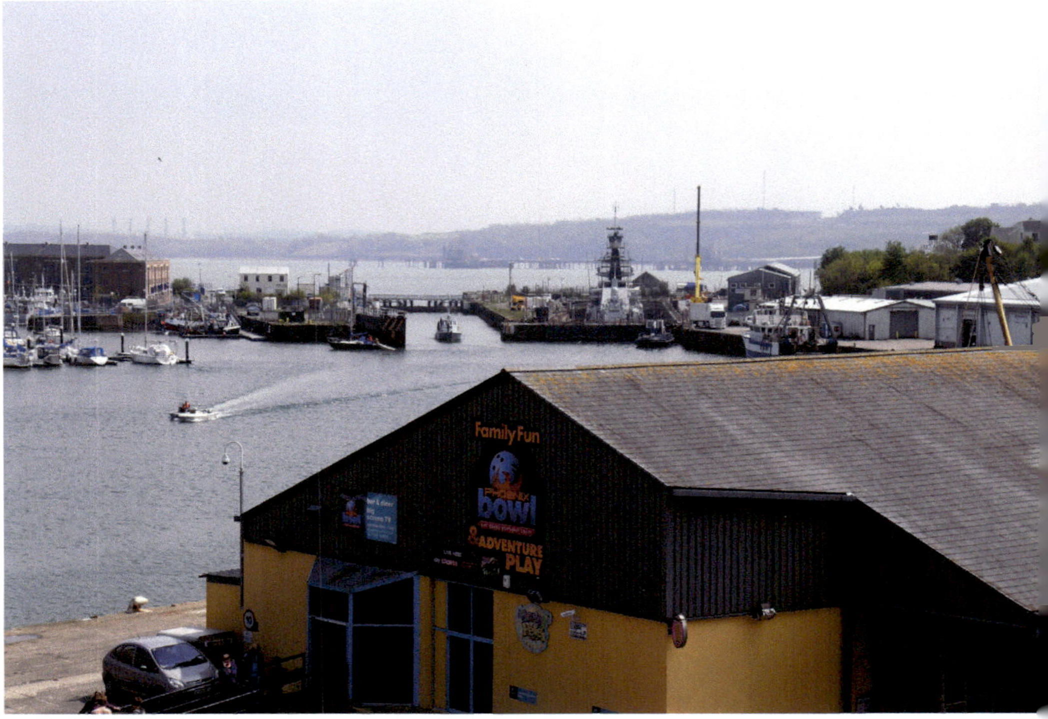

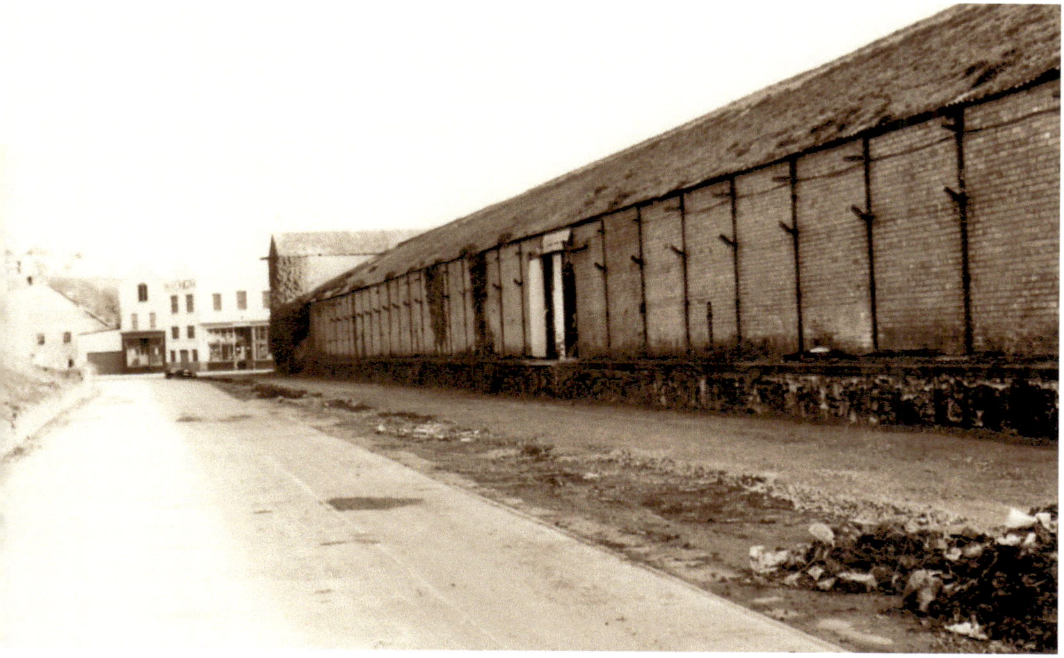

Rear of the Fish Market

The fish market started in the storage sheds built for the transatlantic trade, which never developed. In 1907, the sheds were extended and converted to create the fish market and in the 1930s there was further expansion. Railway loading bays and tracks were built alongside. The Milford Fish Market was acknowledged as one of the best in the UK. In the 1950s, the decline in the fishing trade caused a reduction in the size of the market, and by the early 1990s when this photograph was taken, the decline was complete. In its place now stands Nelson Quay and the red-brick marina-style buildings.

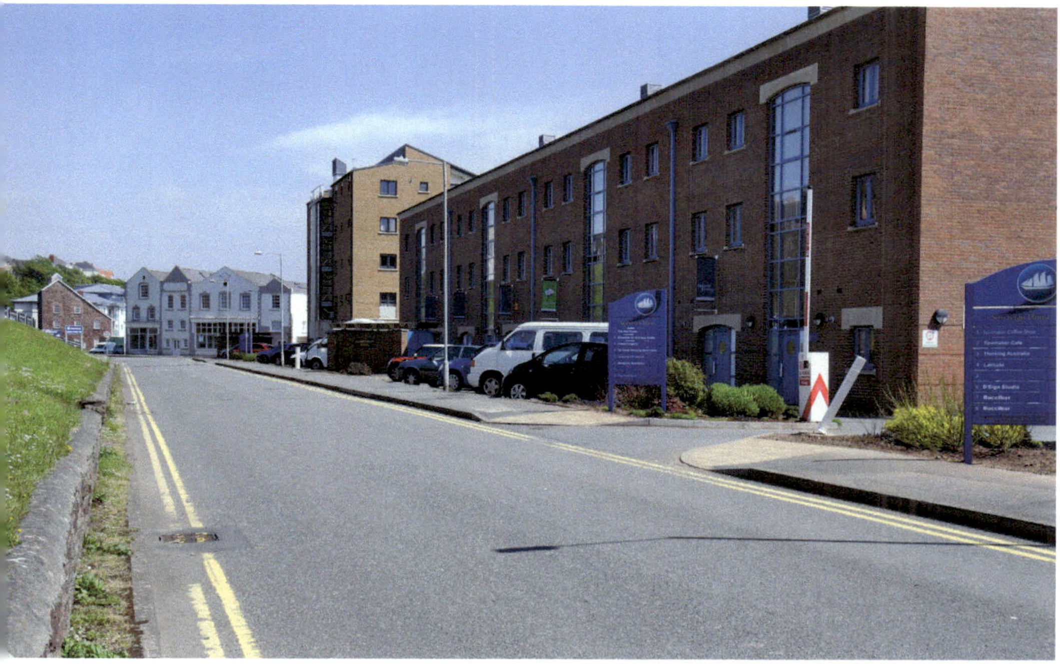

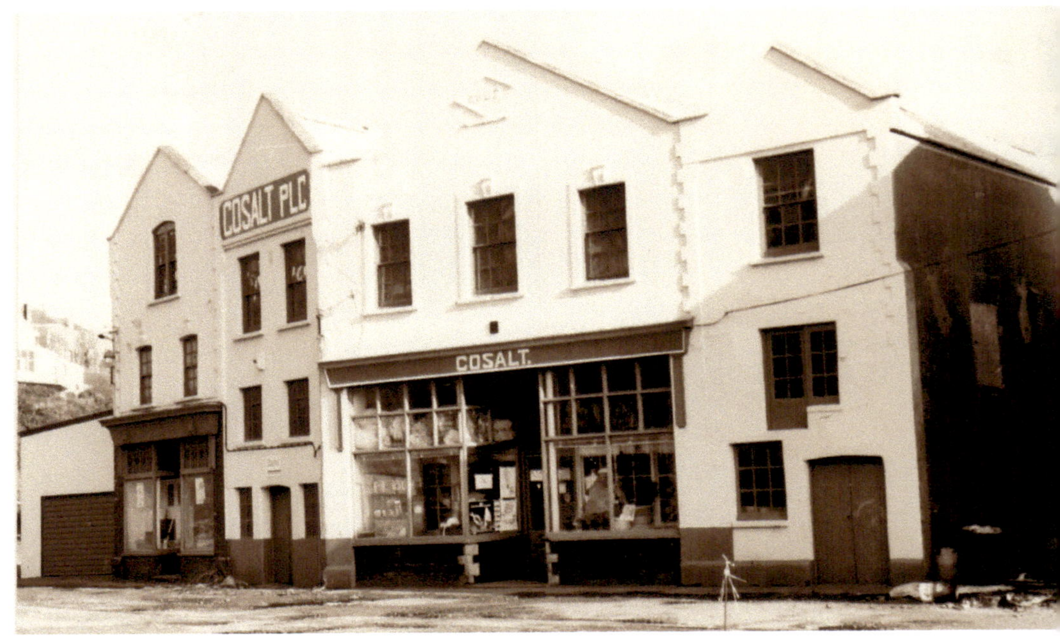

Ship Chandlers' Building

The black-and-white photograph recorded, in around 1990, the Cosalt ship chandlery, one of the notable buildings of Milford Docks. In 1873, a co-operative of Lincolnshire fishing vessel owners formed The Great Grimsby Coal Salt & Tanning Company. It serviced and supplied a variety of products and services required by the fishing and maritime industry: salt to preserve the fish caught, tanning to waterproof sails and rope, coal and clothing. The firm operated in many British ports. The date, 1907, can still be seen at the top of the building. In the coloured inset, it is just possible to see the initials of the company in the leaded light windows of the shopfront. They are still there!

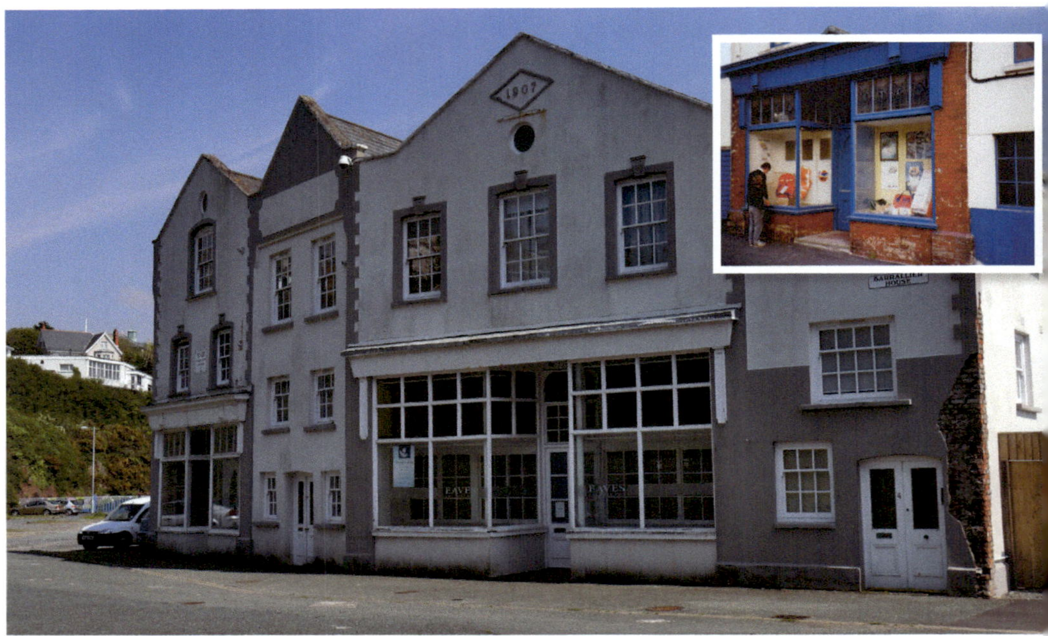

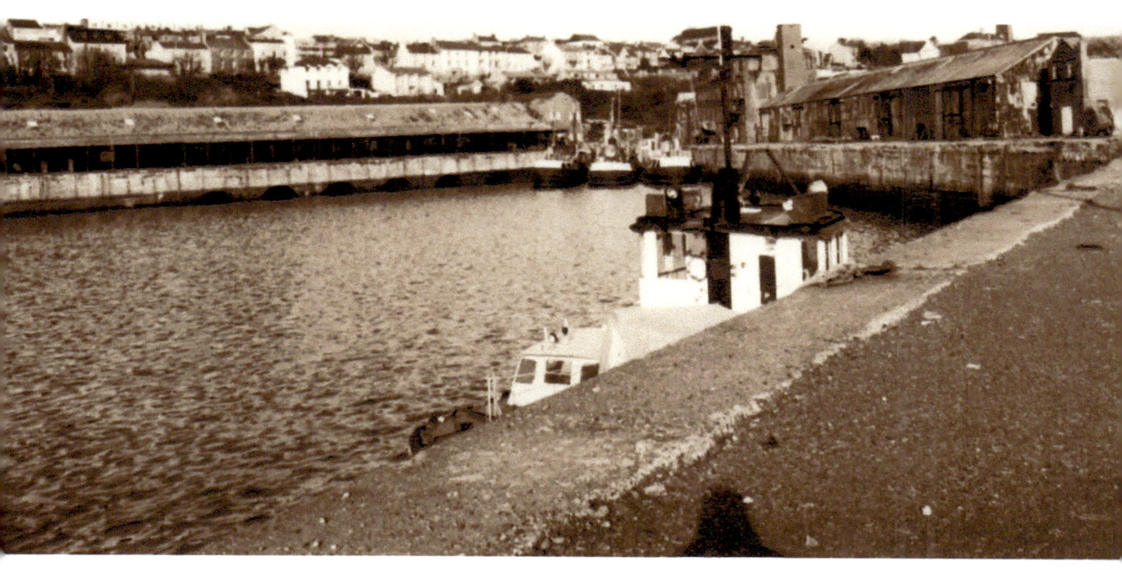

Fish Market

By the end of the 1980s, most of the dock buildings had fallen into disuse. Milford Marina was opened by the Duke of York at the start of the 1991 Tall Ships race and quickly developed to offer facilities for local and visiting yachtsmen. There are now over 300 berths for leisure craft. The inset photograph shows the marina in the very early days of development.

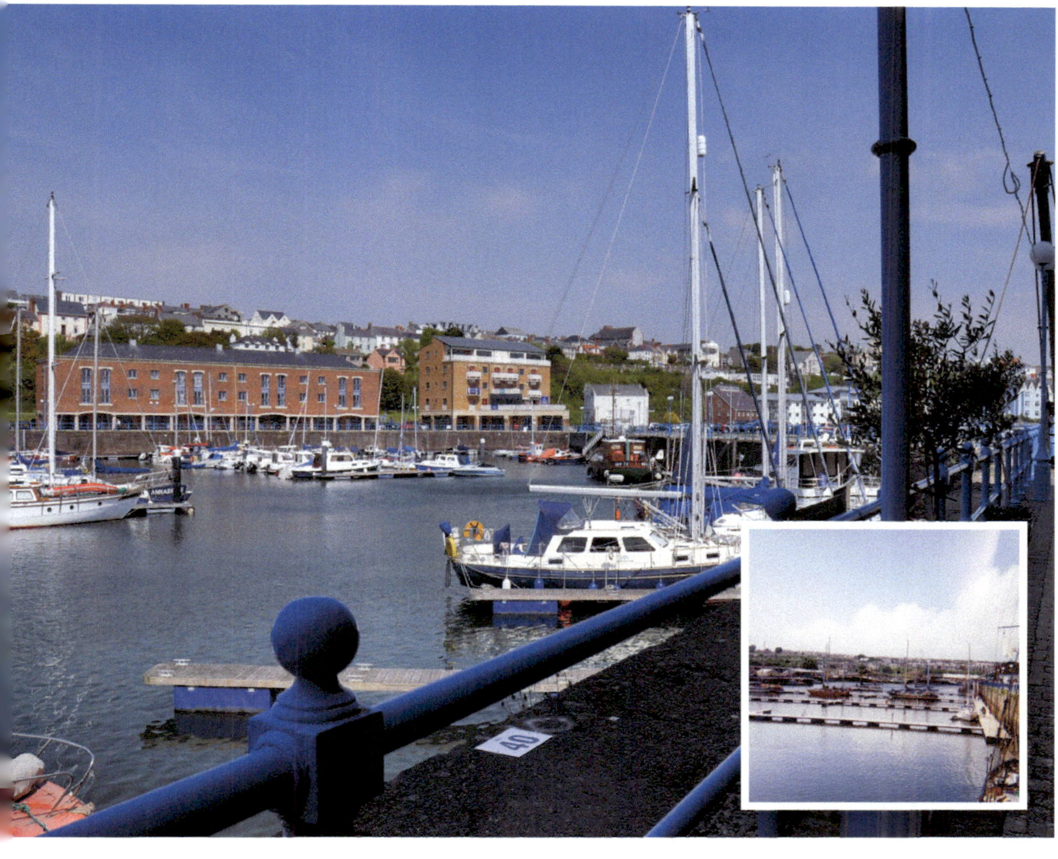

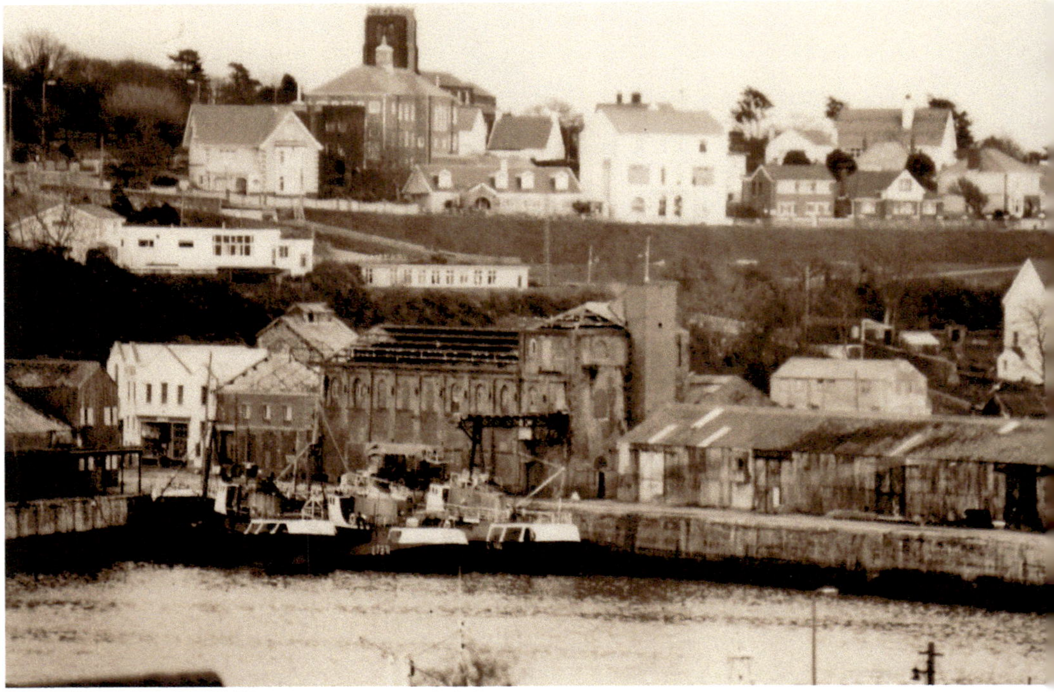

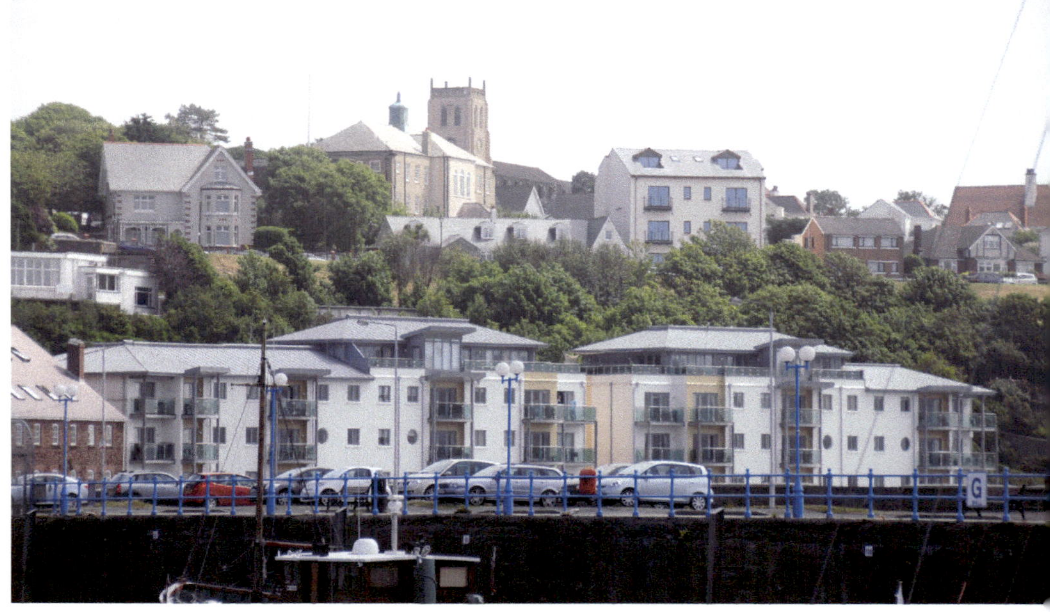

Docks

The 1990 photograph shows the old ice factory on the east side of the docks, which was being demolished as part of the docks redevelopment plans. Although acknowledged as an important part of Milford's history, the construction of the building made it impossible to find it an alternative use in the new, predominantly leisure-based complex. The site on which it stood now forms part of the walkway around the marina. The contemporary photograph shows the Smokehouse Quay development of desirable apartments above Milford Beach.

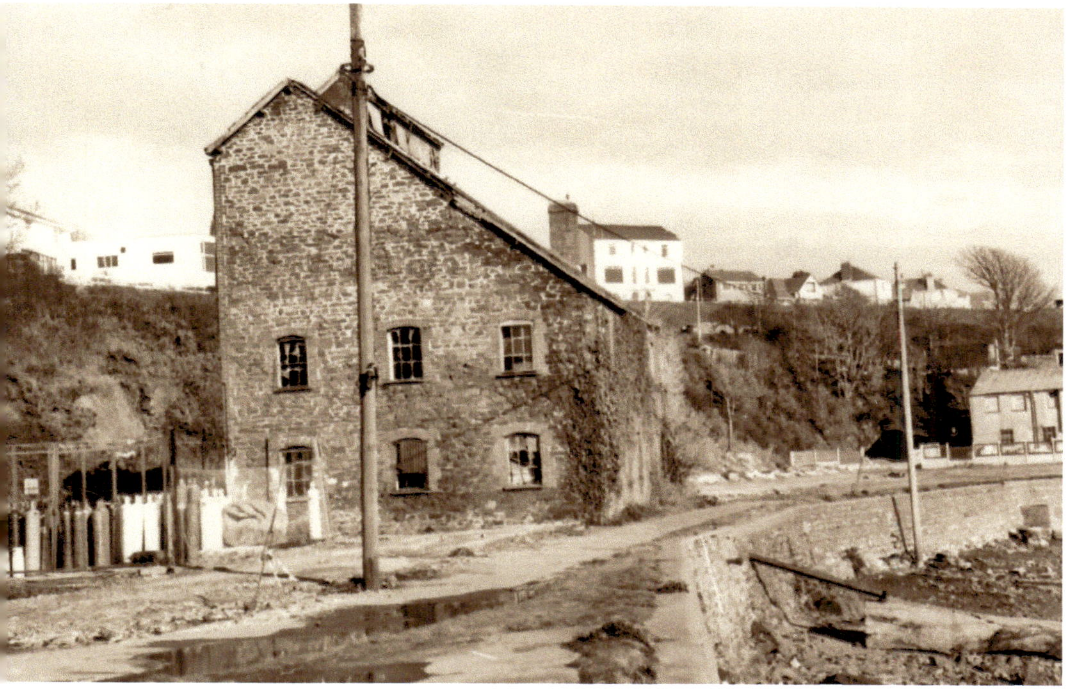

Smoke House

The Smoke House, a rectangular, tall, stone building with a long, sloping roof was built in around 1905, one of several built to satisfy demand for the smoked kipper. The 'Milford Caught, Milford Cured, Excel Kipper, cured with real oak chips' became famous and was greatly in demand nationally. The building has been restored, extra windows added, and converted into offices and apartments.

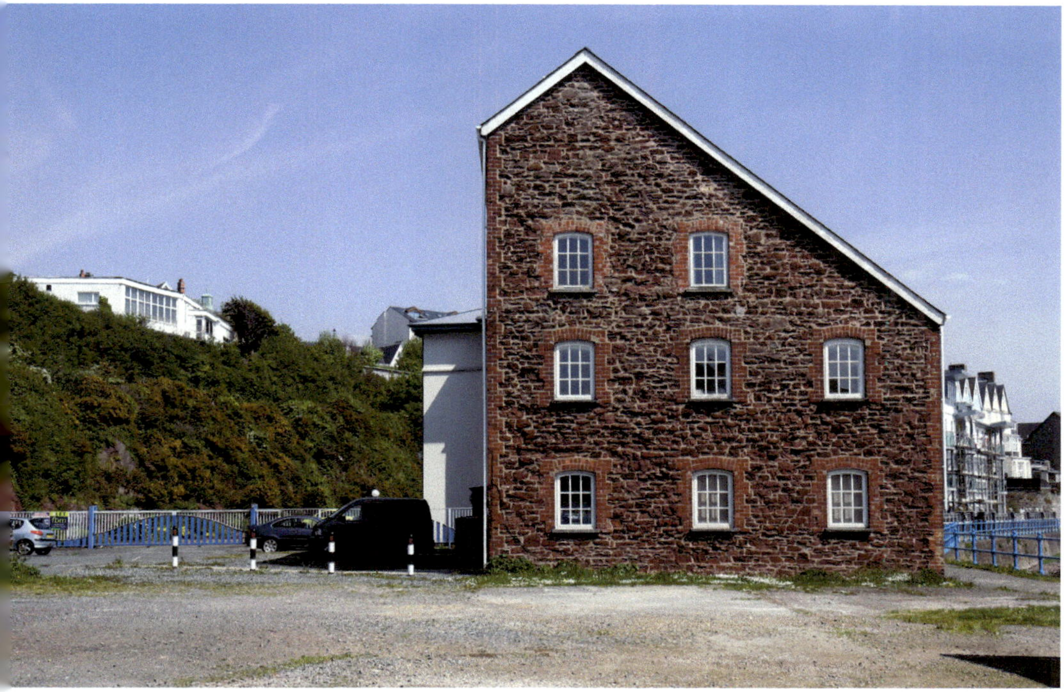

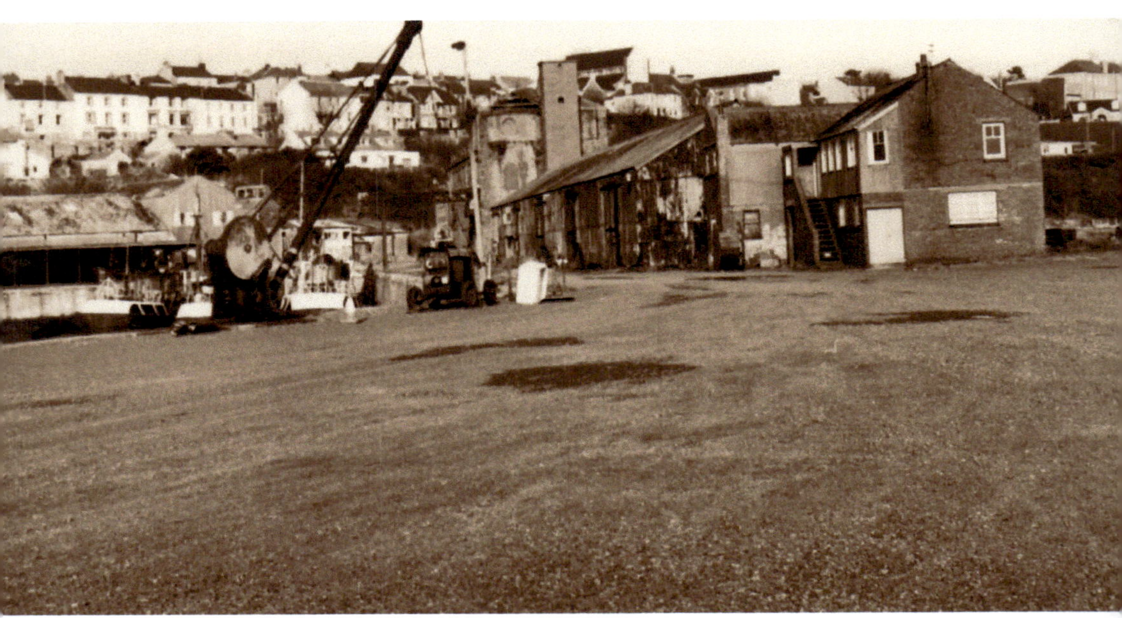

East End of Dock

In 1889, twelve fishing vessels used Milford and about 9,000 tons of fish were landed at the port. By 1908, the capacity had increased dramatically, with over 300 vessels landing almost 45,000 tons of fish. By the 1930s, 1,500 fishermen were always at sea with a similar number employed ashore. It was one of the biggest fishing ports in the UK. However, by the 1970s the annual catch had reduced to 2,000 tons of fish, and only about 200 people were employed in the industry.

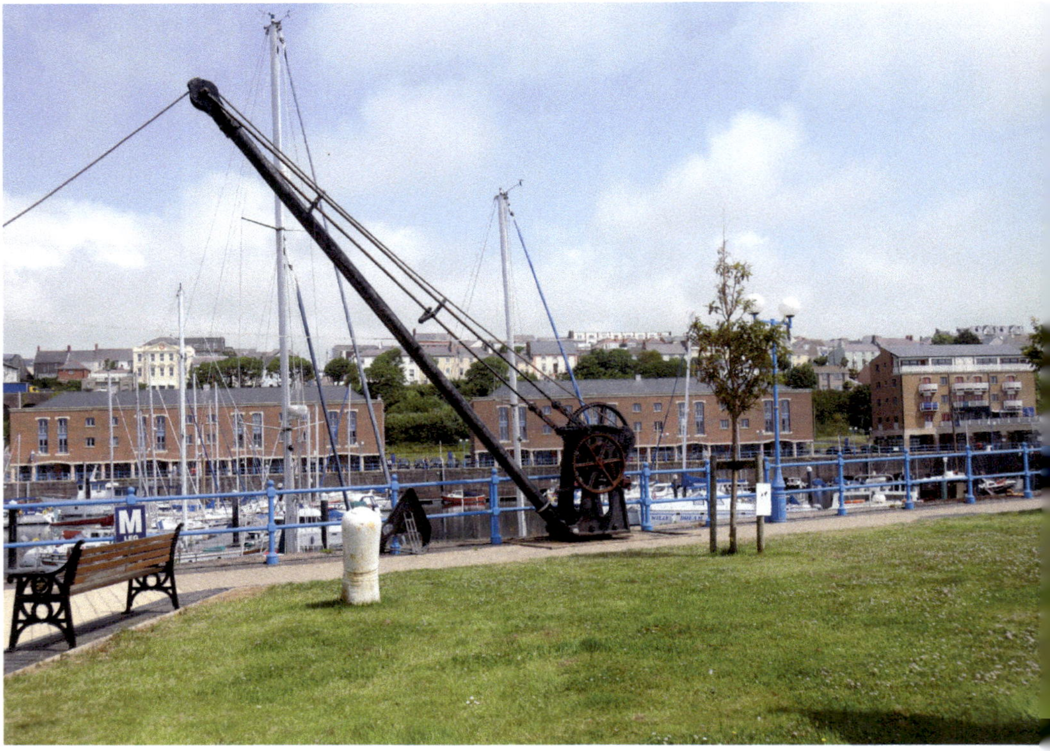

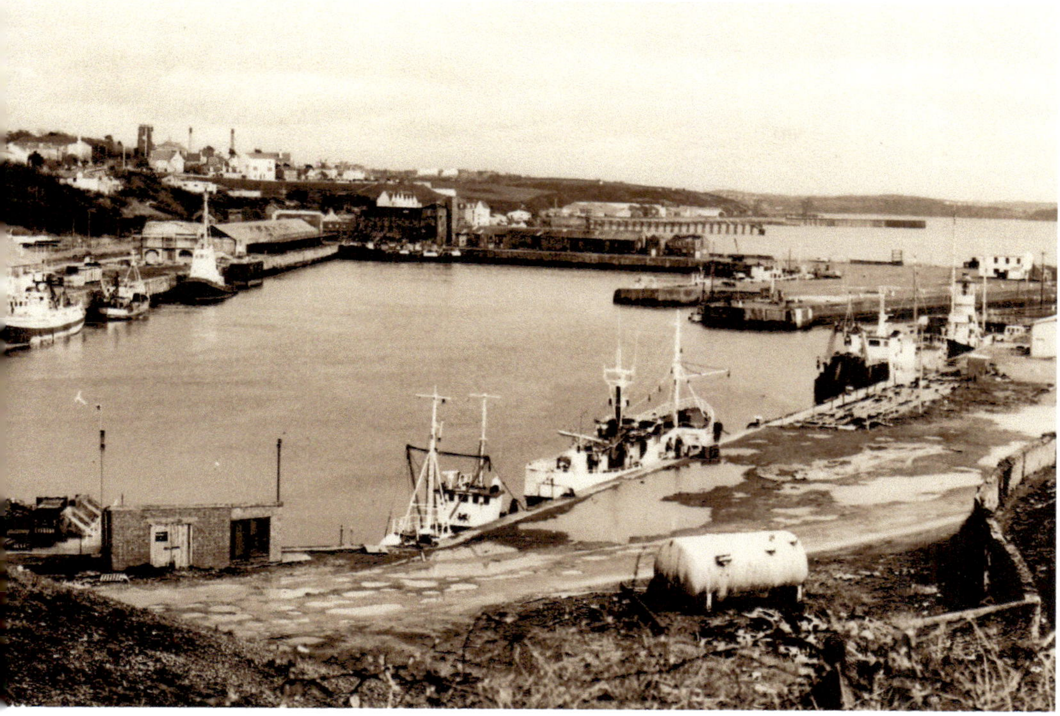

Dock from St Anne's Road

The last twenty years has seen the development from working docks to a leisure attraction. The dock area was crowded with workshops, offices, engineering facilities, chandlery stores and other buildings and apparatus which supported the fishing and maritime industries. The new marina has been designed with leisure and tourism paramount.

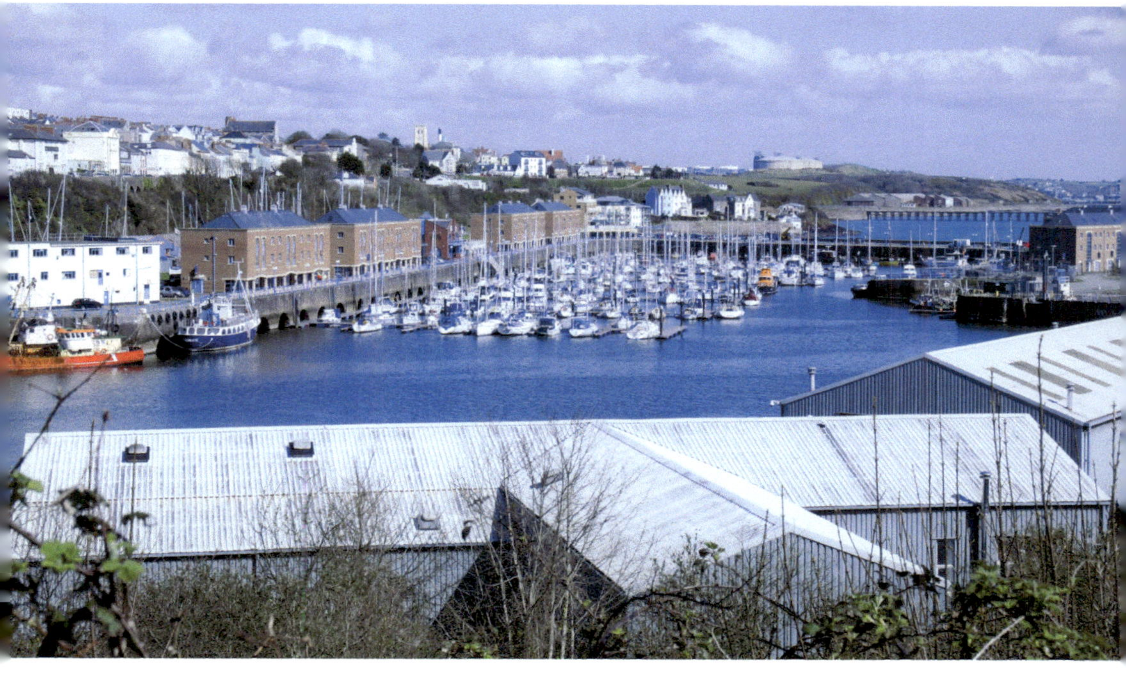

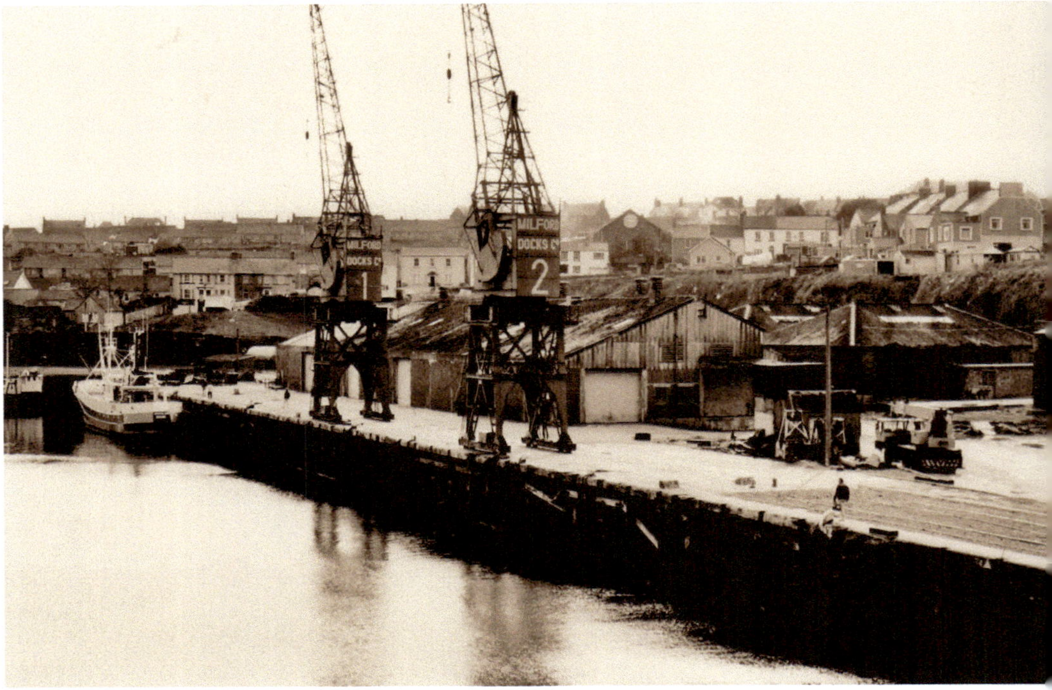

Docks

Although the photographs of the Hakin side of the docks have not been taken from the same angle, the later image shows the large international electronic fish auction hall, constructed in 1998, and one of the large refrigerated lorries that transport most of the catches to Europe.

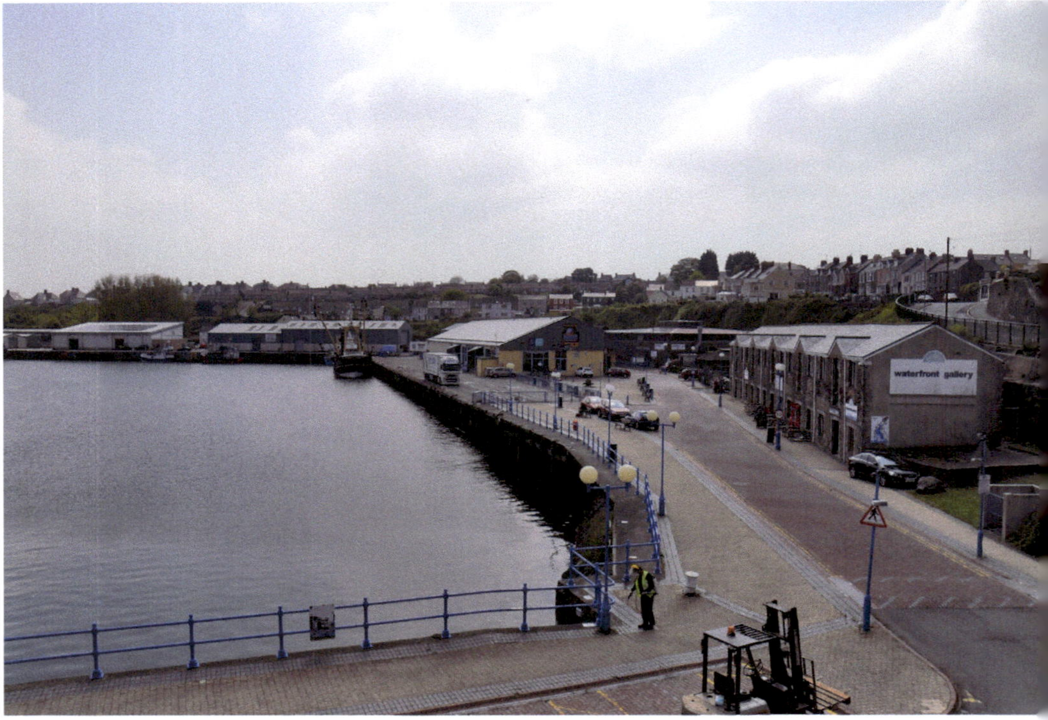

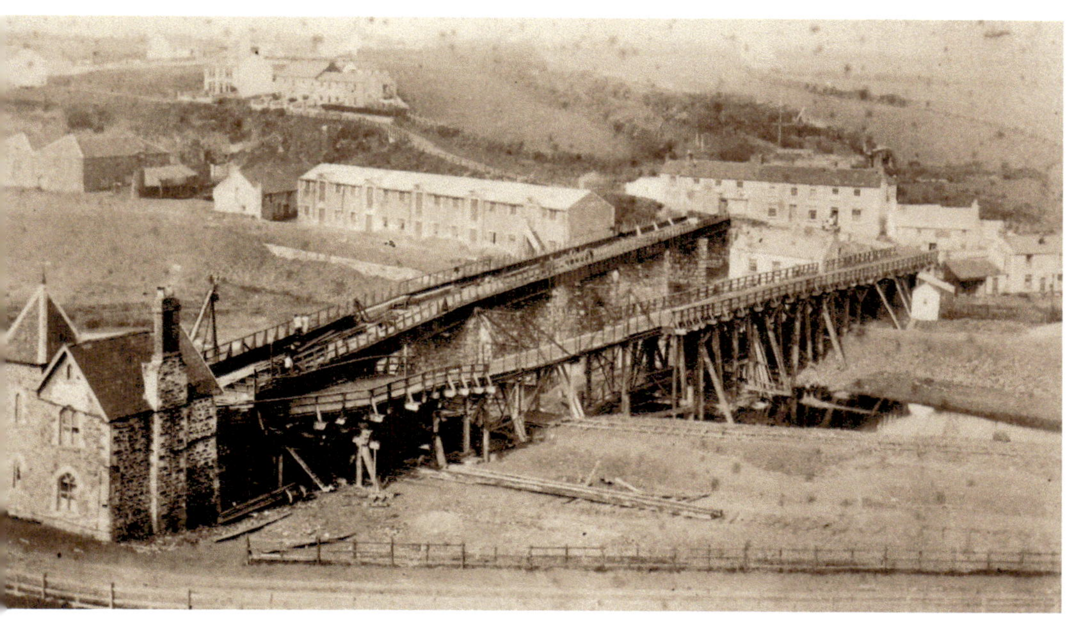

Victoria Bridge

Until 1859, the only way of crossing the water of Hubberston Pill from Hakin to Milford was by stepping stones and wooden planks at low water. The construction of a wooden bridge over the Pill was one of the developments following the passing of the Milford Improvement Act in 1857. The railway, built a few years after, passed under it. This picture was taken in around 1887 when the second bridge (on the left), made of iron, was under construction. The toll house at the Milford end of the bridge is clearly visible. The Sail Loft, on the Hakin side, was restored in 1992, creating a large art and craft gallery on the first floor, and at the same time a brick pavement and public seating were installed in front of the building.

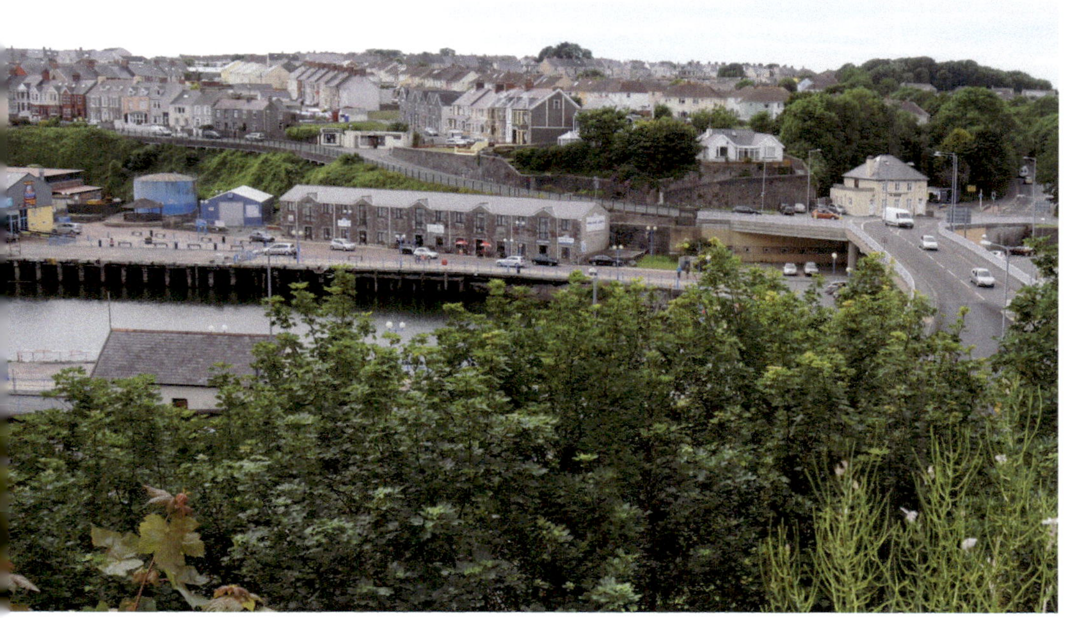

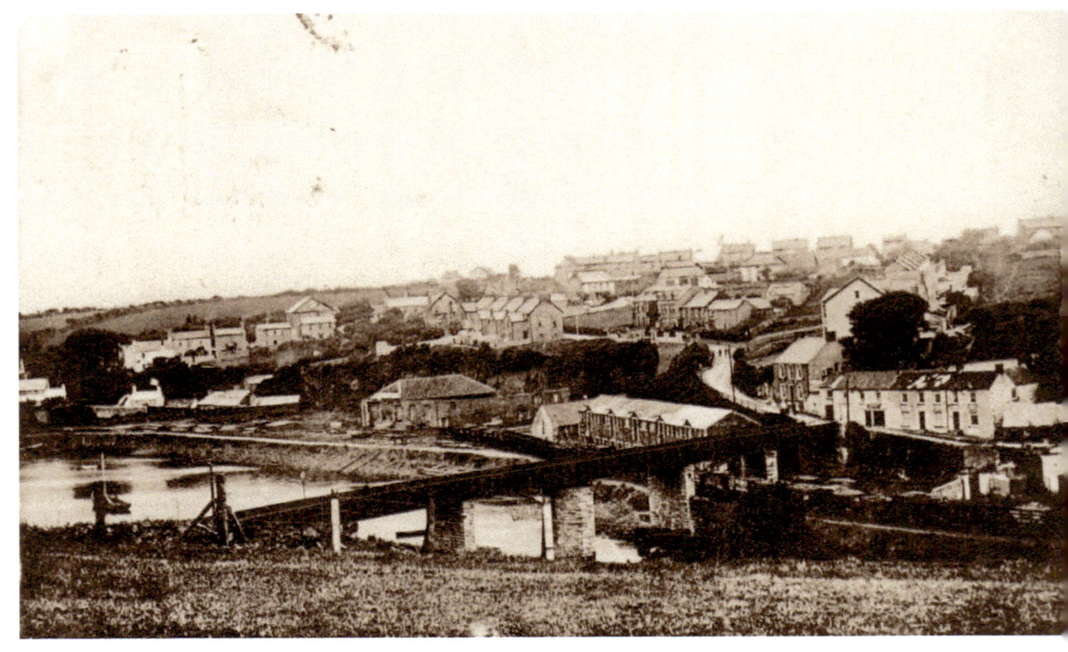

Victoria Bridge

This view of Hakin was taken from the area where the Torch Theatre now stands. Rehoboth chapel was founded in 1840 for Welsh-speaking sailors and workers and is still a place of worship, being part of the Presbyterian Church of Wales. Housing in Hakin has increased greatly. To commemorate King George IV's unexpected visit to the town in 1821, an ornate plaque was erected on a warehouse close to where he landed. In 1859, the plaque was fixed to the toll house. It can now be found at the side of the new bridge, alongside memorials marking the opening of the 1932 and 1989 bridges.

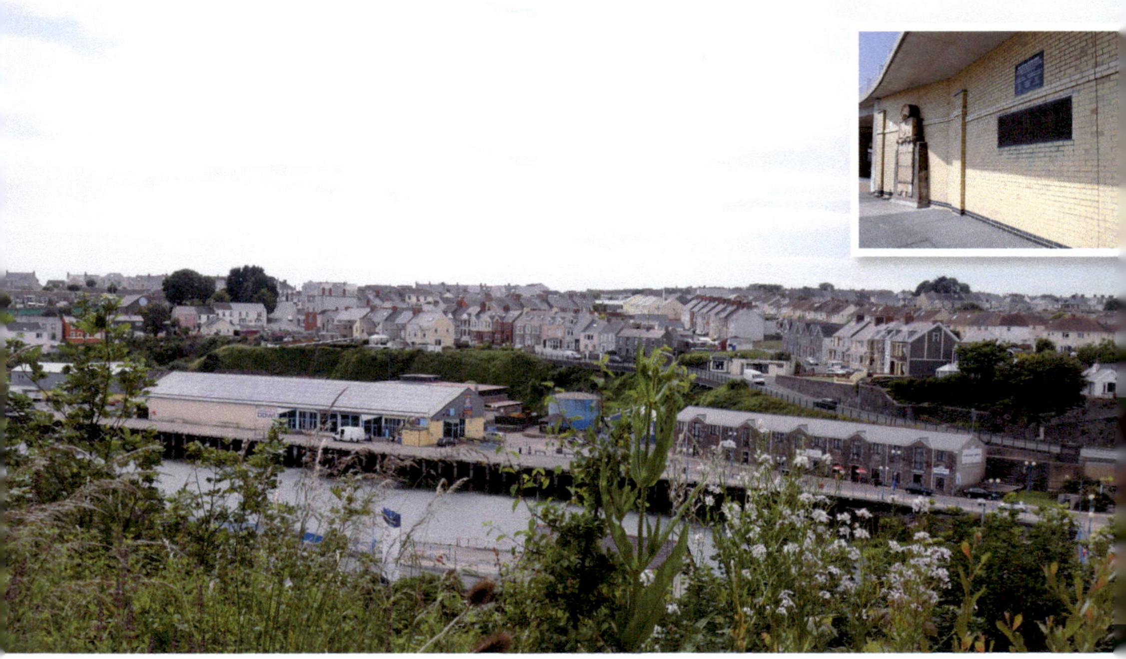

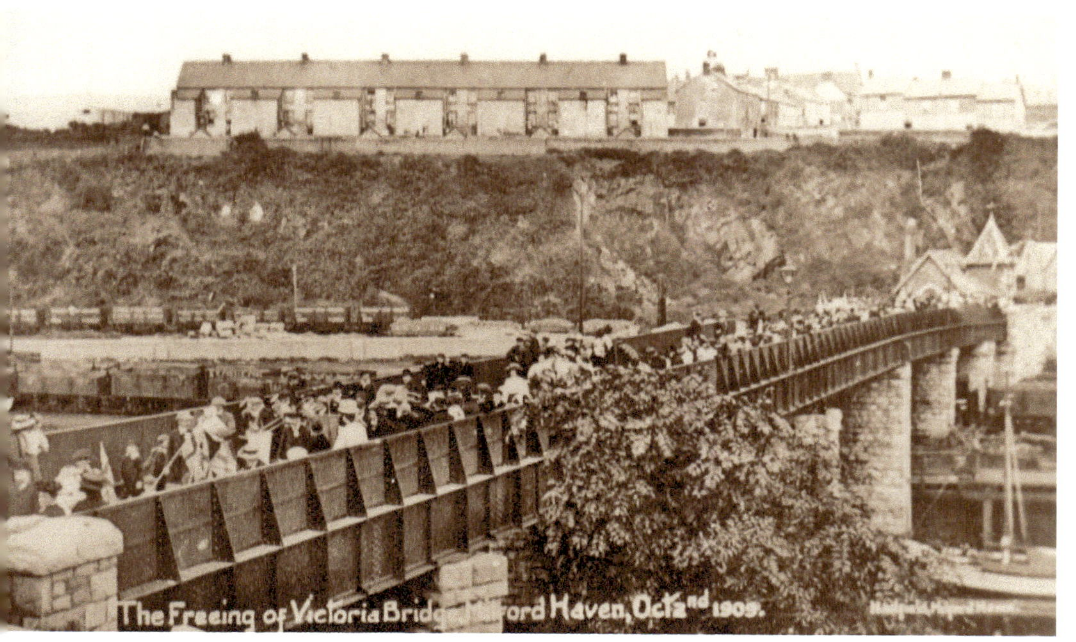

The Freeing of Victoria Bridge

This photograph was taken from the Hakin end of the bridge in 1909 when the toll was abolished. The people of Hakin had strongly objected to the continued imposition of the toll, a halfpenny per person and sixpence for a cart. A letter to the local press in 1905 said, 'It is surely time that this survival of the turnpike age should be done away with. Why should the town of Milford draw a revenue from the poor cottagers and farmers living on the Hakin side, most of them struggling to make ends meet?' There was a celebration when it was lifted and commemorative mugs were presented to all the children of Hakin. The contemporary photograph is taken from a different angle in order to show the Torch Theatre and new housing in St Peter's Road.

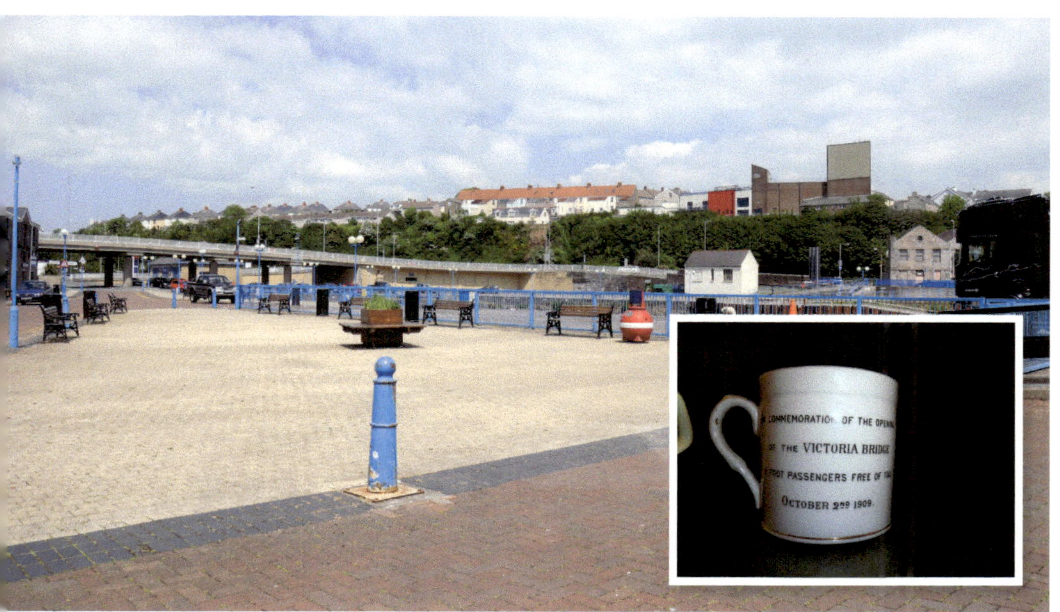

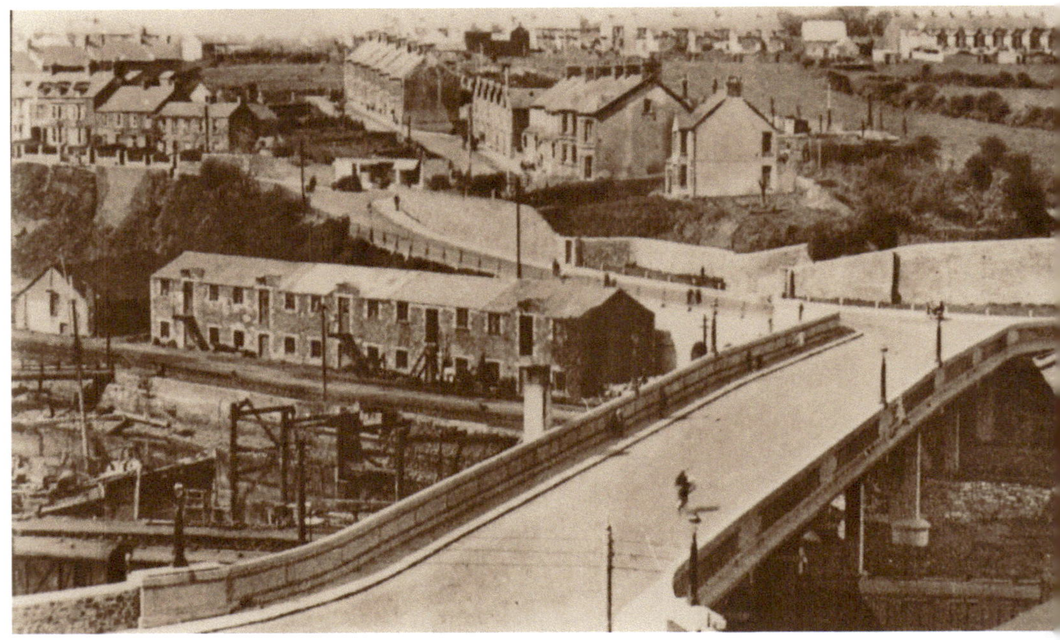

Victoria Bridge

This, the third bridge over Hubberston Pill, opened in 1933, and again a commemorative mug was issued. Some of the local population doubted the safety of the new bridge and eight steam rollers were driven across in convoy to prove its strength. Several properties near the bridge had to be demolished to make way for a new approach road. A large ship is under repair on the slipway to the left of the bridge. Along the top of the view are the backs of the houses in Waterloo Road. The current photograph shows the post-war housing development in St Lawrence Avenue, although Gwili Road and St Anne's Road are little changed.

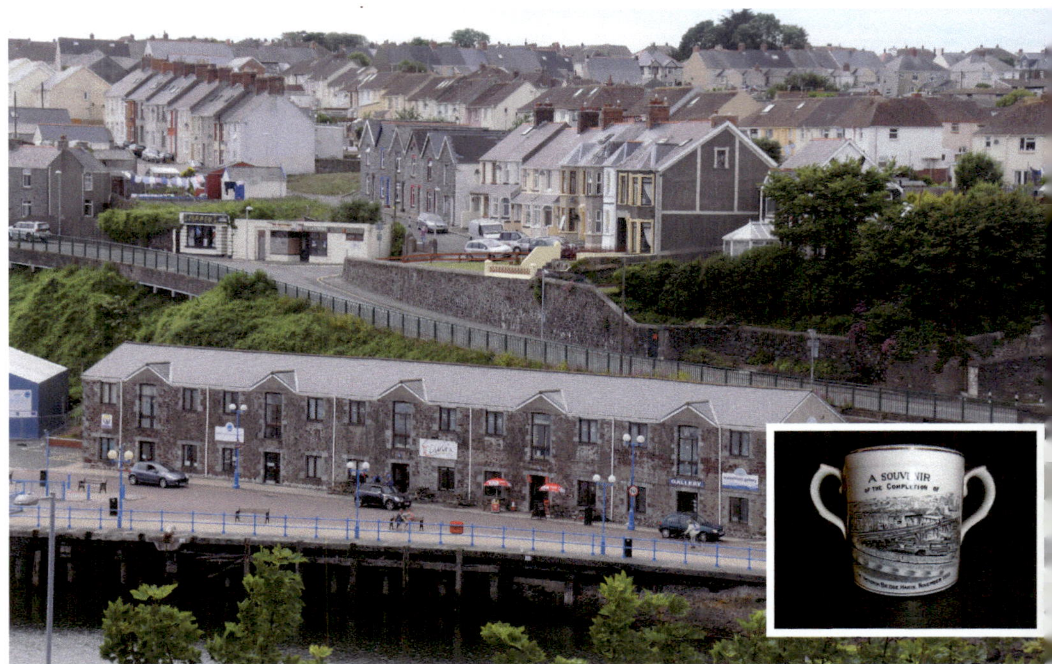

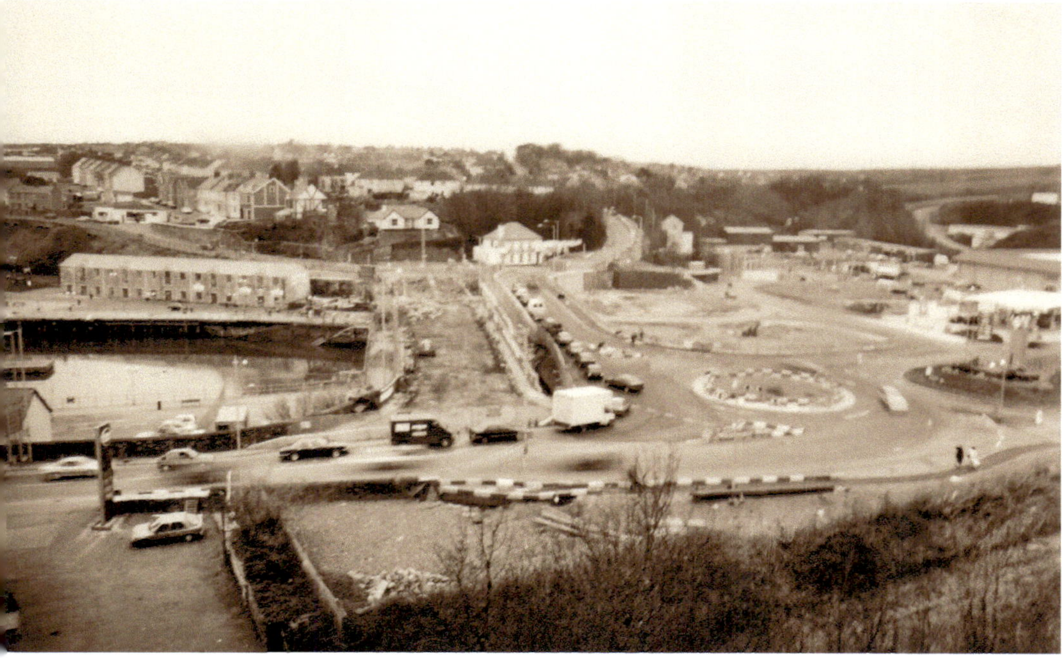

Bridge

In 1996 it was reported that the 1933 Victoria Bridge had major structural problems and it was necessary to replace it with the fourth bridge to span the Pill. This new bridge linked Hakin with a new roundabout serving the docks, railway station and the development at Havens Head. The photograph shows the traffic on the new bridge, alongside the older structure.

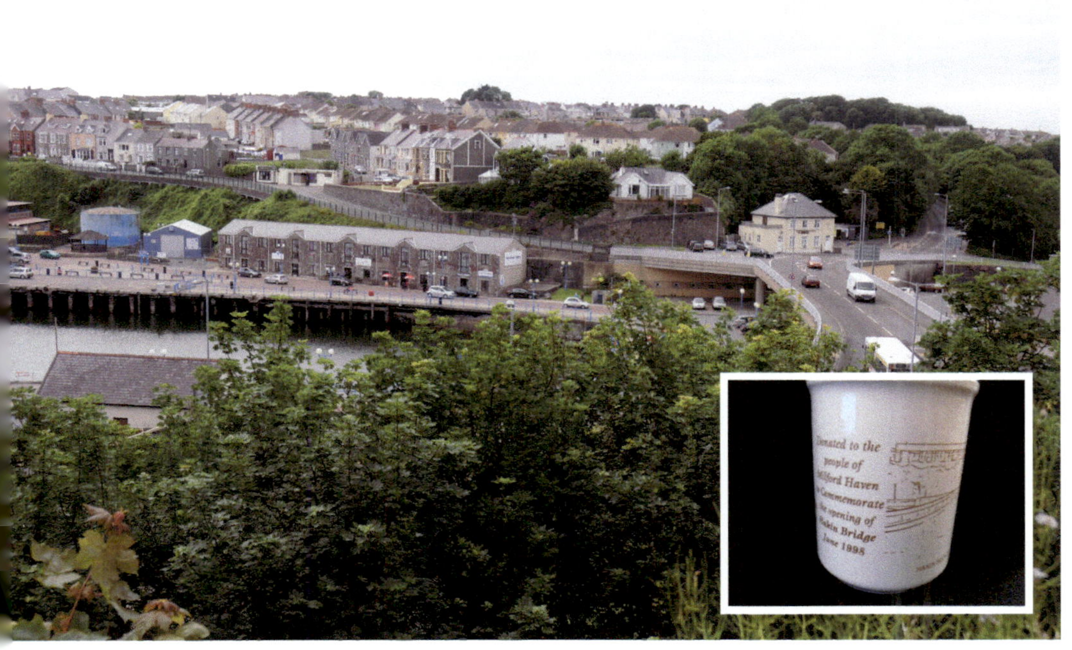

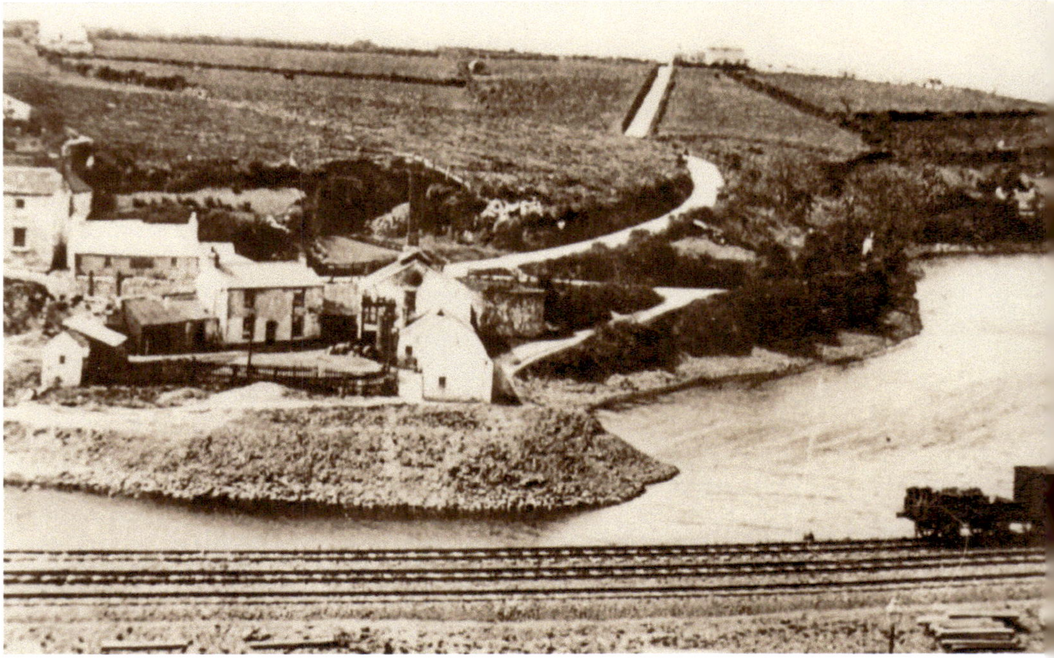

Hakin

This picture clearly shows the water of Hubberston Pill at Havens Head. The area now accommodates the retail and business parks. The railway lines in the foreground extended into the docks complex. The steep St Lawrence Hill (known locally as Captain James' Hill, as his home was at the top) leads up to Hubberston. Many local houses were built from stone taken from the quarry, which can now be seen just behind the Bridge Inn.

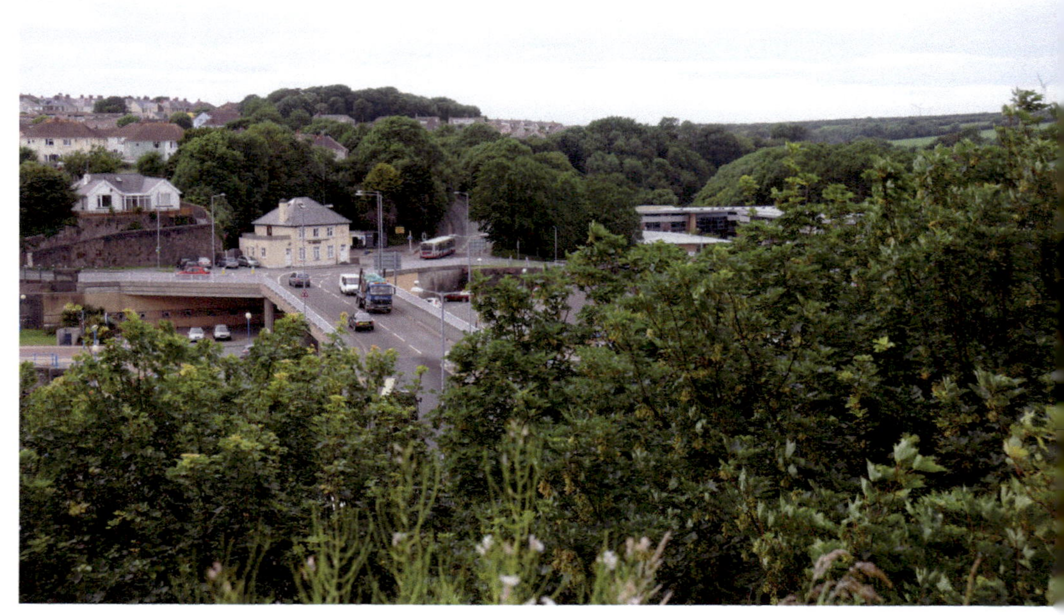

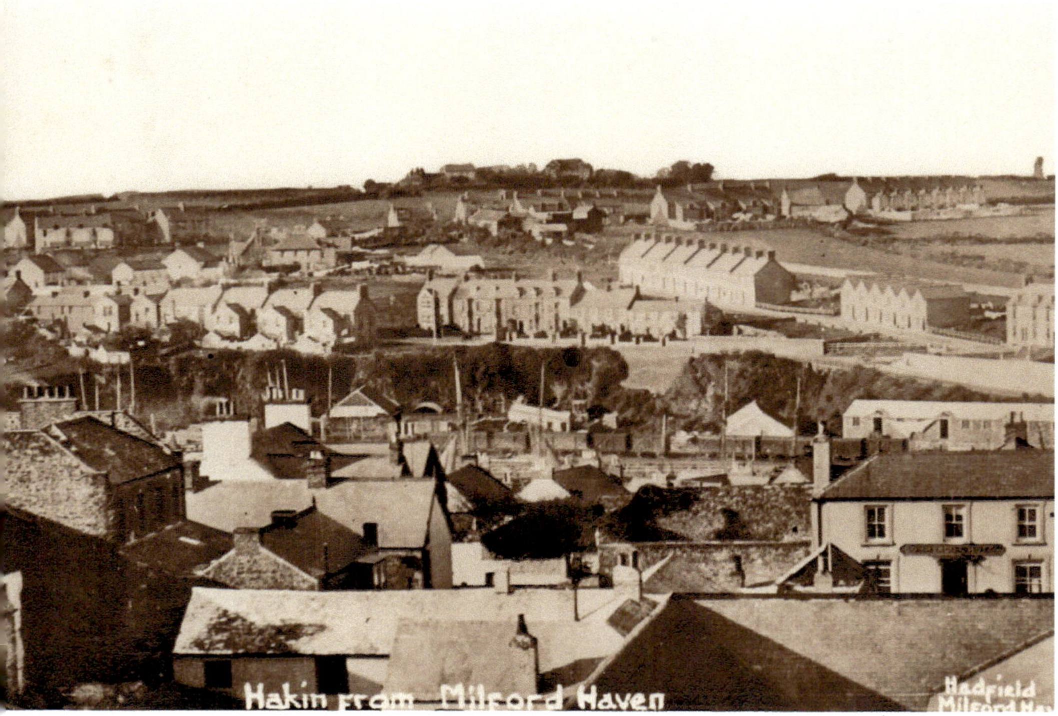

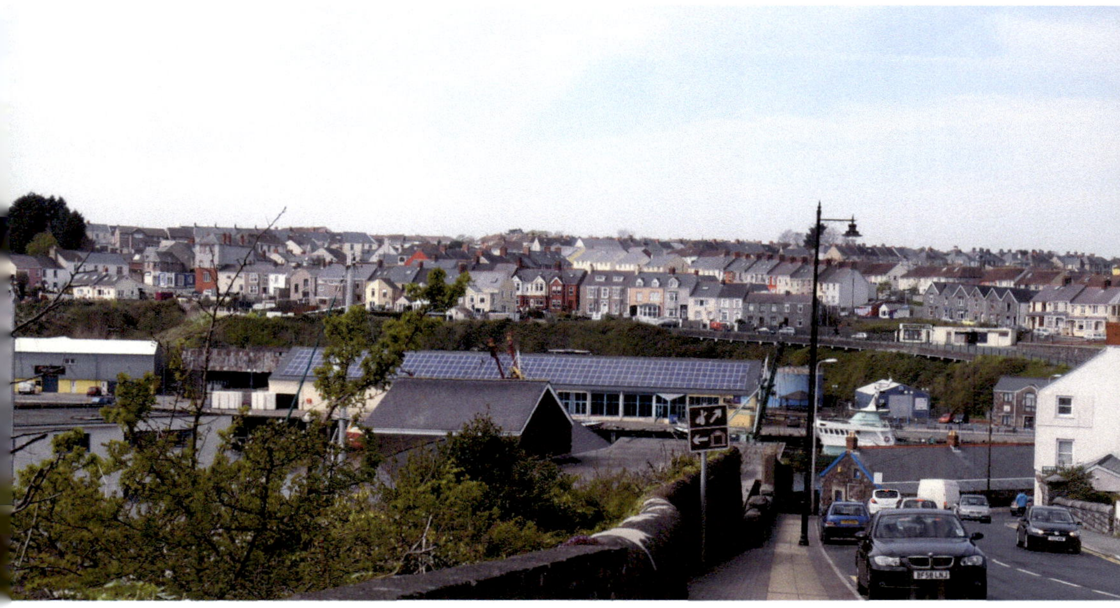

Hakin from Milford

The most striking feature of the earlier postcard is the sparsely built-up area in Hakin. Along the top it is possible to make out the observatory and the adjoining large house, now known as Observatory Hall. Nearby, one side of Waterloo Road, where several terraced houses were built around the turn of the twentieth century, runs either side of Dairy Park Farm House. Development in Gwili Road, St Anne's Road and the Ropewalk is well underway. The contemporary photograph shows the large amount of housing built over the last century.

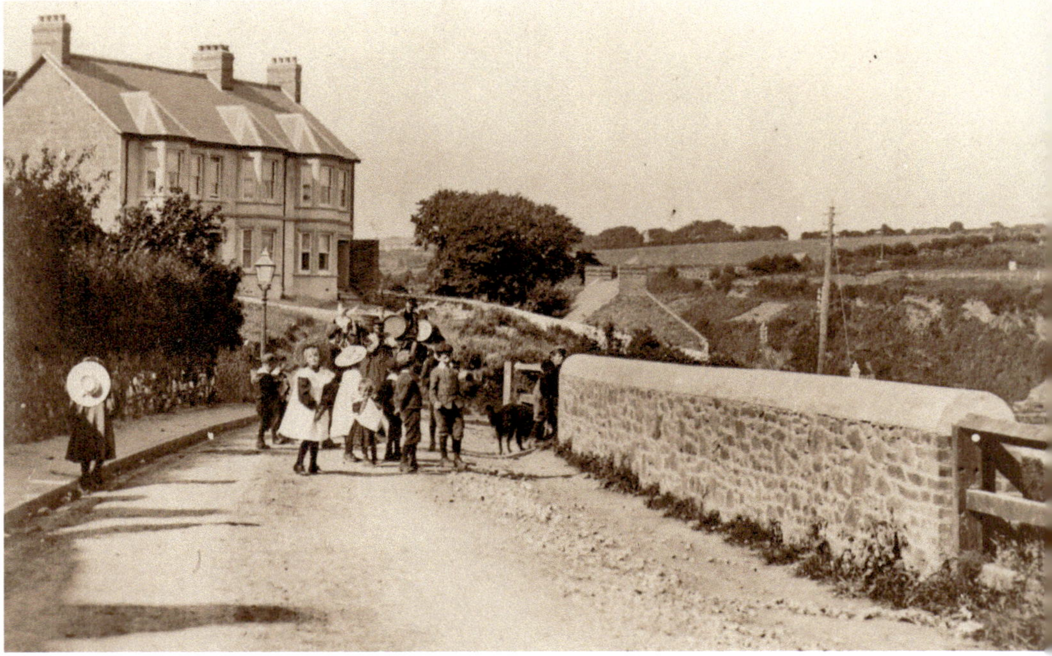

Gwili Road

This view of houses in Gwili Road from St Anne's Road with a group of young people would have been taken in the early years of the twentieth century. The 1911 census shows that, almost without exception, the workers in every household were involved in trades linked to the sea, such as deep sea fishermen, ships' engineers and master mariners. Many of them had moved to the town from Scarborough, Hull or Yarmouth.

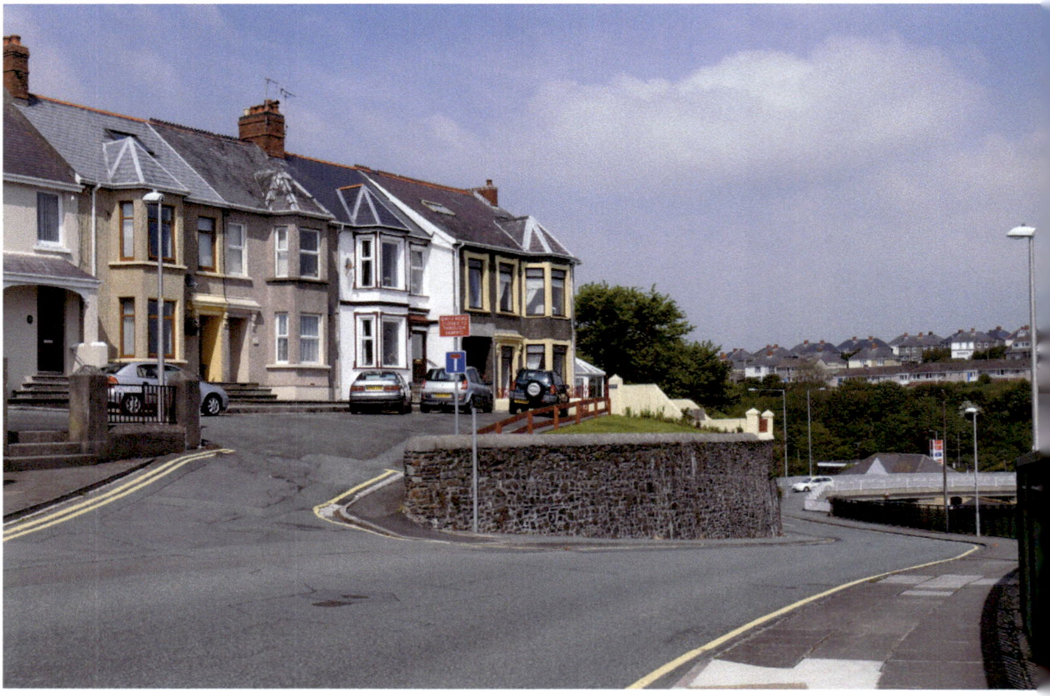

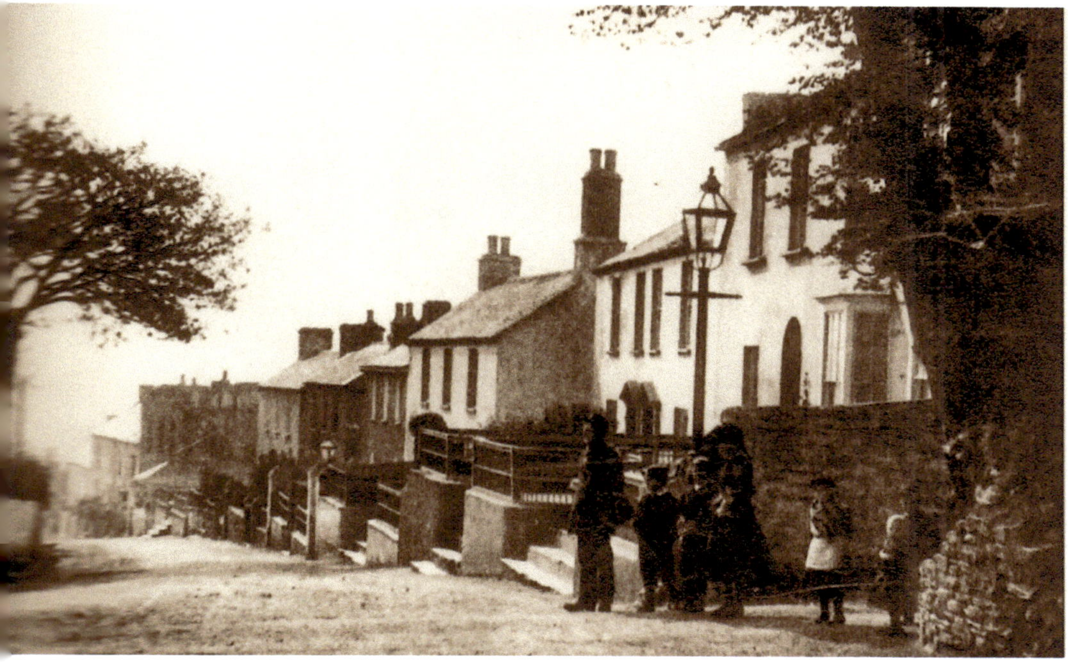

Hakin

This photograph was taken at the junction of Lower Hill Street and Spikes Lane in around 1900. Significant changes have been made to this residential area over the century, which runs down to the Hakin dockside. Known just as Hill Street in 1901, the census of that year records a population of about 150 in the street, with occupations such as shipping cashier, dock gatekeeper and net braider.

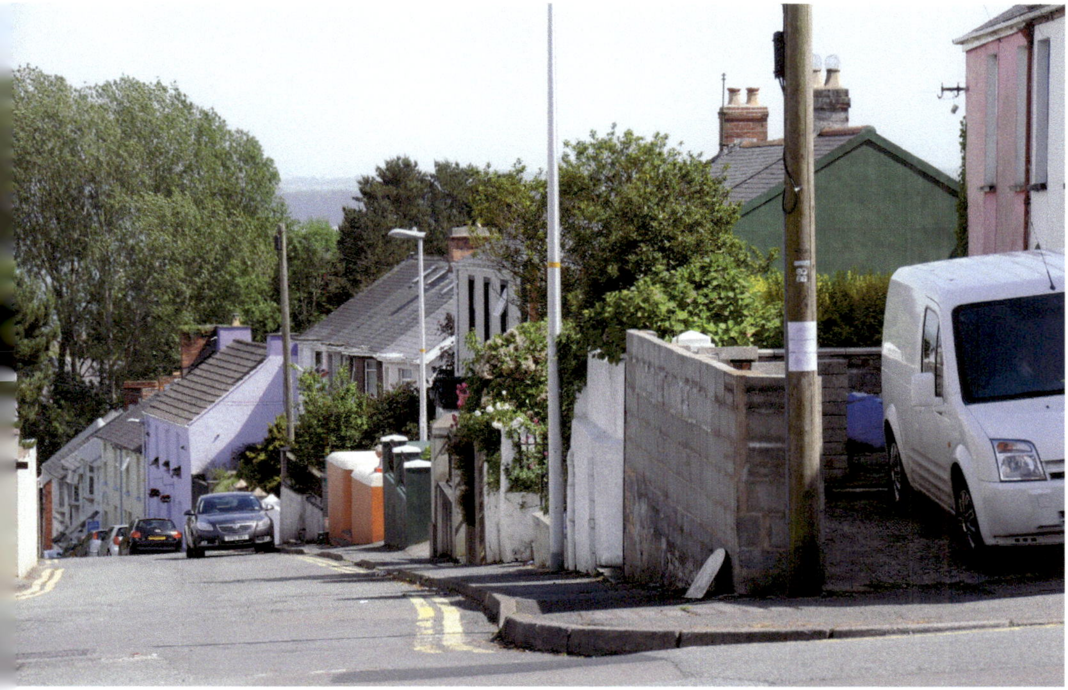

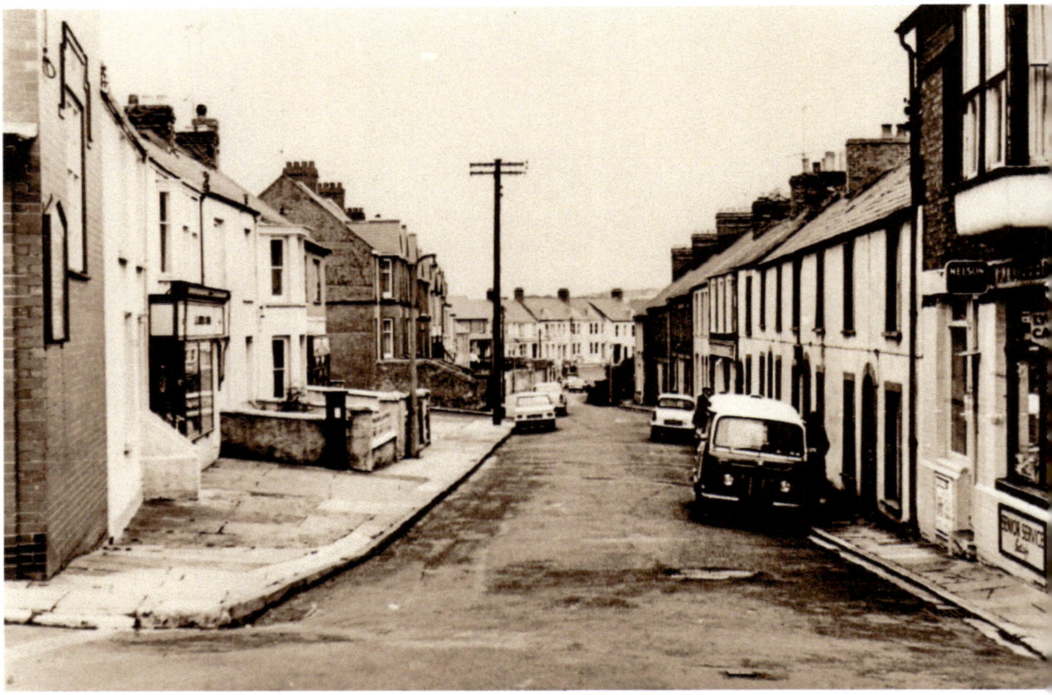

St Anne's Road

Until the latter part of the twentieth century Hakin supported a variety of small shops such as newsagents, a bakery, off licence and general stores. These shops in St Anne's Road, together with several on Waterloo Square, closed many years ago. A post office, fish and chip shop and a general store have survived, as has the post box in St Anne's Road!

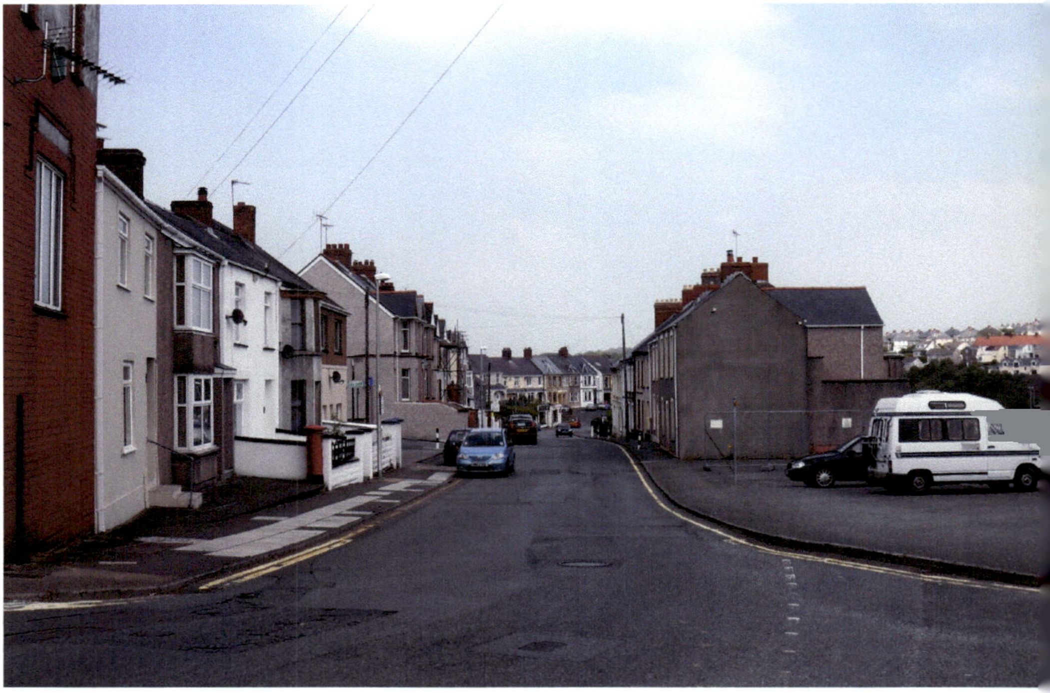

Observatory

Overlooking the Haven, this octagonal two-storey dome, with slit openings for telescopes, was intended to be the centre of Charles Greville's proposed 'College of King George the Third'. He intended including lecture rooms to teach mathematics, military and naval and civil engineering, ship construction, navigation, surveying and drawing. According to Fenton, published in 1811, an astronomer had already been appointed and so 'Milford can boast of an observatory furnished with a most extensive apparatus of instruments by the first makers'. Unfortunately, the project was abandoned after Greville's death in 1809. It now lies in ruins, but is recorded in the name of the adjoining Observatory Hall.

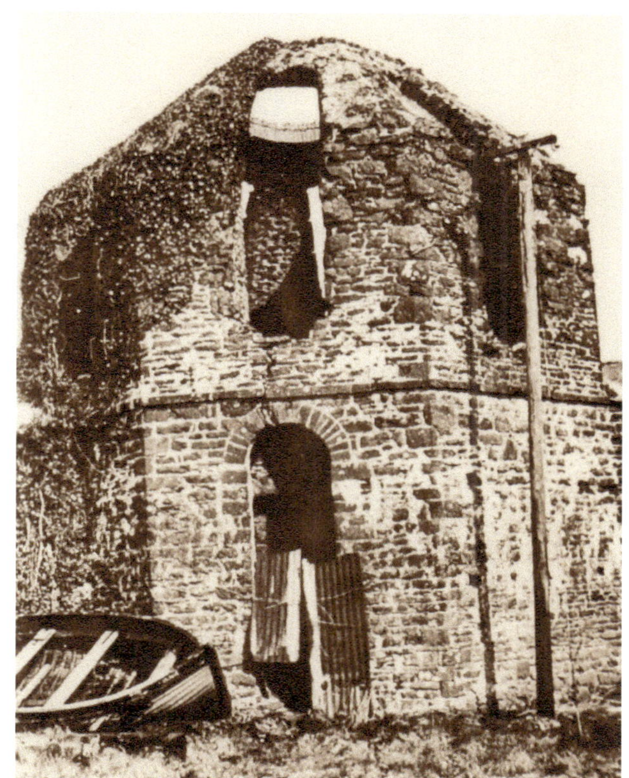

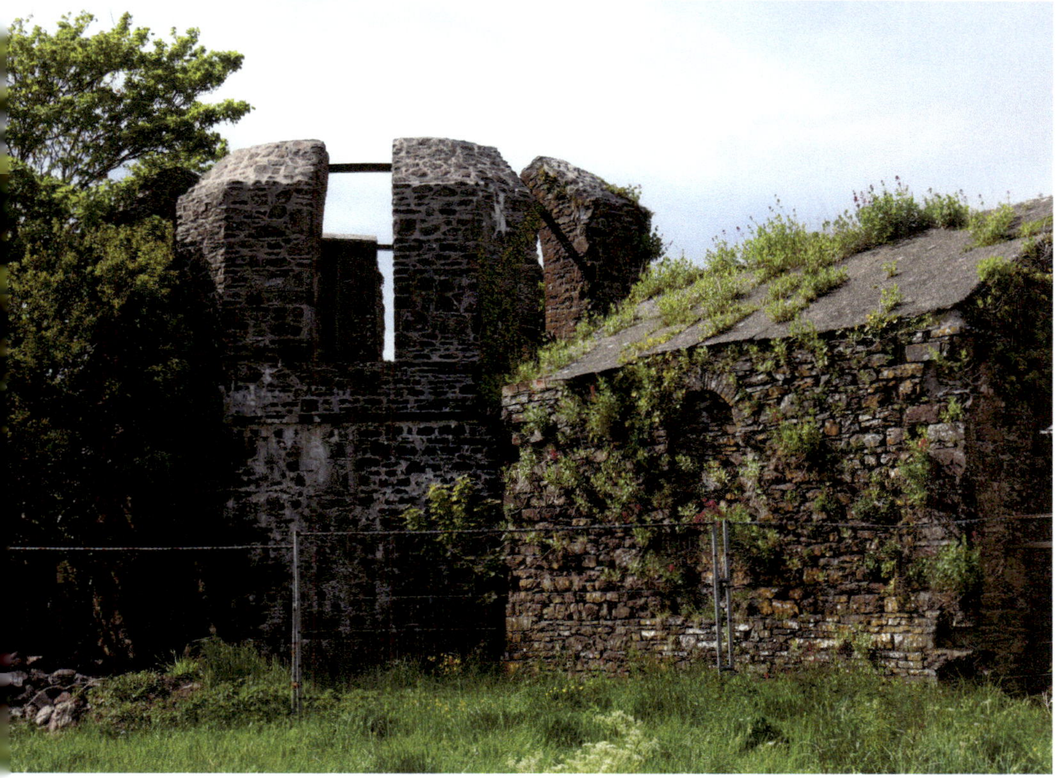

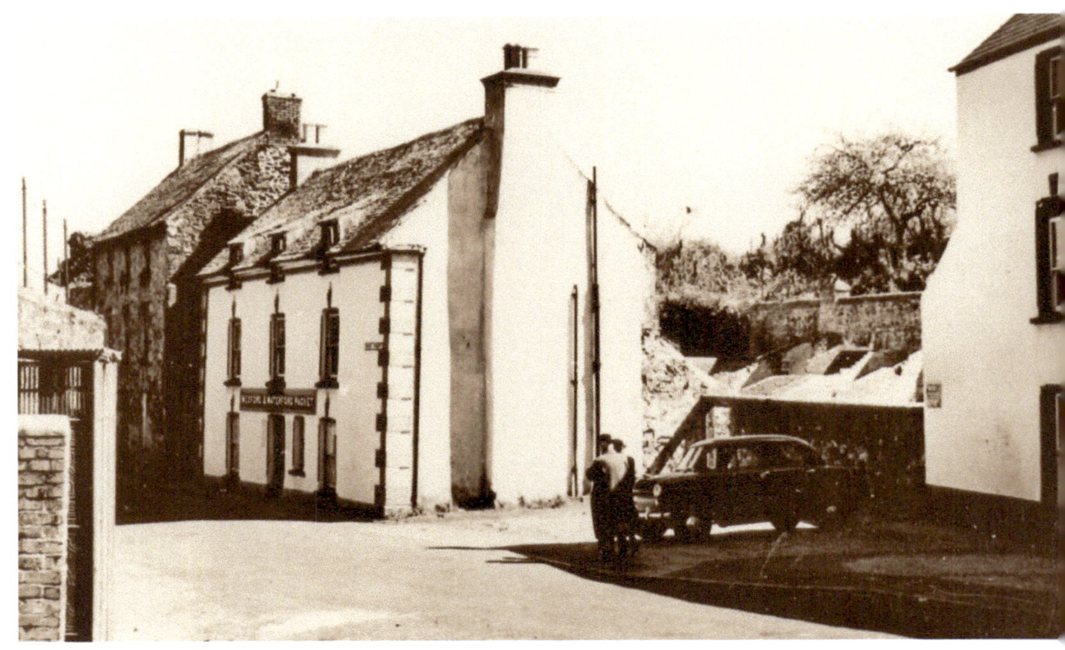

The Waterford & Wexford Packet

Hakin was a thriving port long before the town of Milford was created. Among the ships landing there was the Irish Packet, carrying mail to and from Waterford. The Waterford and Wexford Packet was one of the oldest public houses, marking the northern end of Point Street. It closed in the early 1950s, around the time that Point Street was demolished. In the earlier picture, the wall of the Heart of Oak public house in Lower Hill Street is just on the right. This area was used for the filming of some episodes of the BBC TV programme *The Onedin Line*. A new house has recently been built where the car is parked in the earlier photograph.

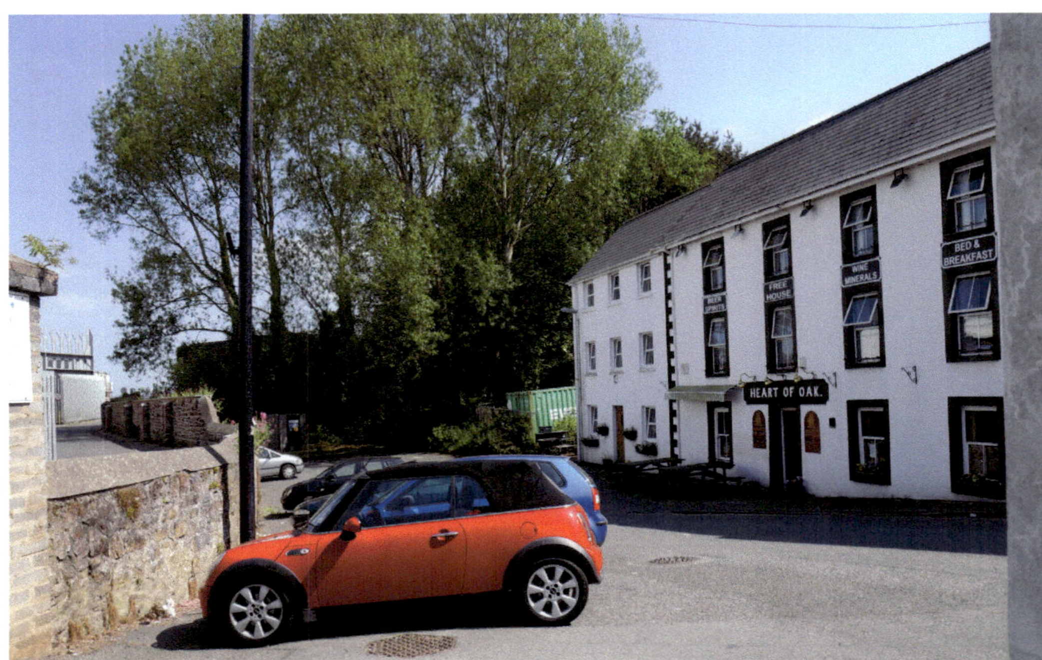

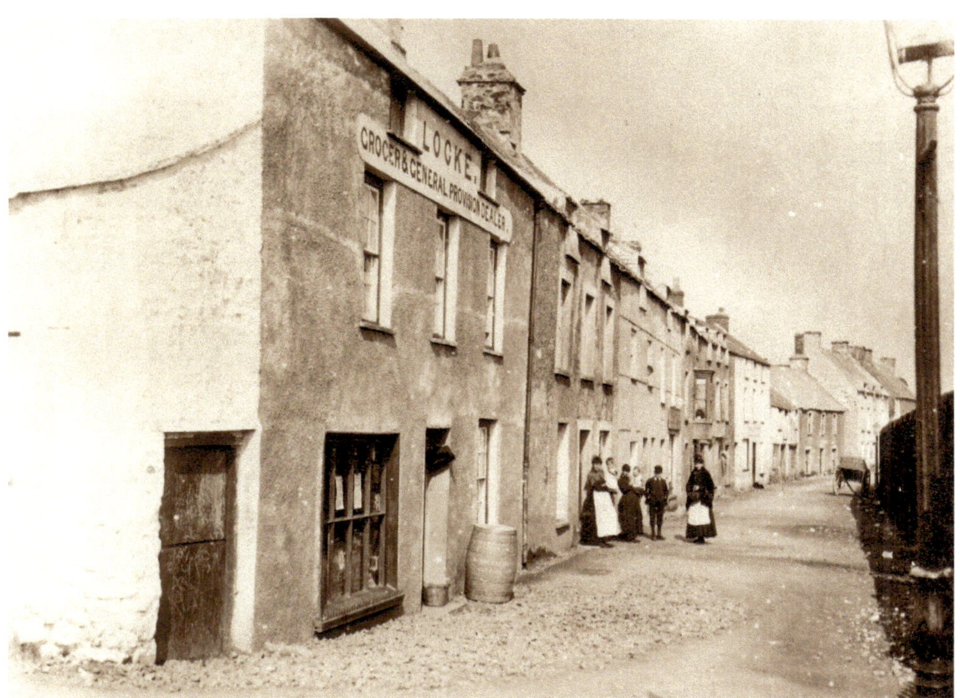

Point Street

Point Street linked the Kings Arms, which is prominently situated on Hakin Point, and the Waterford and Wexford Packet. The photograph dates from around 1890. When the dock was built, the waterfront on the Hakin side became part of the docks and Point Street was fenced off, cutting off the view and access previously enjoyed by the inhabitants of the street. The Locke family occupied their grocery and general provision shop from before 1841 and were still there at the 1911 census.

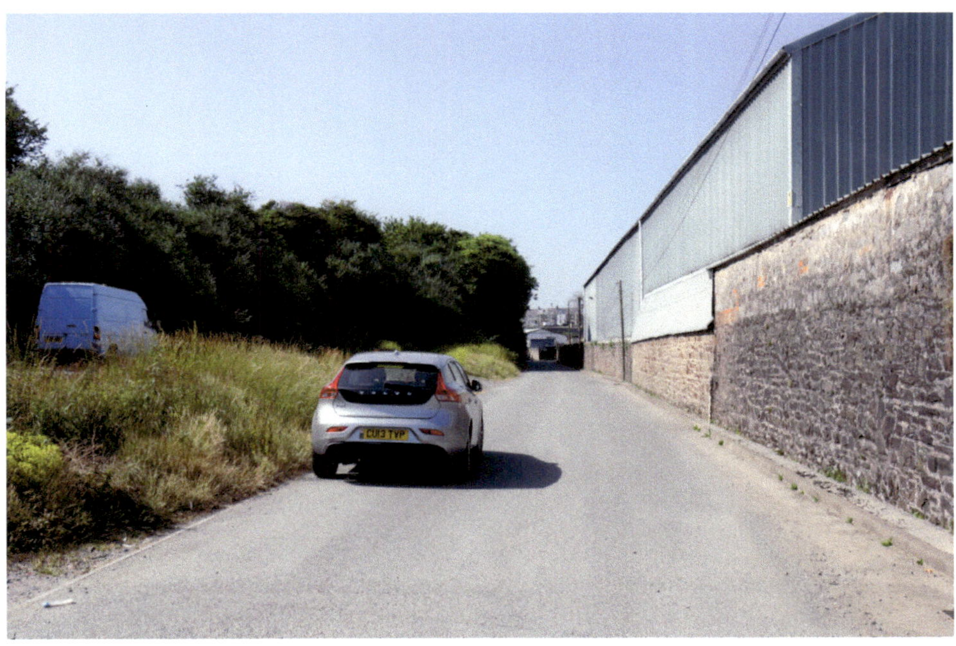

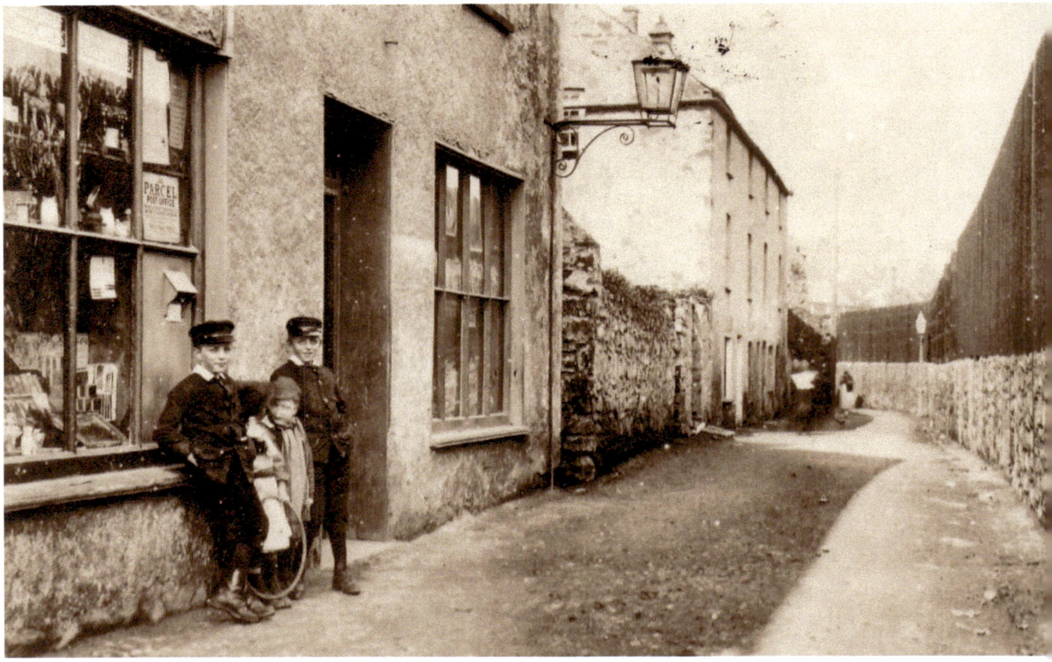

Point Street

Hakin (or Haking as the village was sometimes known) was part of the parish of Hubberston and included the thriving and distinctive dockside community of Point Street. In 1871, the street was home to almost sixty families, the majority of whom were employed in shipbuilding and allied trades. Most of the inhabitants were born in the parish and many families were to remain in the street well into the twentieth century. There were at least ten public houses in Point Street as well as the post office pictured.

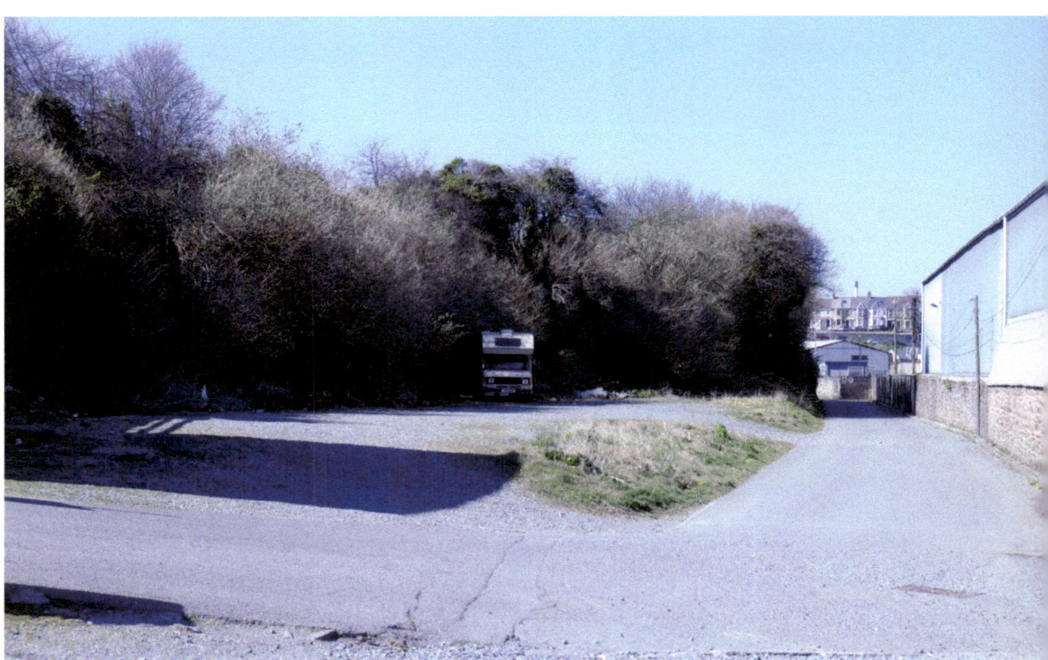

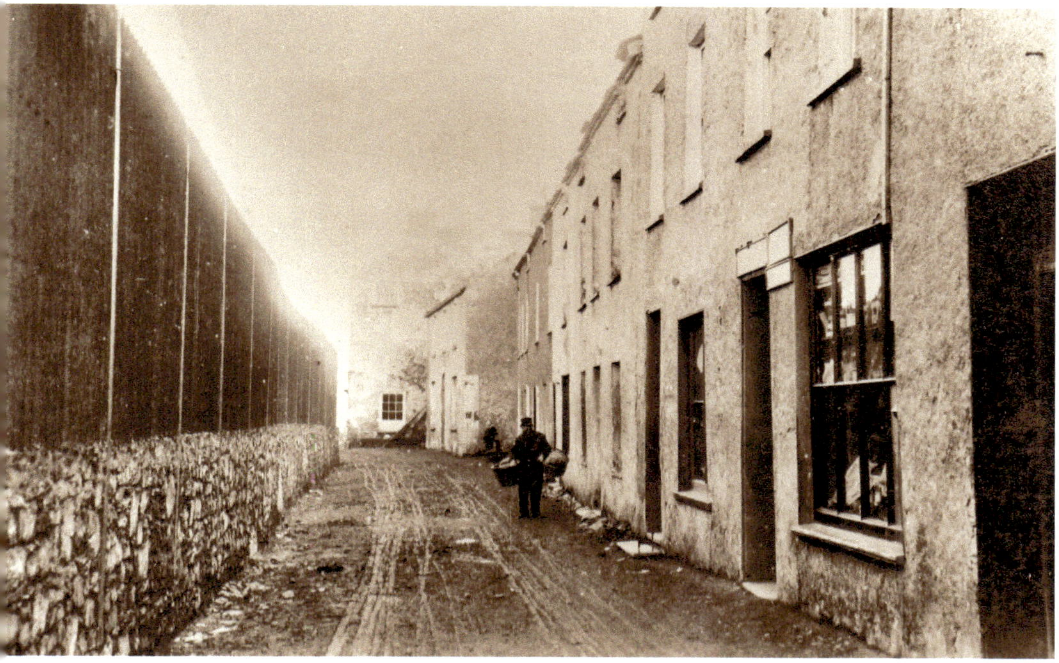

Point Street

A few of the buildings on the east side of Point Street had been demolished when the dock was originally built. In the 1950s, the Dock Company published plans to extend the size of the dry dock in order to repair large tankers. As a result, the rest of the street was subject to compulsory purchase. All the buildings were demolished, but the expansion never happened and a large empty space is all that remains.

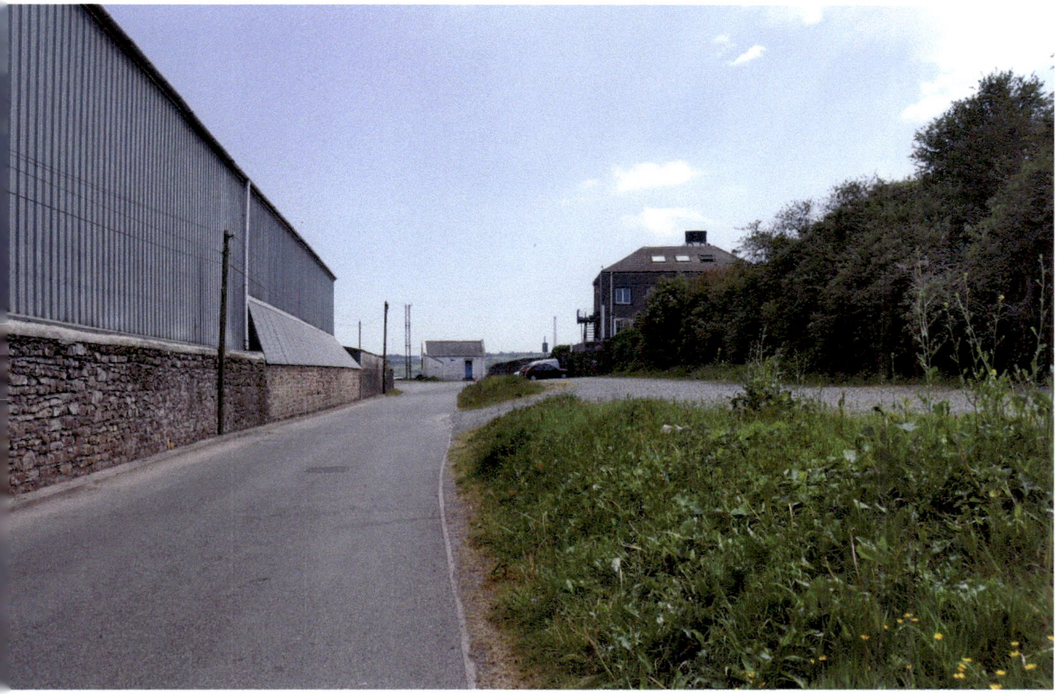

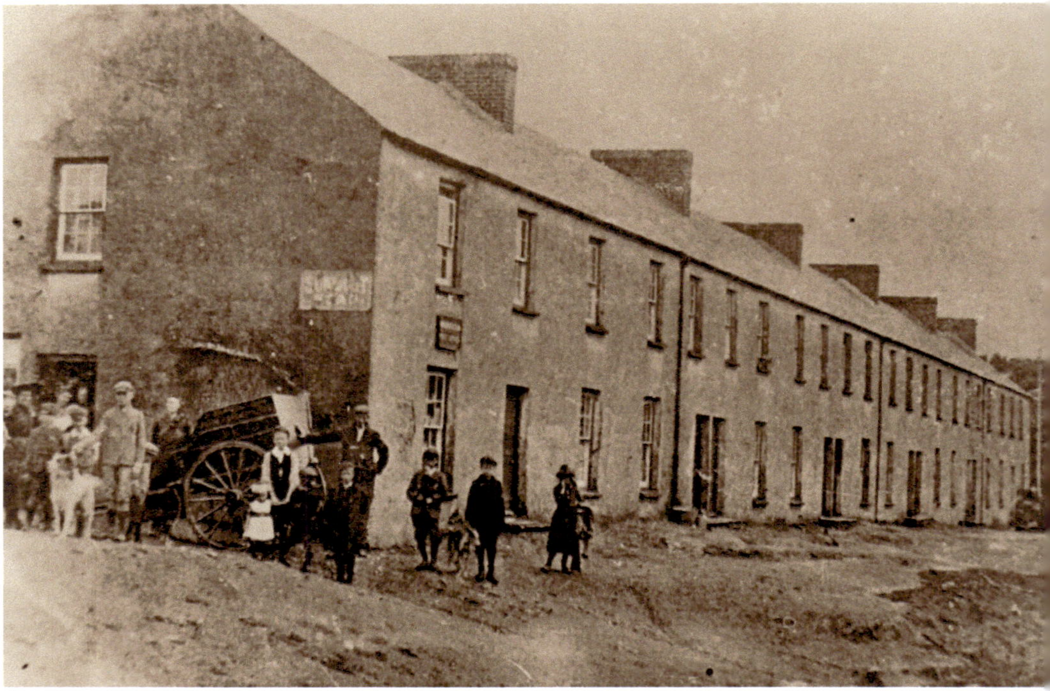

Green Terrace, Hubberston

The row of houses known as Green Terrace is situated close to the thirteenth-century Hubberston parish church, dedicated to St David. The picture was taken in around 1900, when the post office and corner shop, nearby bakery and dairy supplied most of the needs of the community.

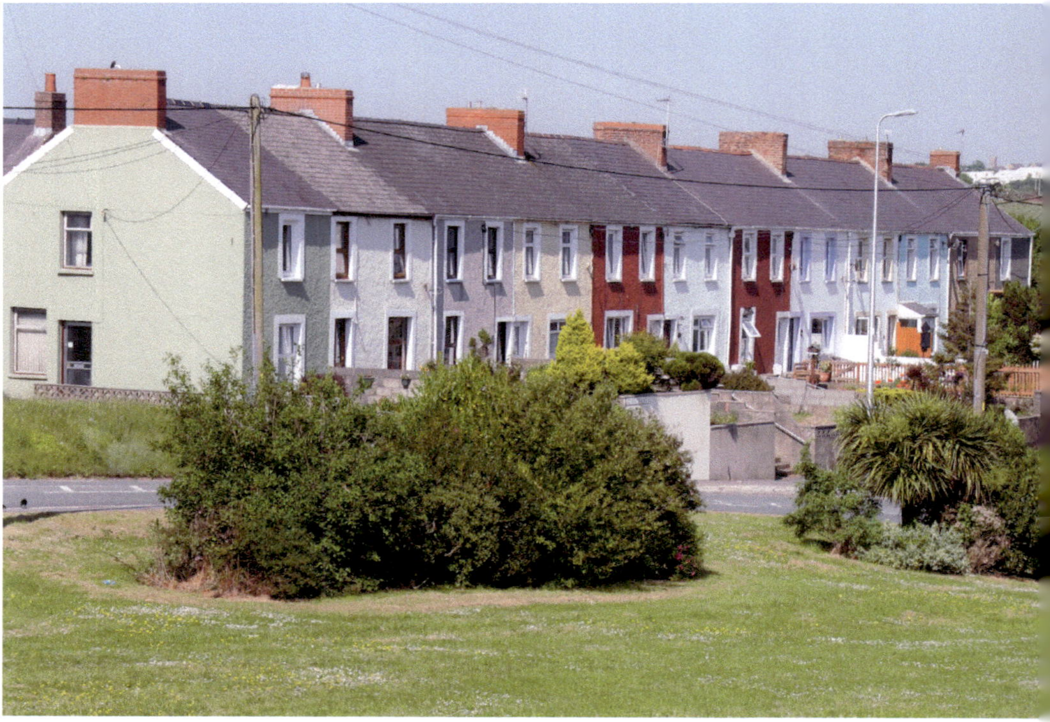

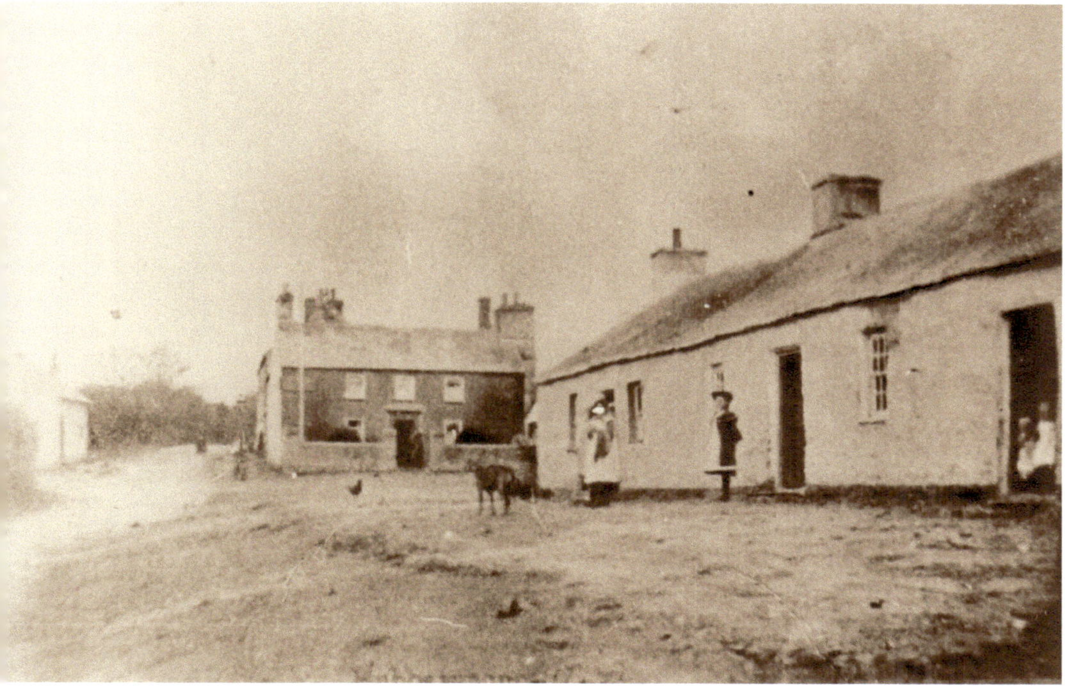

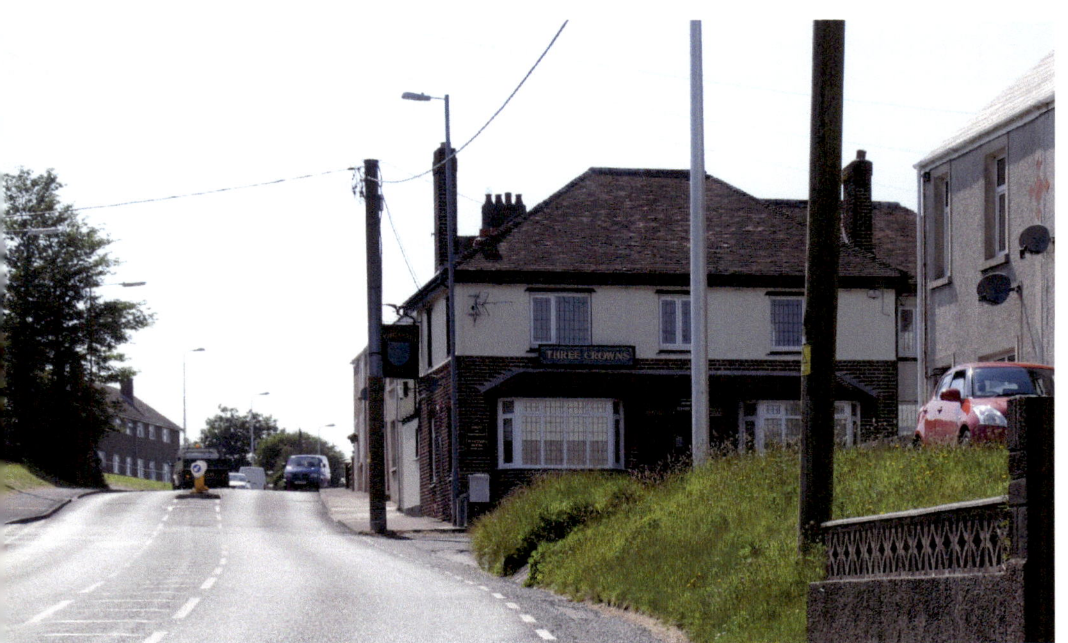

Hubberston

The Three Crowns public house, previously known as The Weary Traveller, was on the road from Hakin to Herbrandston. Since the 1920s, the population of the area has continued to expand with council, housing association and privately owned houses. A few hundred yards beyond the Three Crowns is the Milford Haven Golf Club, which is currently celebrating its centenary, although the course dates from 1933. Just beyond is a very large housing development, The Fairways, which is being built on land that was previously occupied by the Esso Club.

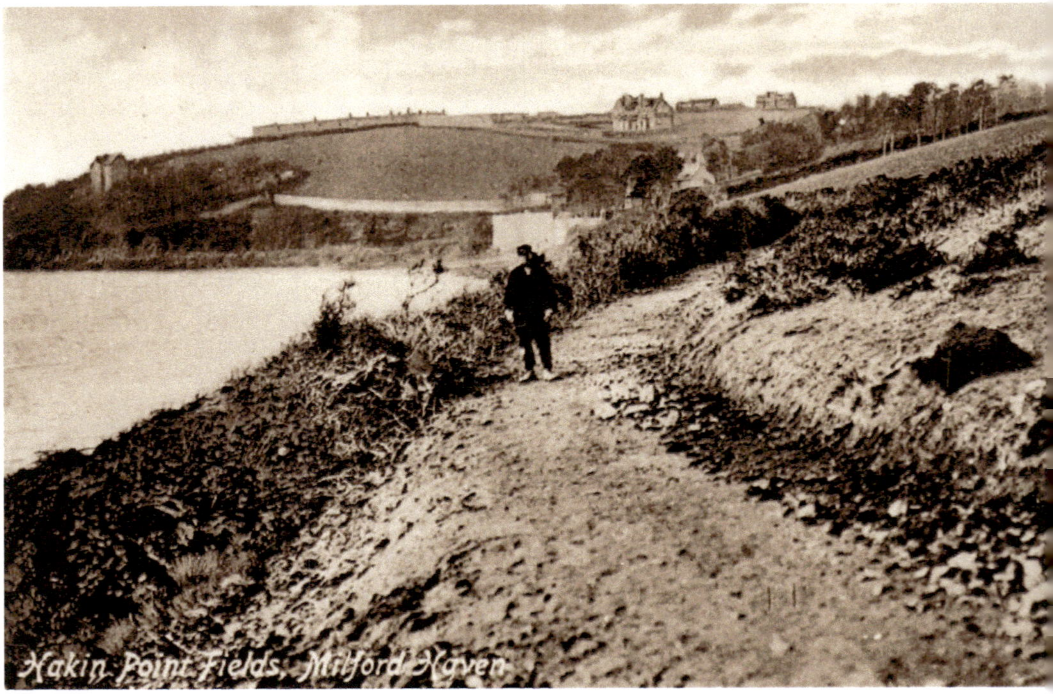

Point Fields

The early Point Fields footpath has been developed into an attractive walk along the Hakin cliffs from Conduit (also known as Conjuic) Beach to Hakin Point. The views of the waterway from this area are spectacular. The isolated house on the headland is Gorsewood, which now gives its name to Gorsewood Drive. The headland now houses the offices of the Milford Haven Port Authority, which controls the safety and navigation of all maritime activity in the waterway.

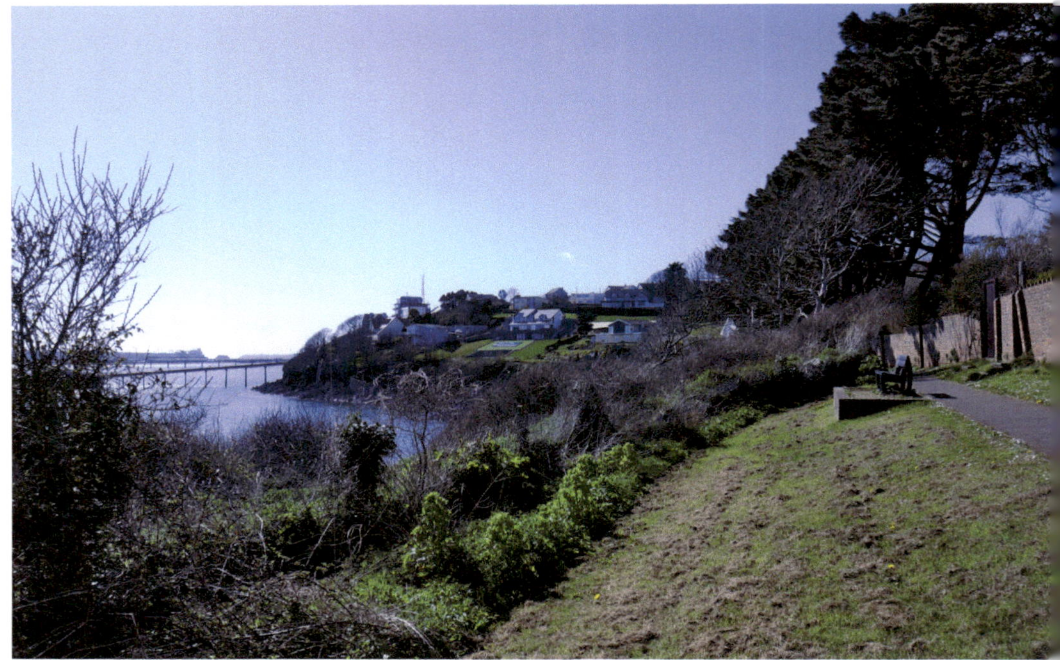

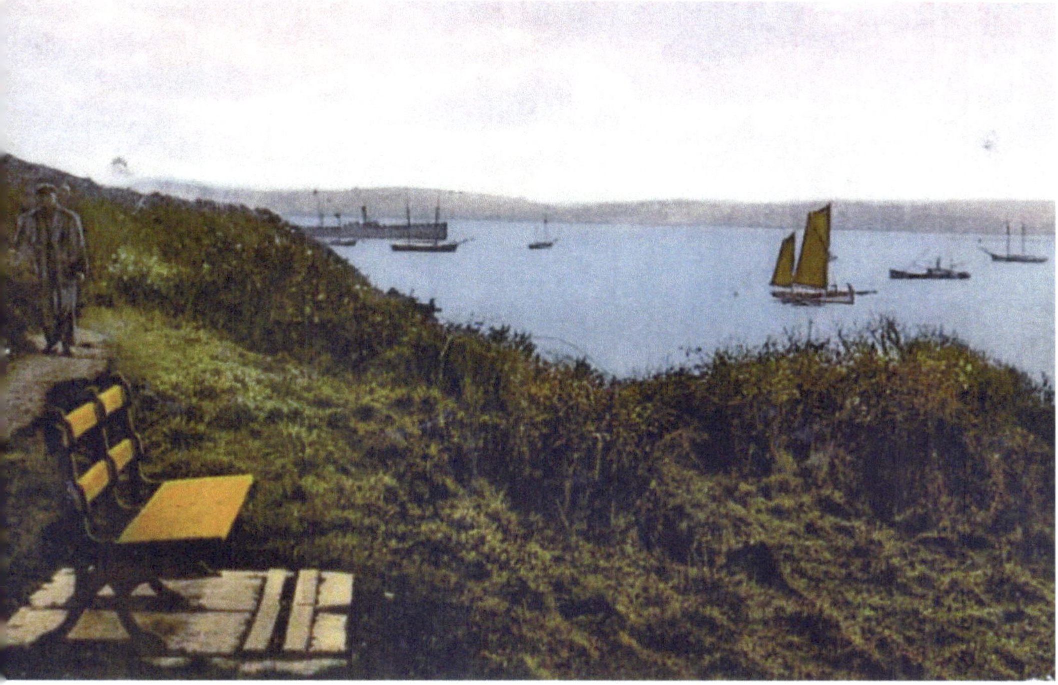

Point Fields

Fears of invasion led the government to place a defensive gun battery on Point Fields in the eighteenth century. The seven guns were never fired in anger, but did mark the landing of King George IV at Milford in 1821. Looking east in the twenty-first century, it is possible to see the Dragon LNG Terminal at Waterston and the new power station on the south side of the Haven.

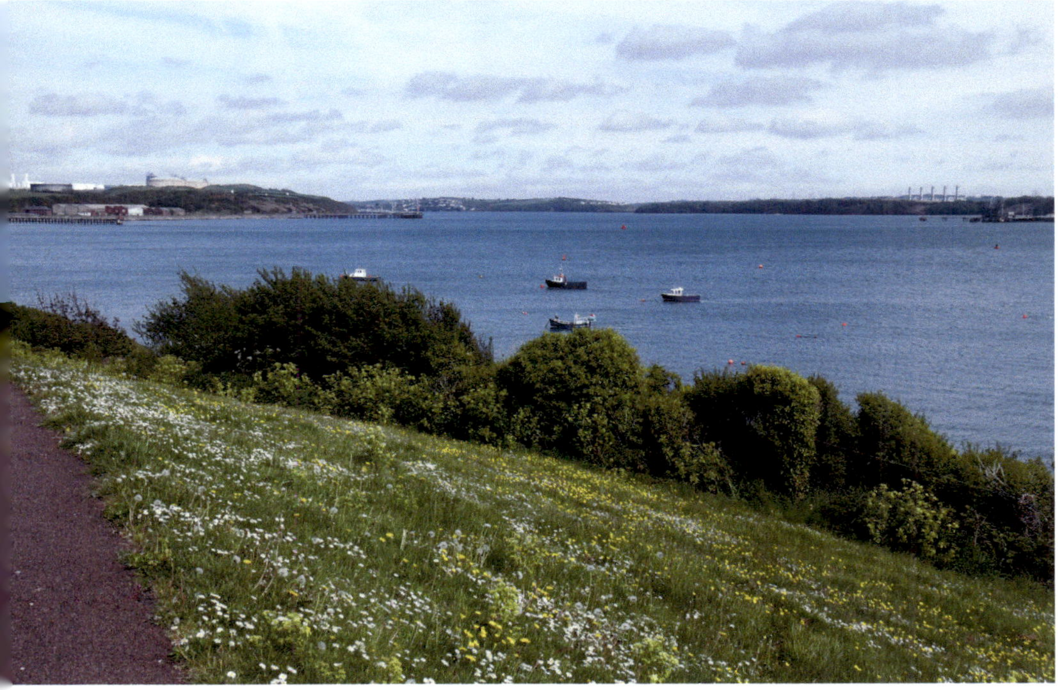

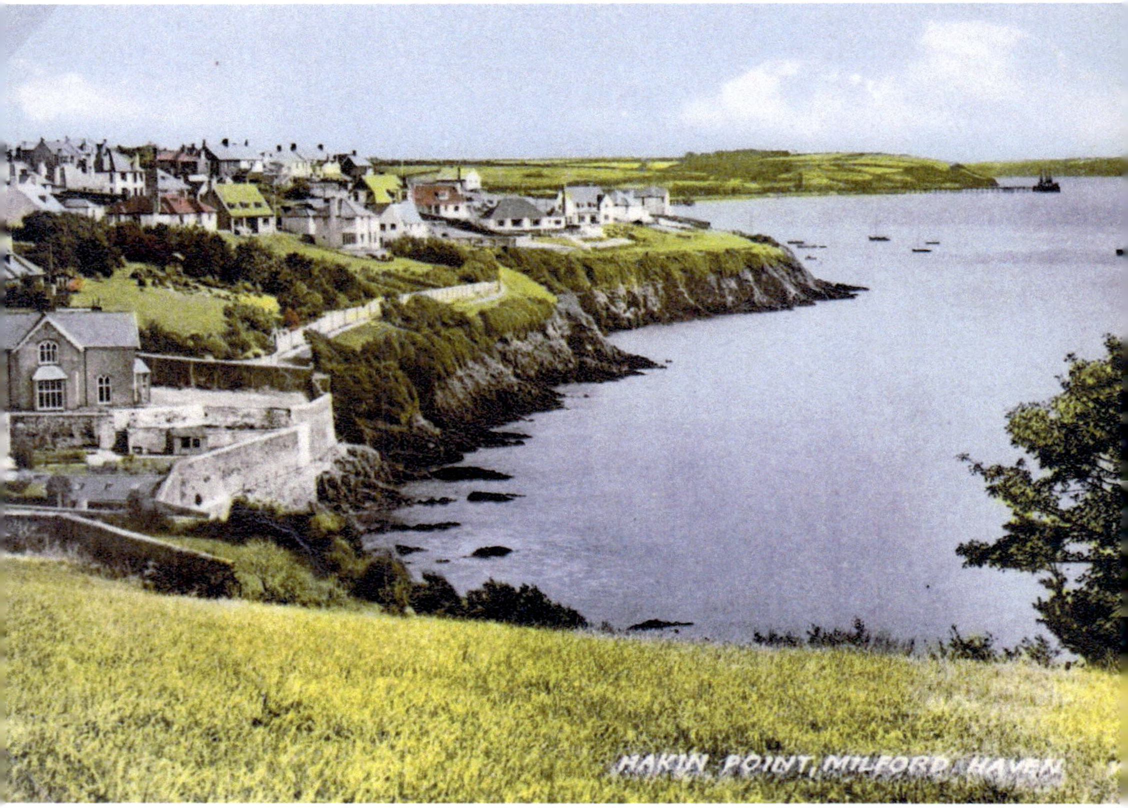

Hakin Point

This card was posted in 1955, and shows Conduit Beach and Point Fields as far as Hakin Point. Many of the houses in this desirable residential area date from the 1920s and 1930s, reflecting a time of comparative prosperity in the area.

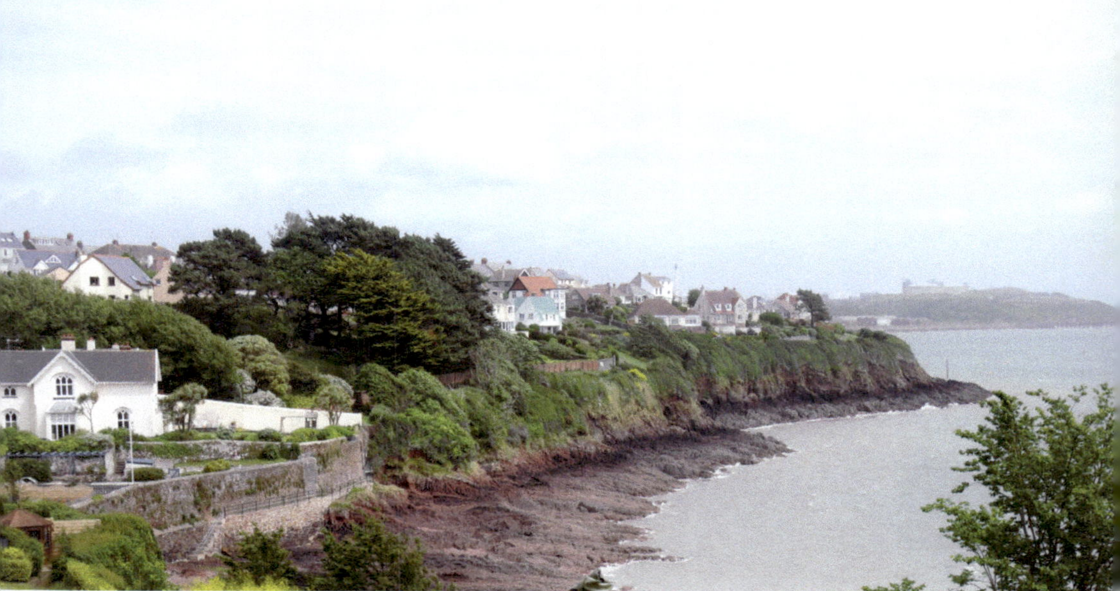

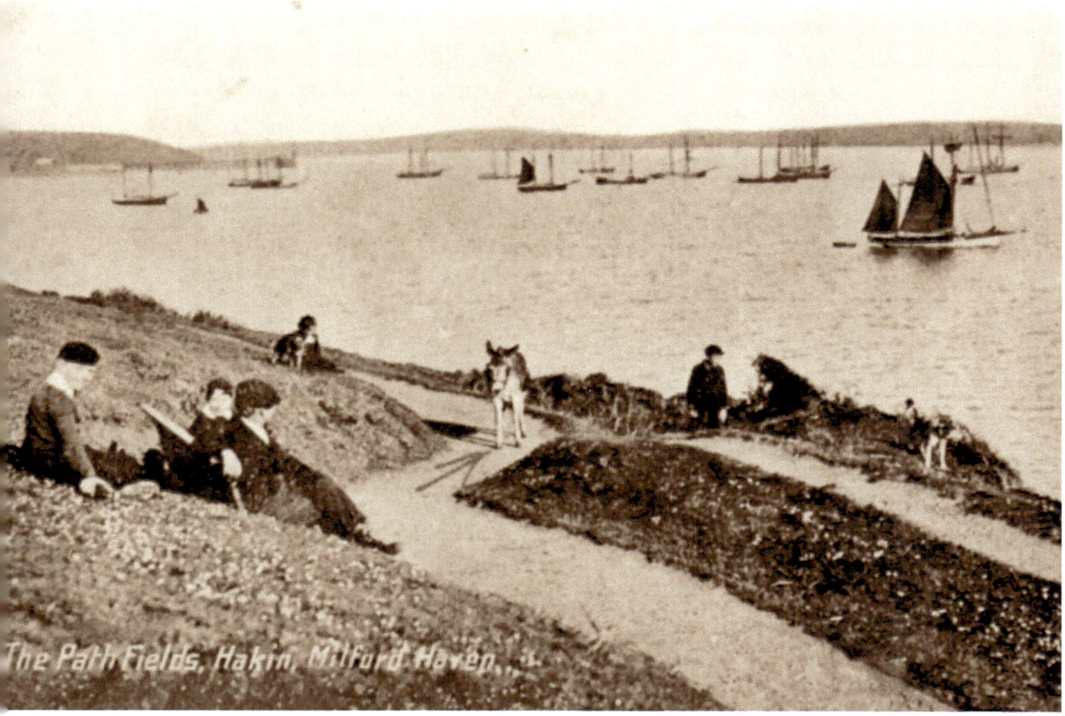

Point Fields

This early picture shows some of the sixty-six trawlers and 150 fishing smacks that formed the Milford fishing fleet in 1904. Much of the clifftop is now overgrown.

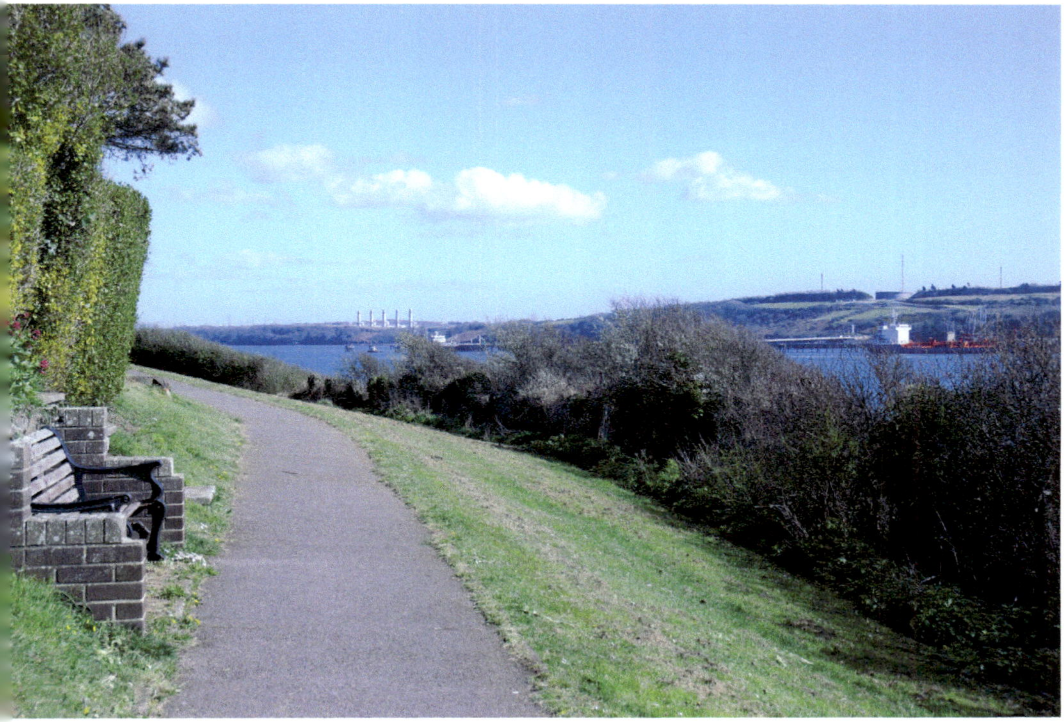

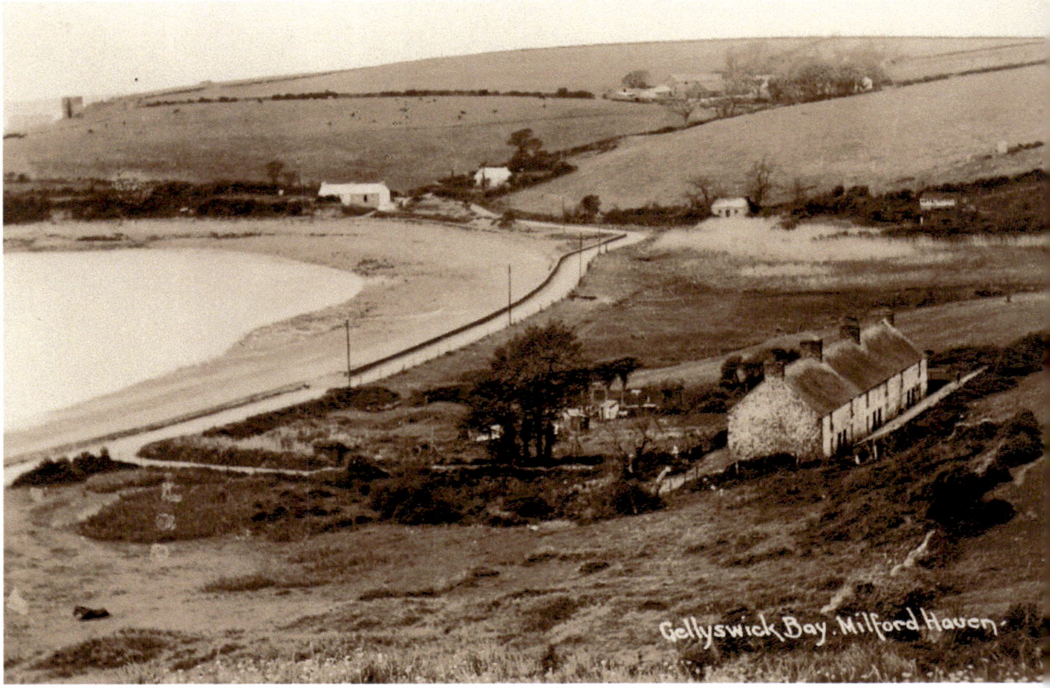

Gellyswick Bay

The sand and shingle beach of this sheltered bay has always been a favourite location. Since the late 1950s, it has been the home of the Pembrokeshire Yacht Club and a popular venue for water sports. Their clubhouse and boat park have replaced the old cottages and there is a slipway on the beach. The Murco jetty extends from beyond the headland.

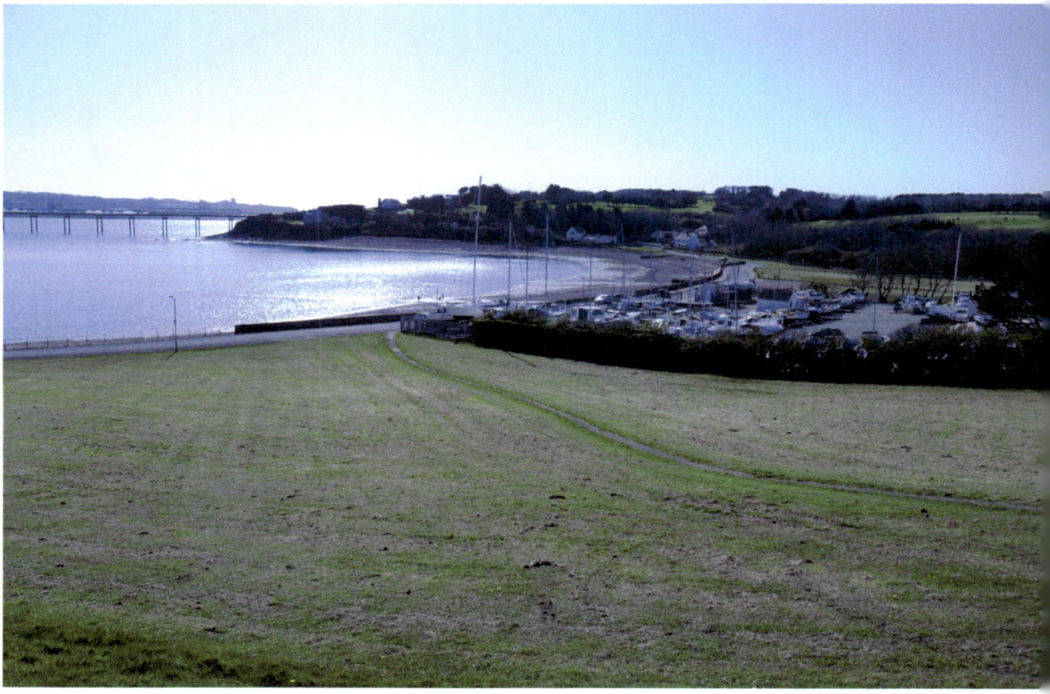

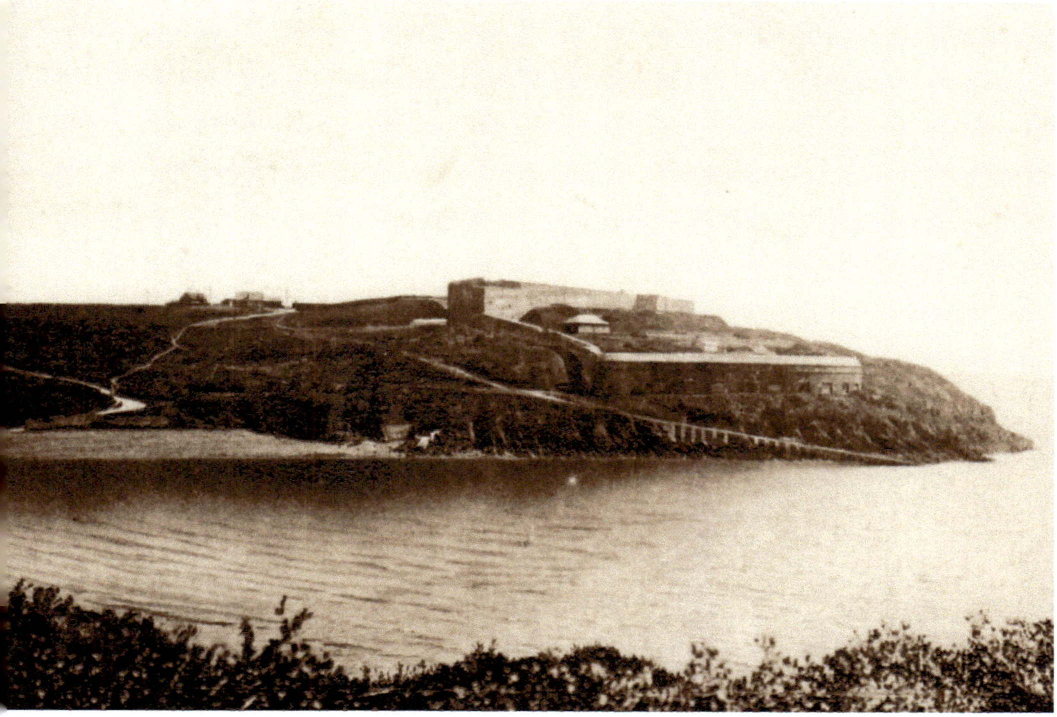

Hubberston Fort

Hubberston Fort was one of the most extensive nineteenth-century fortifications built in Europe. Completed in 1865, its guns dominated the waterway with a view stretching from Pembroke Dock to the mouth of the Haven. It was manned during the First World War, while in the Second World War it was used as part of a large American Army camp.

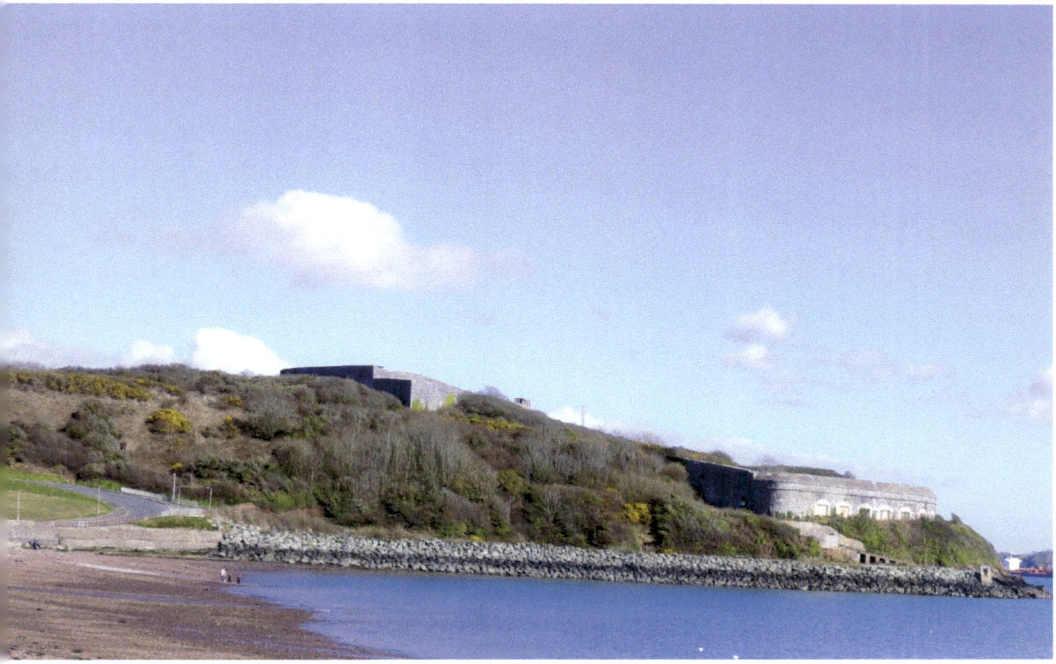

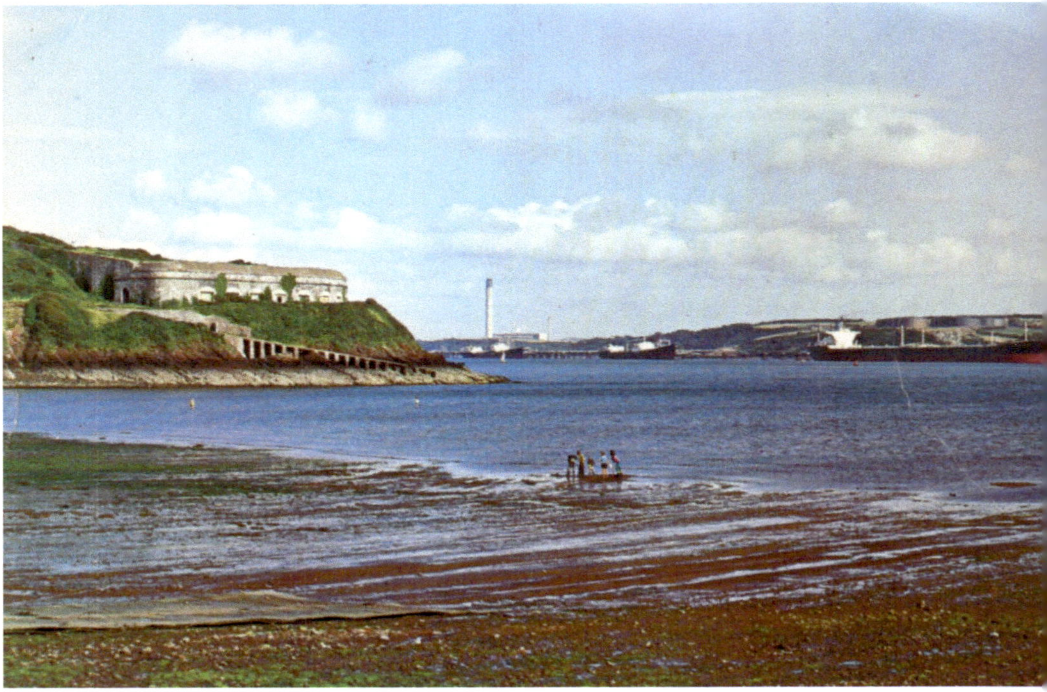

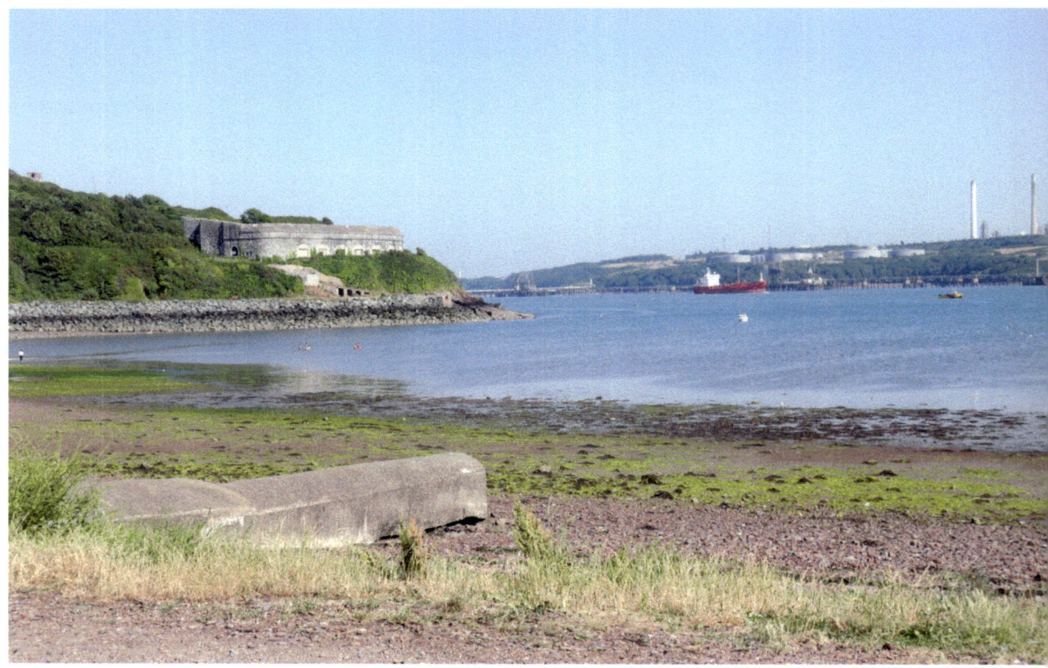

Hubberston Fort

In 1885, the Royal Pembrokeshire Militia was relocated from Haverfordwest to Hubberston Fort, which became the recruitment depot for the 24th Regiment of Foot. It included a large barracks, capable of accommodating up to 250 men. In 1908, the militia regiments were disbanded and the active life of the fort ended. Much of the fort is now derelict, and in 2011 it was named as the fifth most endangered archaeological site in the UK.

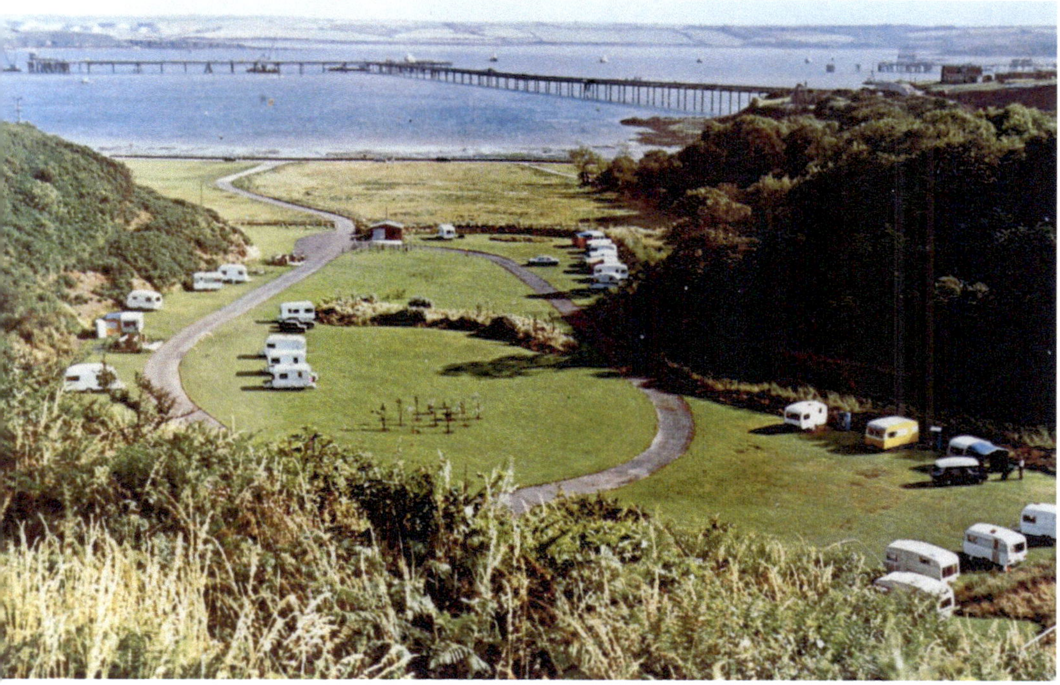

Gellyswick Caravan Site

In the 1970s, the Gellyswick Caravan Site, situated alongside the yacht club, was widely advertised but there is no trace of it today. Much of the site is now overgrown, as the photograph below shows. The Murco refinery's jetty protrudes into the Haven. Nor is there any trace of Gellyswick mansion, which stood on high ground above the bay. It was demolished in 1981 as its owner, the Esso Oil Company, no longer required the property, which they had used as offices while their new site was developed.

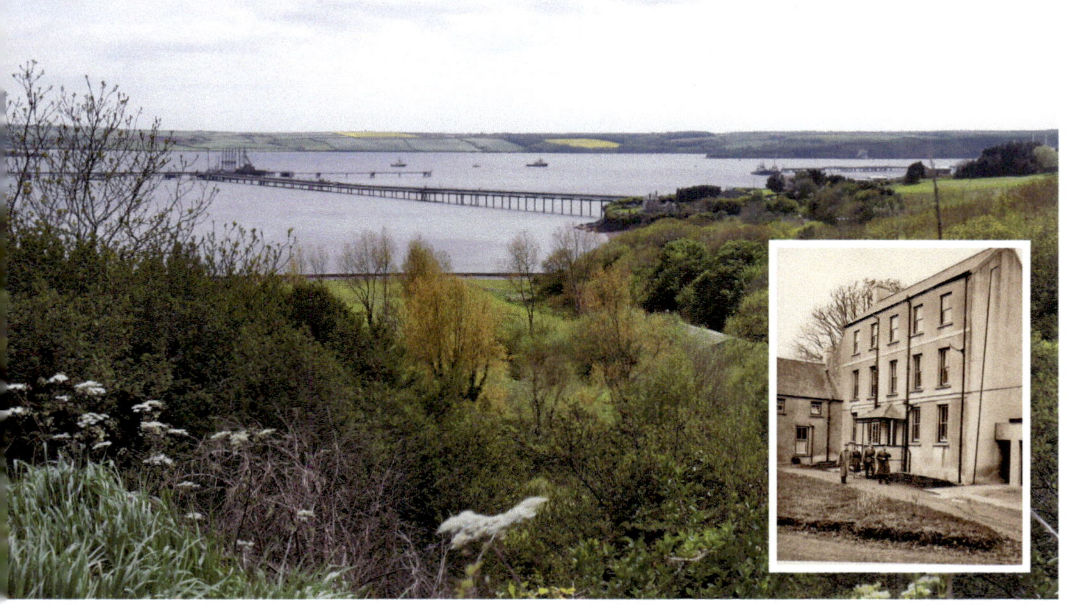

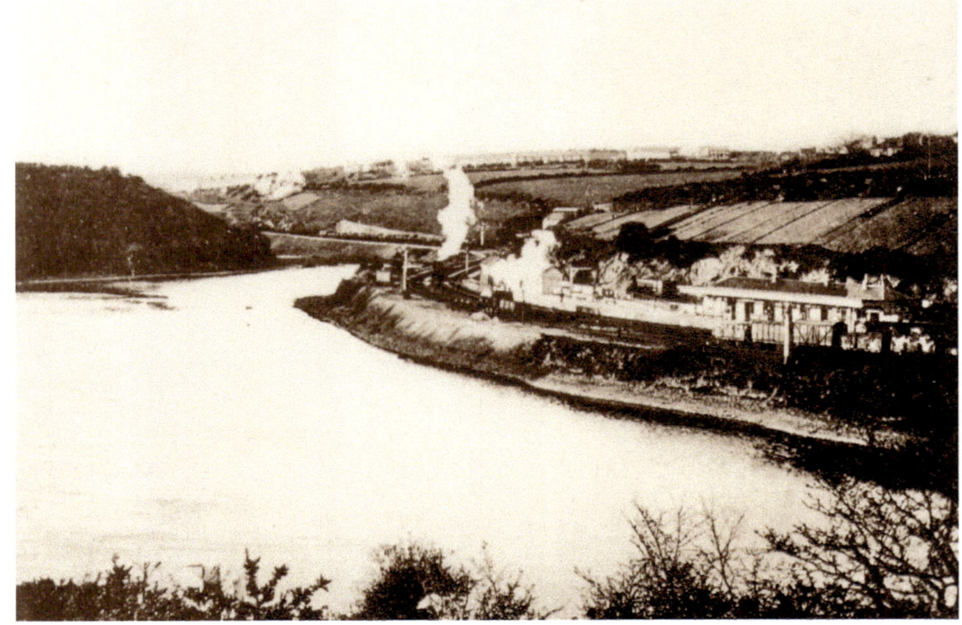

The Railway Station

This early photograph shows the railway station and the line running alongside Havens Head and Hubberston Pill. Work on building the railway line from Johnston to Milford Haven began in 1858, and was eventually completed in 1863 when the terminus was a simply a single short platform and goods sidings. The line was extended and connected with the docks in 1875. The station building followed later. In 1924, a length of 300 yards of the Pill was filled in and the main line diverted to ease a steep gradient. In the modern photograph, it is just possible to see the railway line beyond the filling station and retail park.

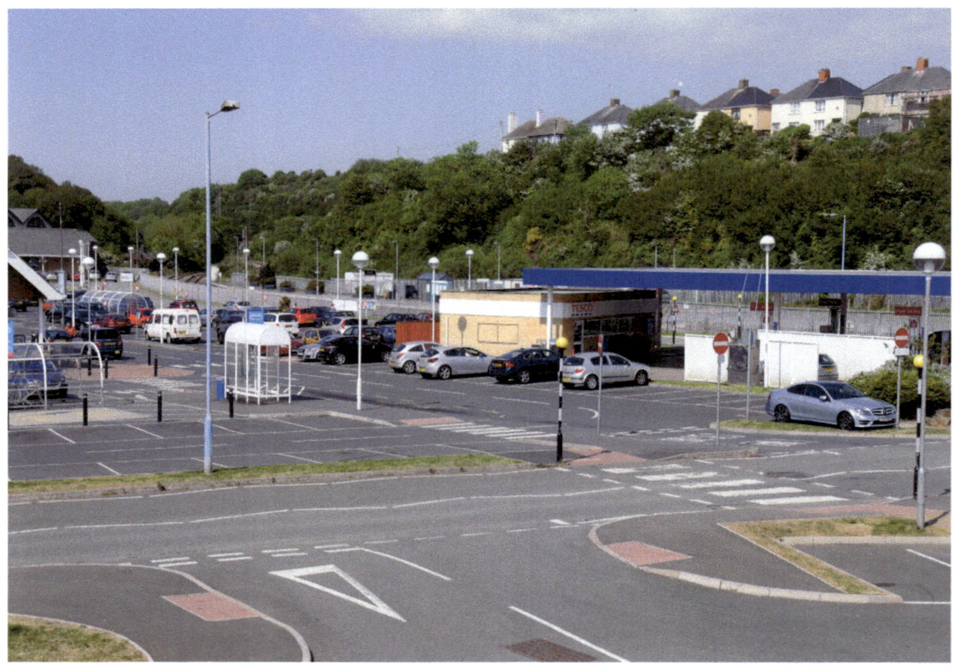

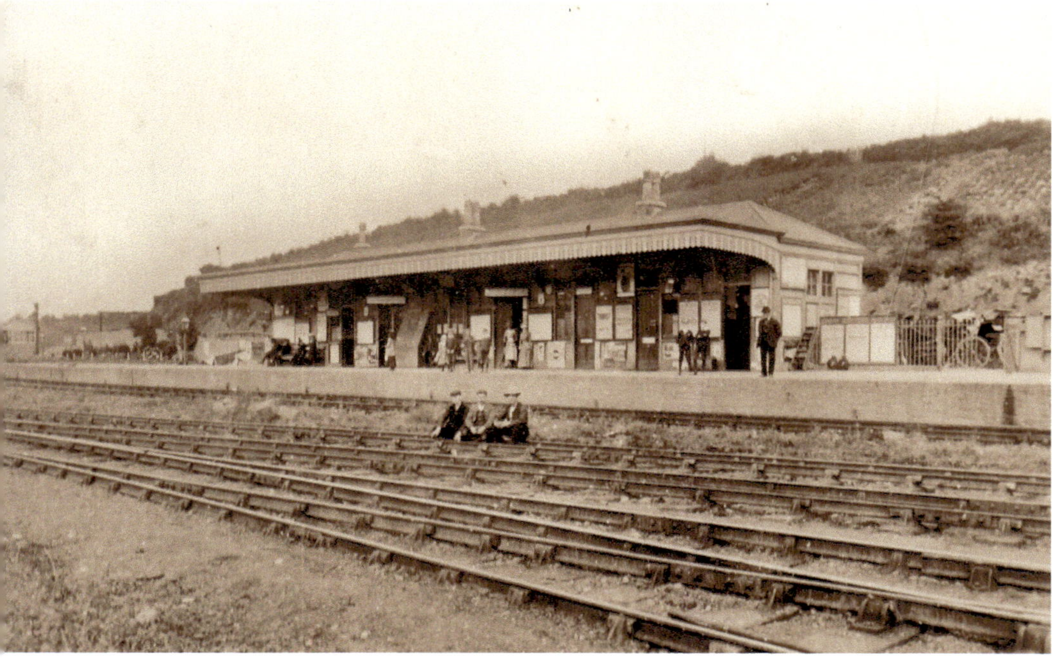

Station

The station building in around 1890 would have included the ticket counter, waiting rooms with large coal fires, and a canopy to protect those waiting for their trains from rain and wind. The building was demolished over thirty years ago. Instead, a bus shelter now provides some protection from the weather and tickets are purchased in a Portakabin. The railway station is now overlooked by houses built in St Peter's Road.

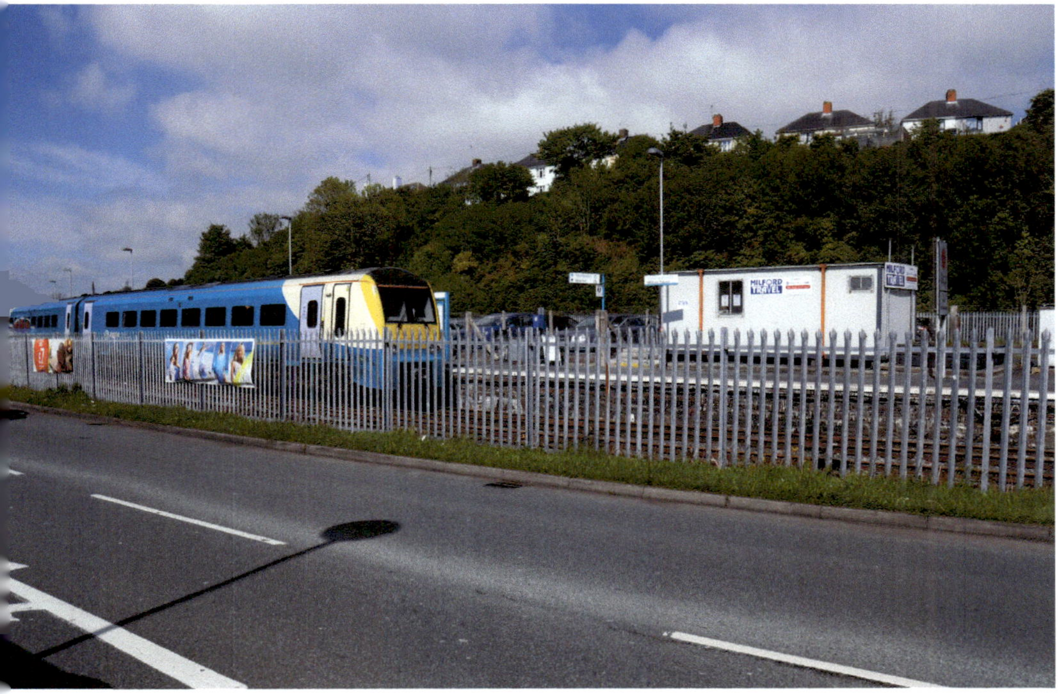

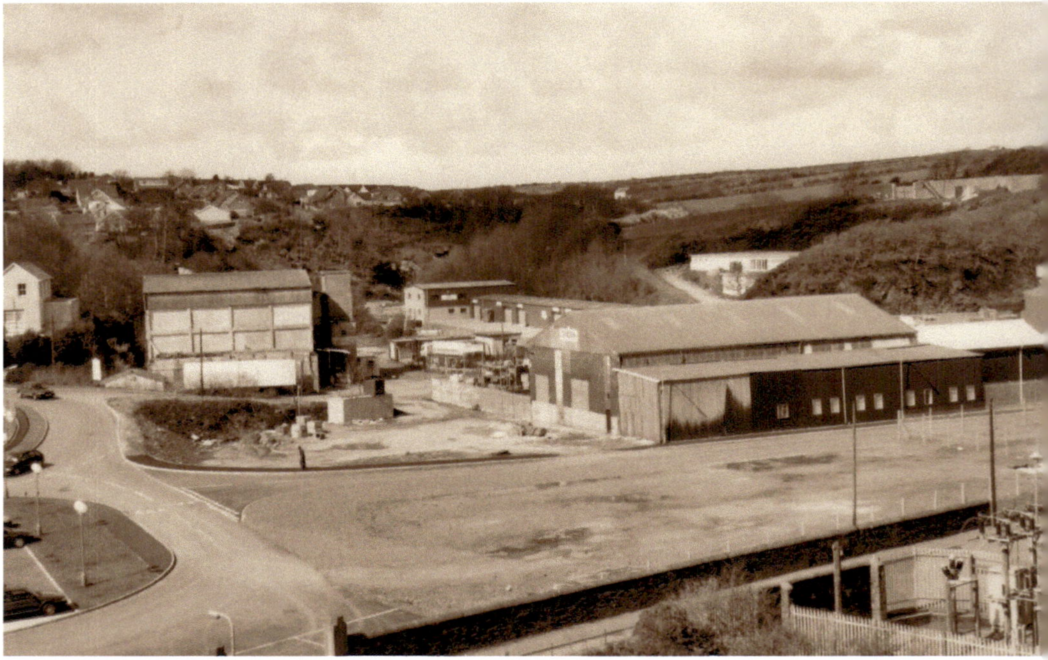

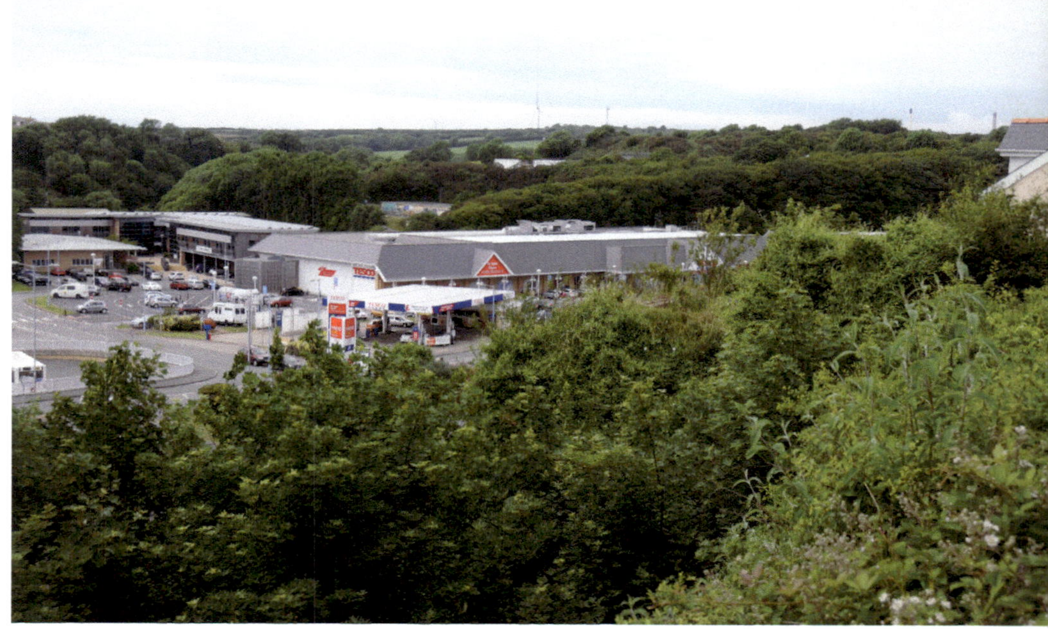

Havens Head

This photograph was taken in 1997, just before work began on building the new Havens Head Retail Park, part of the Milford 2000 plan. The building on the left is a freezer plant, one of the first factories built after the Second World War. The large warehouse was occupied by Jewson's builders' merchants, and just above it was a practice golf range. These were replaced by a large retail park dominated by the Tesco supermarket and filling station. The business park incorporates the Cedar Court suite of offices and a new County Library.

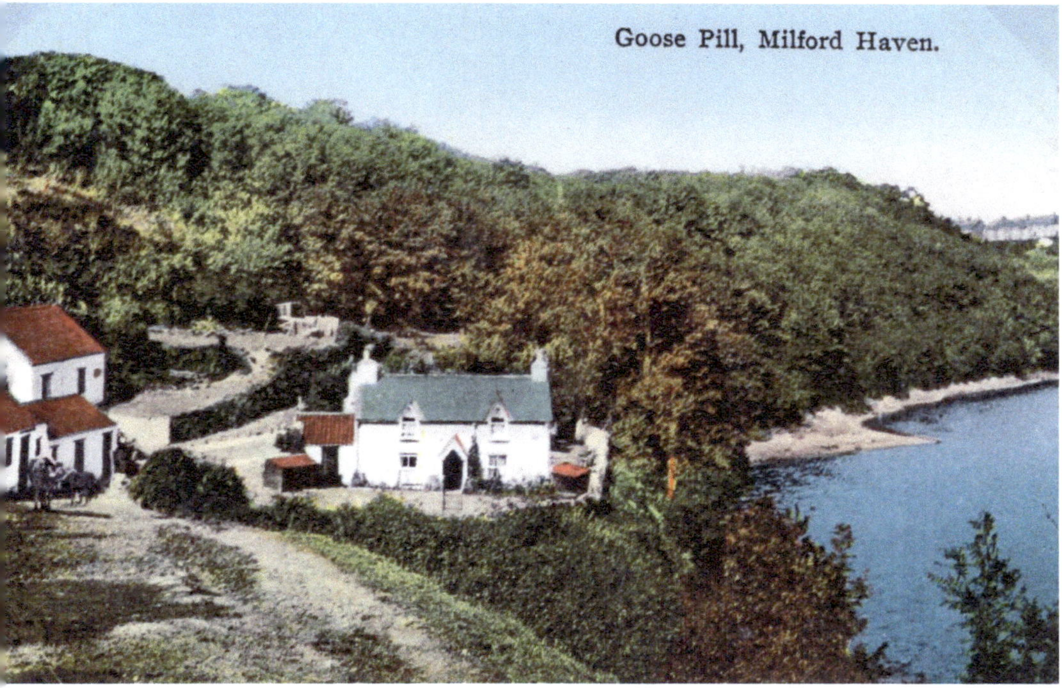

Goose Pill

Goosepill Farm and the cottage have gone. Walking along the nature trail from its start behind the Havens Head Retail Park, there are occasional glimpses of the waterway and railway line on the opposite bank. The path forms a link between Milford and the old priory, and would have been the route used by workmen employed in the box factory and saw mill, which made an important contribution to Milford's marine industry. At one time, there were oyster beds in this area.

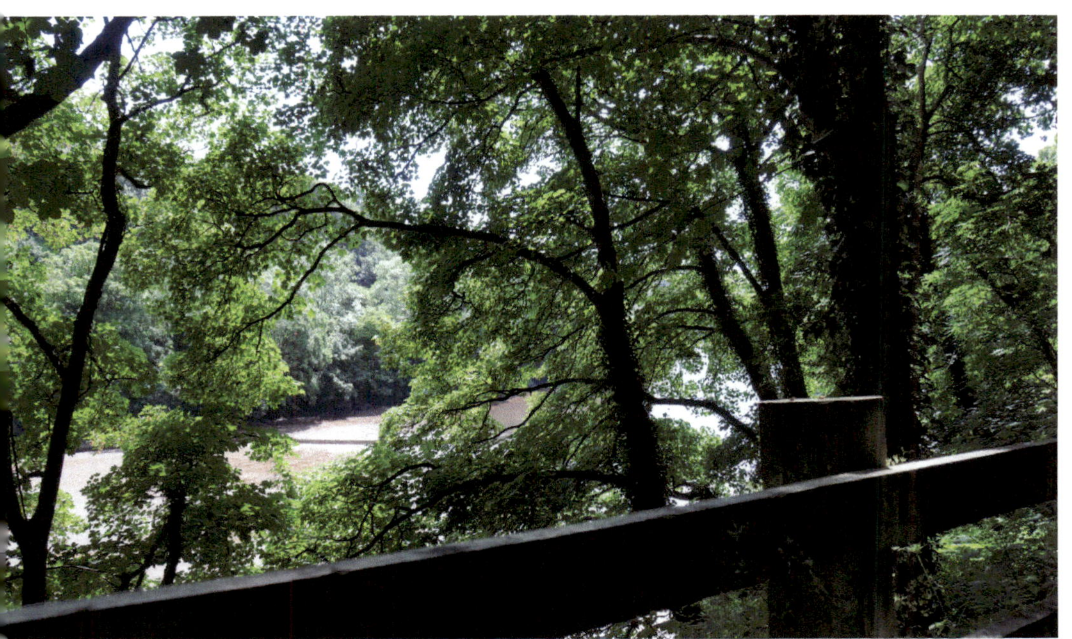

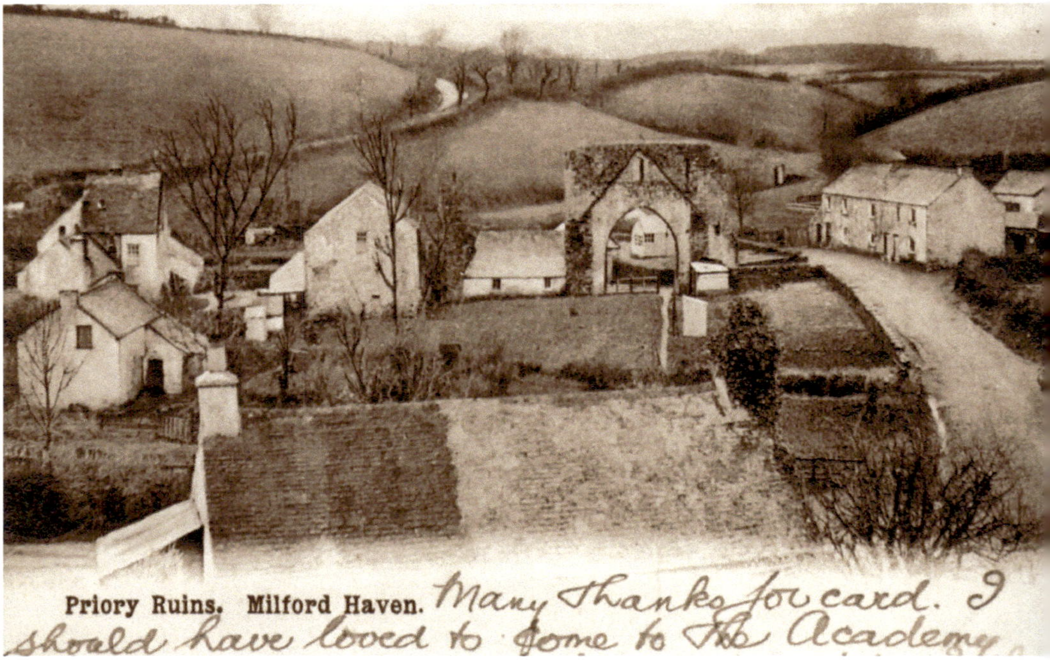

Priory Ruins. Milford Haven. *Many thanks for card. I should have loved to come to the Academy*

Priory Ruins

The medieval priory, a Benedictine foundation, was dedicated to St Mary and St Budoc (Bishop of Dol in Brittany). Founded in 1170, it had links with the priory at St Dogmaels. It was dissolved in the Reformation. The arch of the chancel of the church dominates the ruin. Now in private ownership, considerable restoration work has recently been completed.

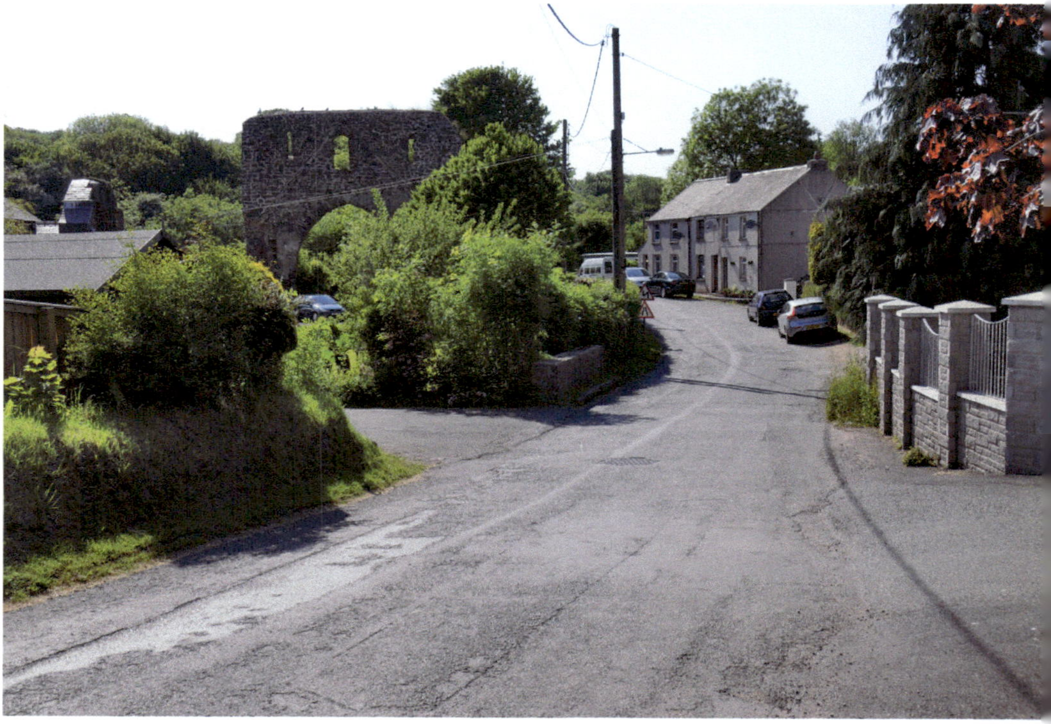

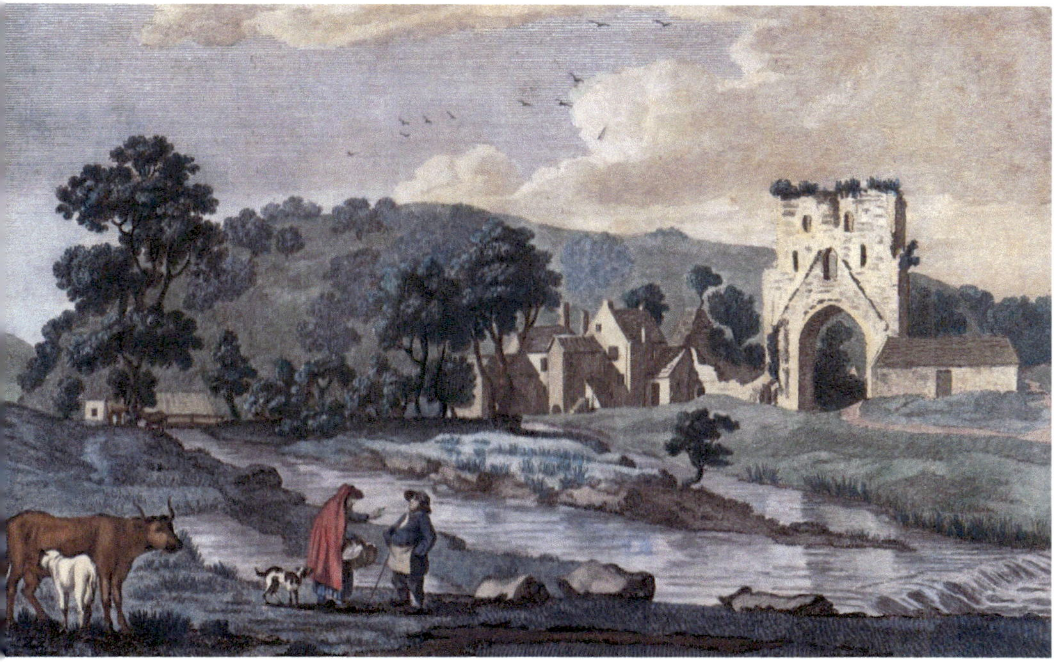

Priory Ruins Print

The early print records the small settlement around the priory, built near the upper reaches of Hubberston Pill, north of the town of Milford. The present community is known as Lower Priory. It is a popular area, especially the Priory Inn, which is adjacent to the priory itself.

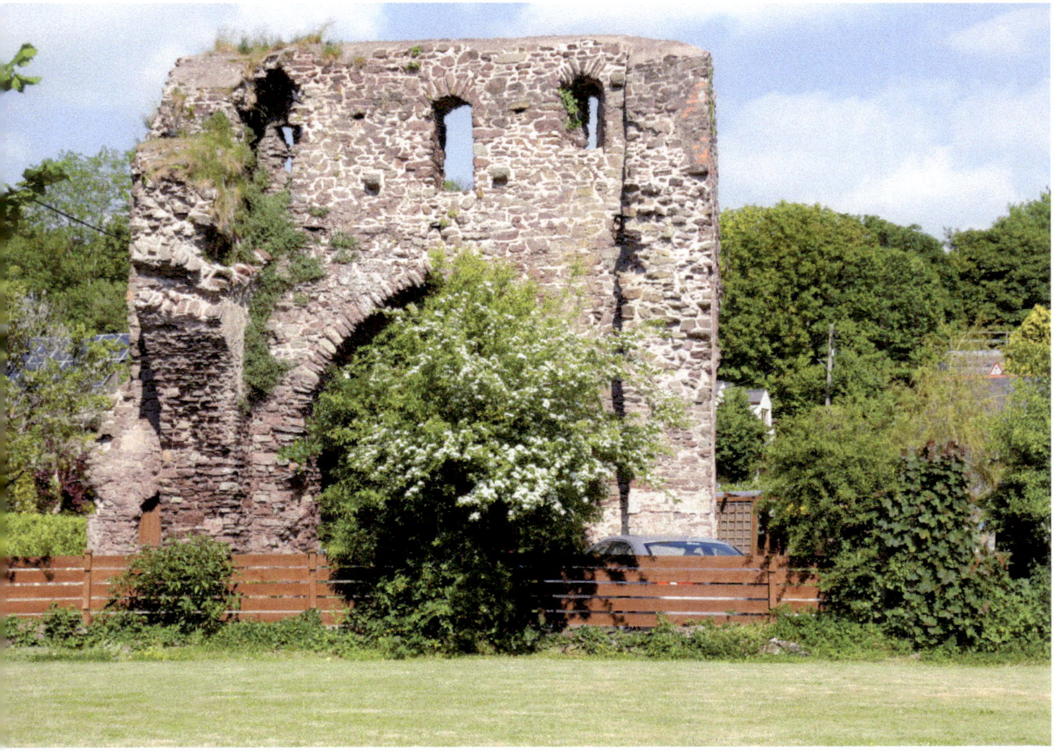

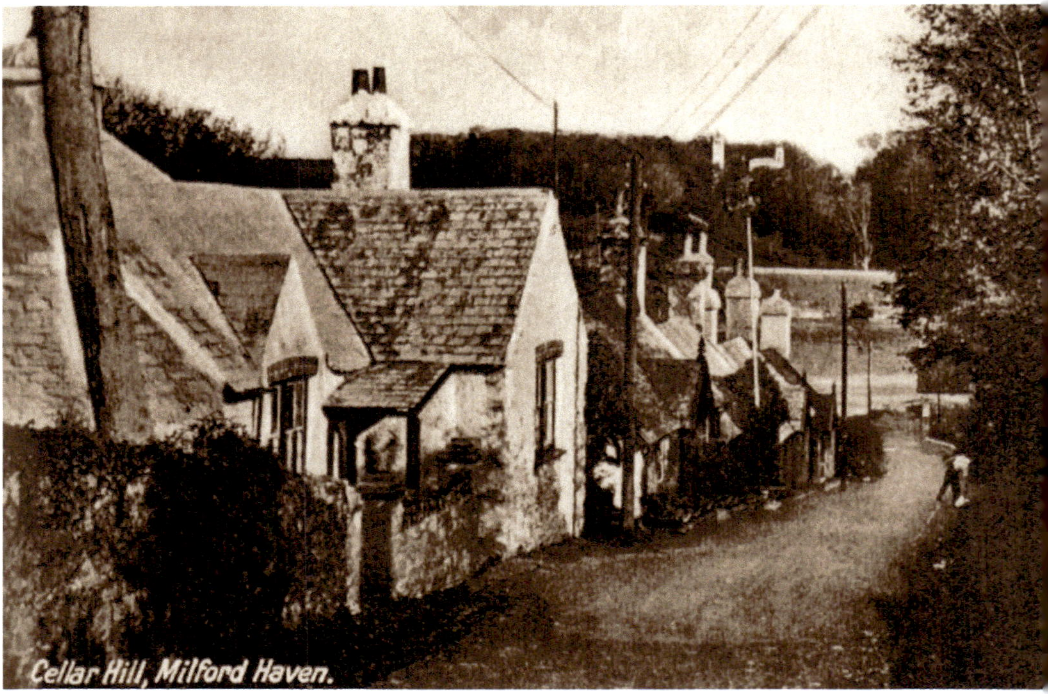

Cellar Hill

Cellar Hill is the road that links Milford and Castle Pill. On the hill is a row of some of the oldest and most picturesque cottages in the town, probably built by boat builders employed at the Pill and by the immigrant American whalers, who supplied whale oil for London's street lighting.

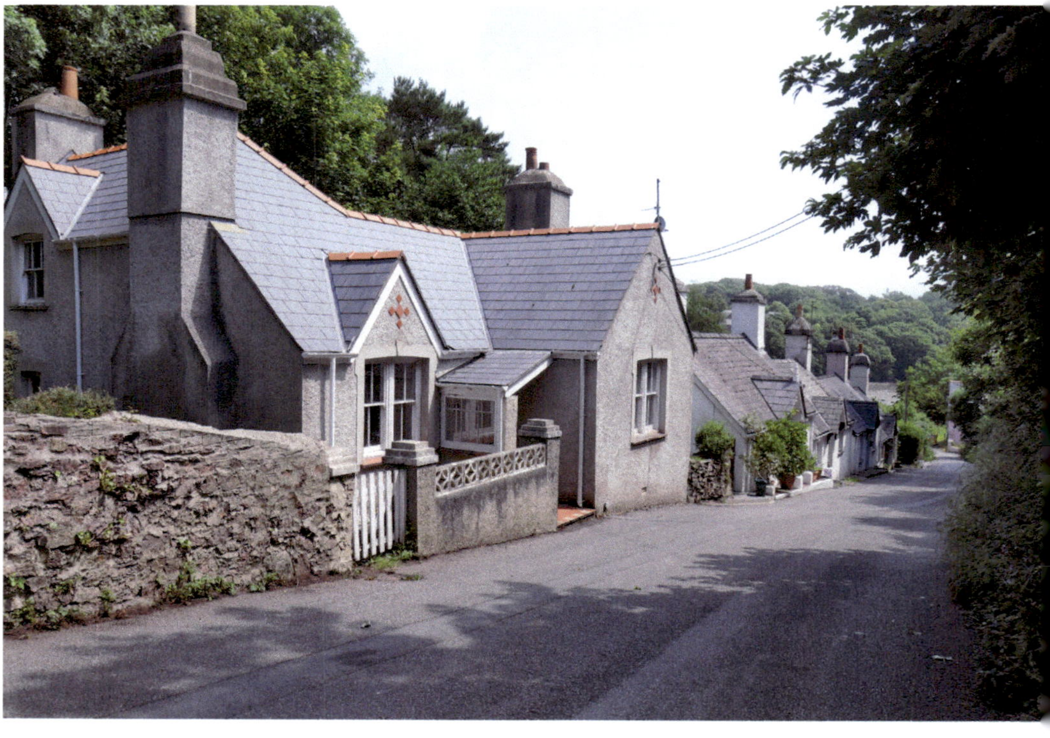

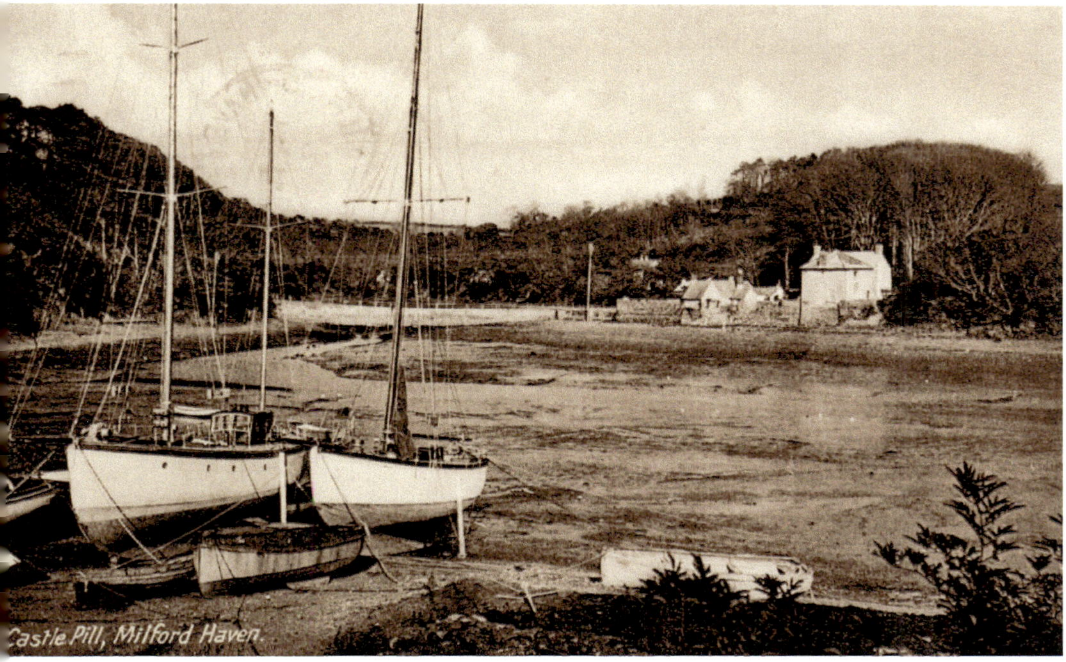

Castle Pill

Castle Pill is situated at the east end of Milford, and is approached from Cellar Hill. At the far end of the picture is Black Bridge. The original bridge was opened in 1858, made of wood and coated with pitch and tar for protection. It was replaced by the concrete bridge in 1921, part of the road connecting Milford and Neyland.

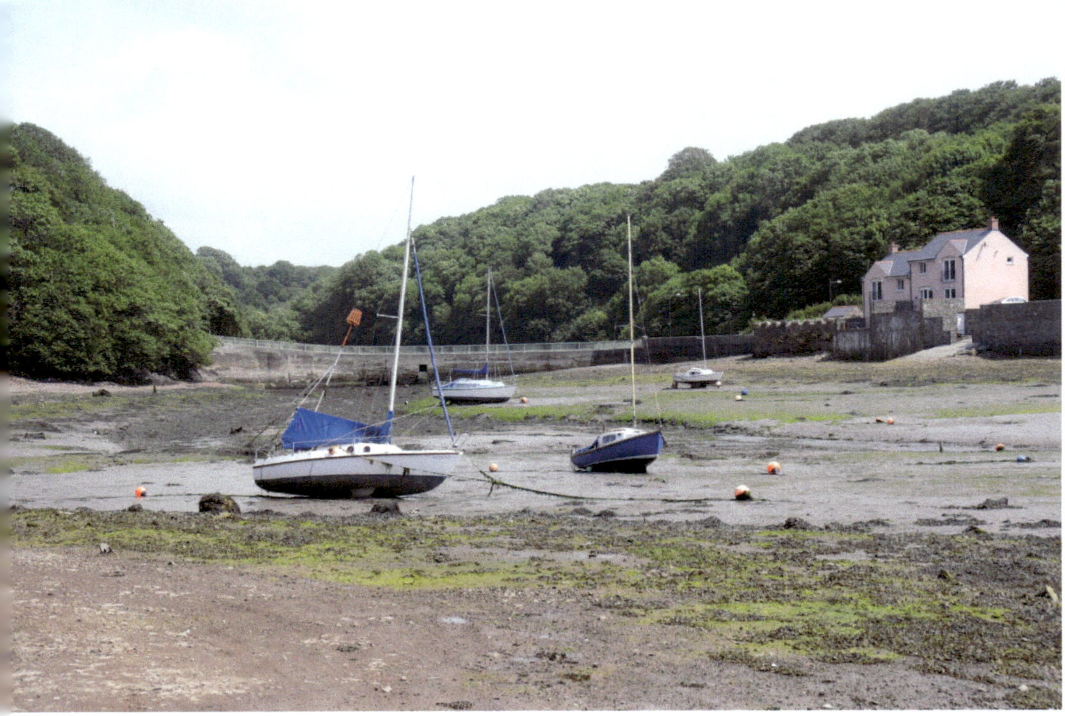

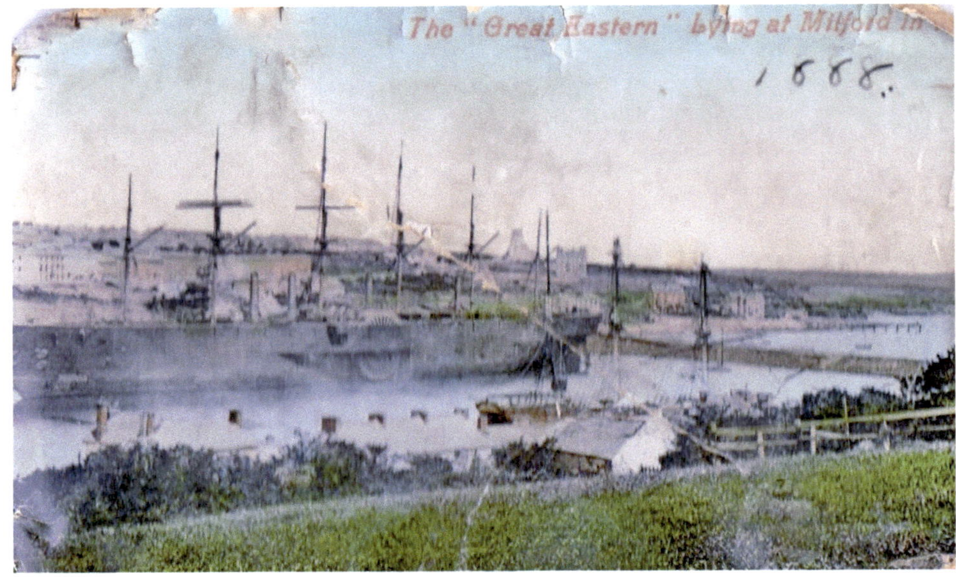

Great Eastern

This huge ship first visited Milford in 1861. Following work laying Atlantic cables, it returned for refitting in 1875 and spent many years moored below and parallel to Hamilton Terrace. Two marker stones were set in the dock wall to record the length (692 feet) of the ship. She eventually left in 1886, sailing to Liverpool to be scrapped. The Port Authority is now strongly promoting the town of Milford and Pembrokeshire as a cruise destination. Too large to enter the dock, the ships moor on Milford Shelf and tenders transport the passengers to a fleet of buses on land. Behind the ship is the Valero oil refinery.

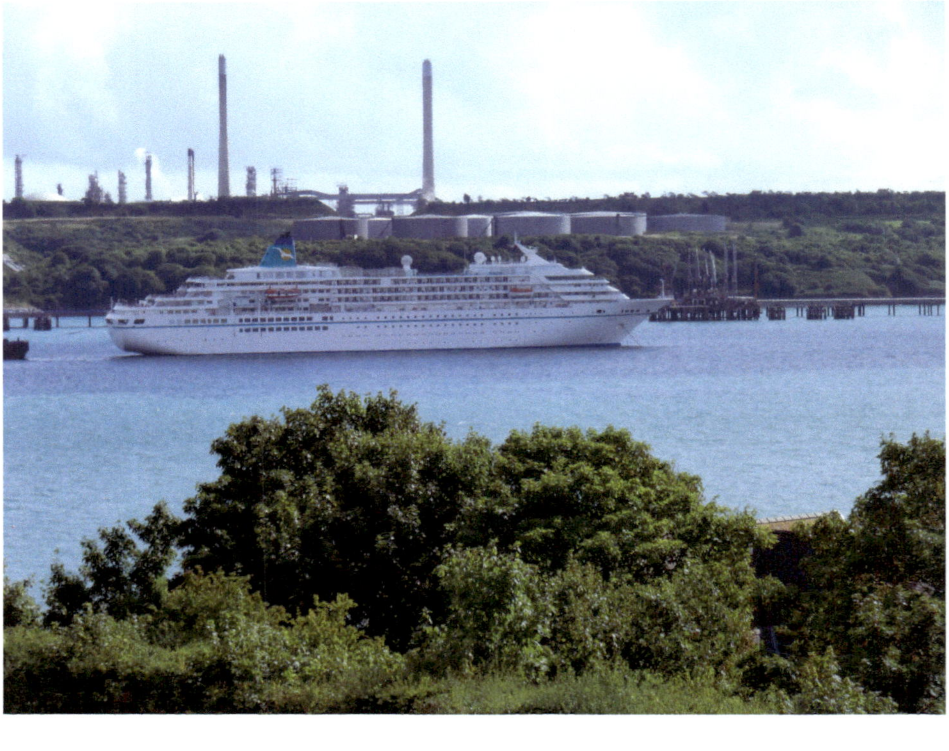

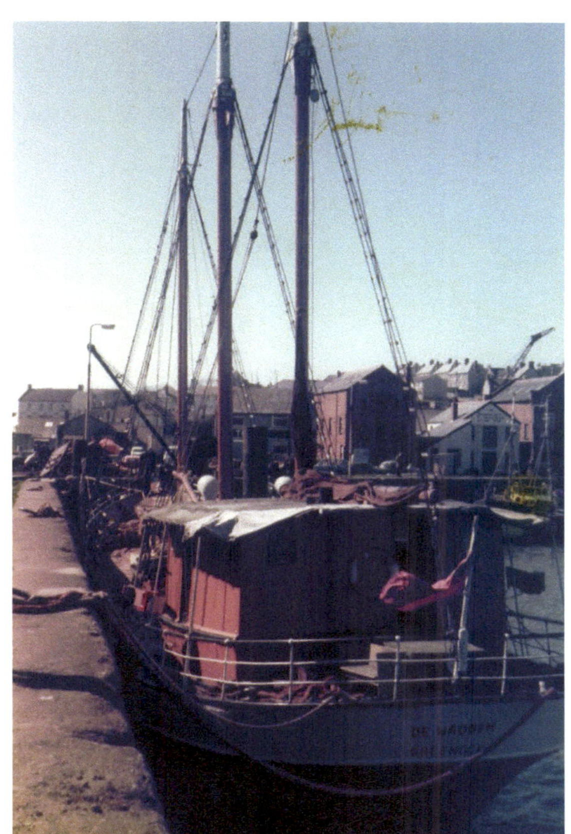

The Onedin Line

Several episodes of the 1970s BBC Television series *The Onedin Line* were made at Milford Docks, and the three-masted schooner *De Wadden* often sailed into the docks. Built in 1917 in the Netherlands, she is now undergoing conservation at Liverpool. The original dock buildings provided an ideal setting for the drama.

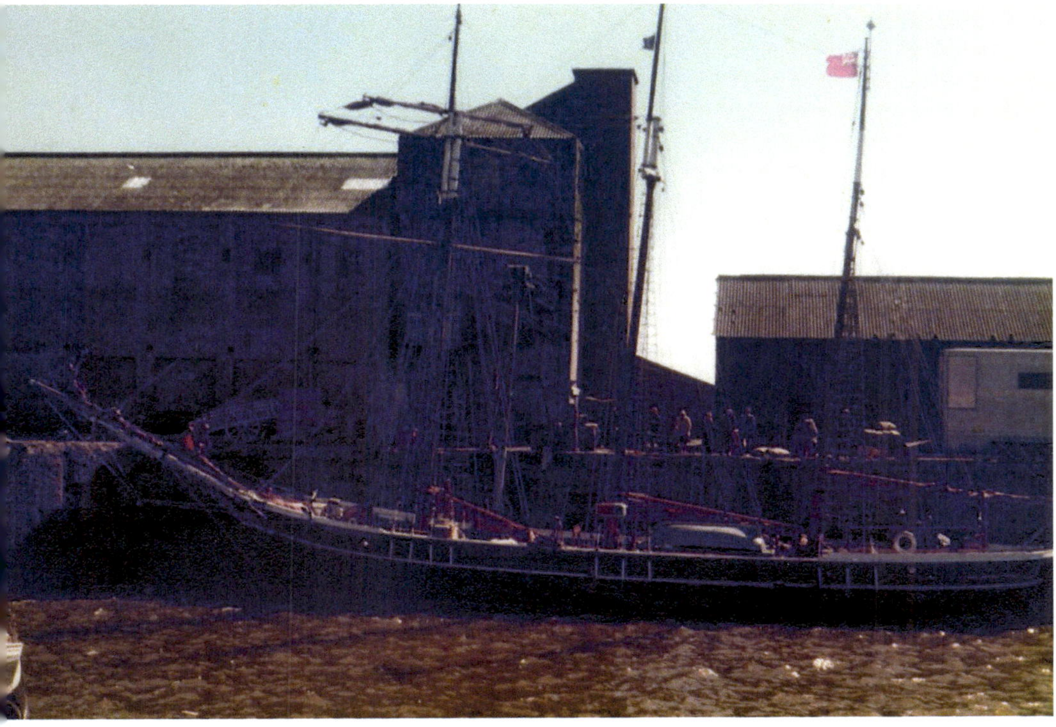

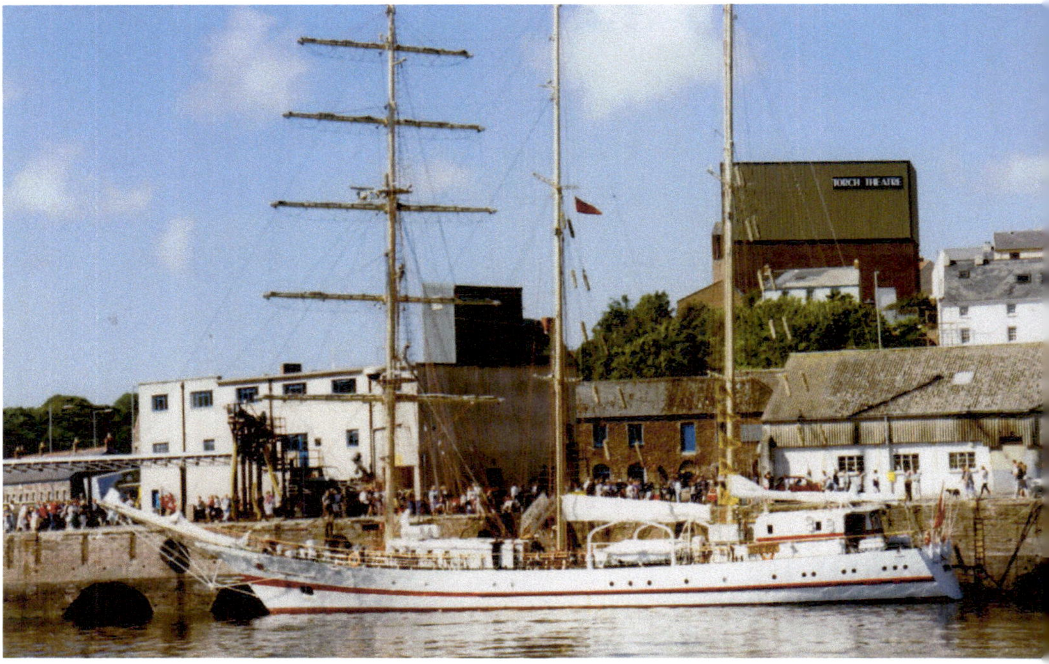

Visiting Ships

The 1991 Cutty Sark Tall Ships Race signalled the start of a new era for the dock, with a new emphasis on leisure. Many of the visiting ships sailed into the docks and took part in the spectacular Parade of Sail. It gave the area widespread publicity and a high profile. Naval vessels are regular visitors to the port.

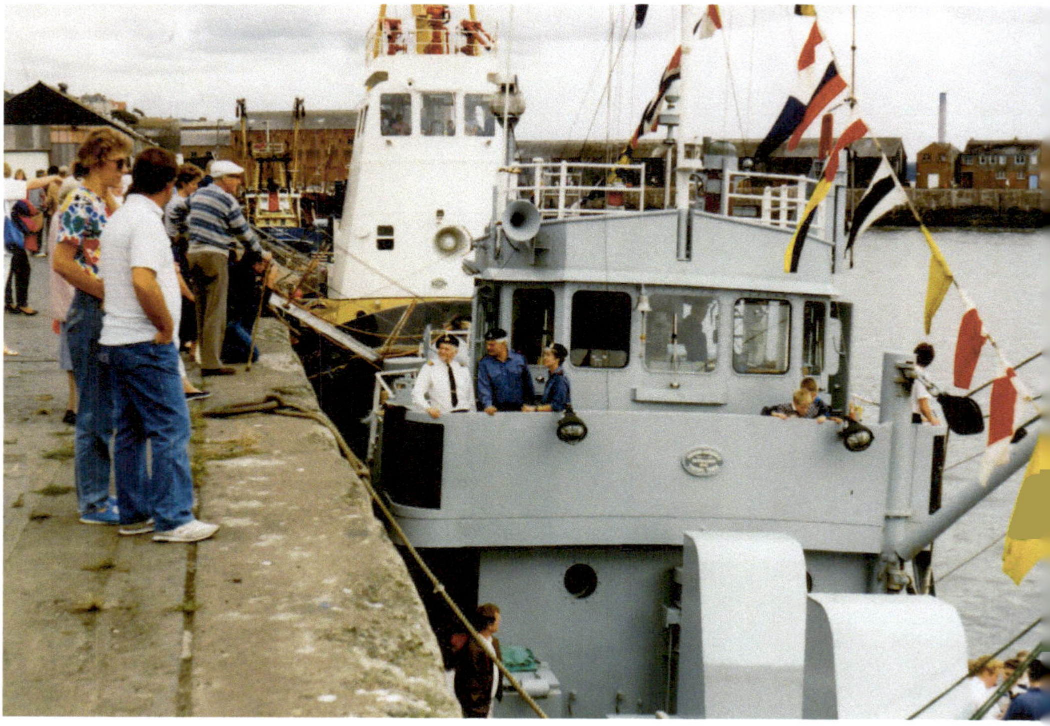

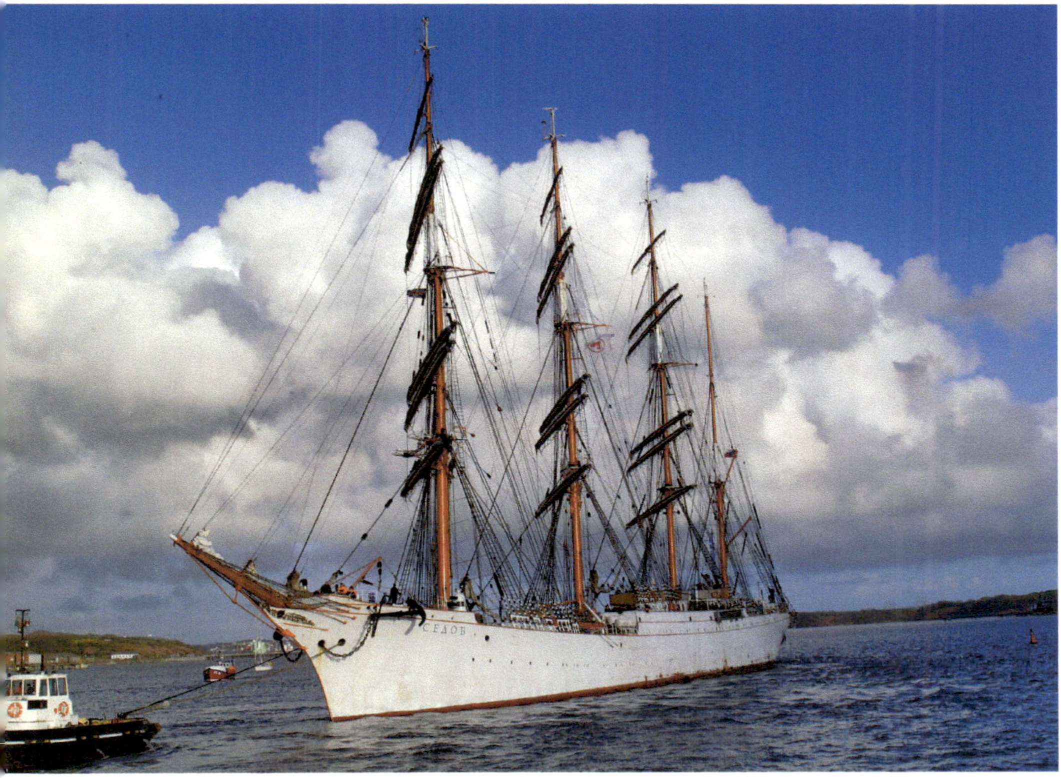

Visiting Ships

The many sailing ships visiting the
redesigned dock and marina have included
the *Dunbrody, Sir Winston Churchill* (Sail
Training Association), the *Picton Castle*, the
Grand Turk, the *Sedov* from Russia and *Dar
Mlodziezy* from Poland. A biennial Sea Fair
Maritime Festival is based on the marina.

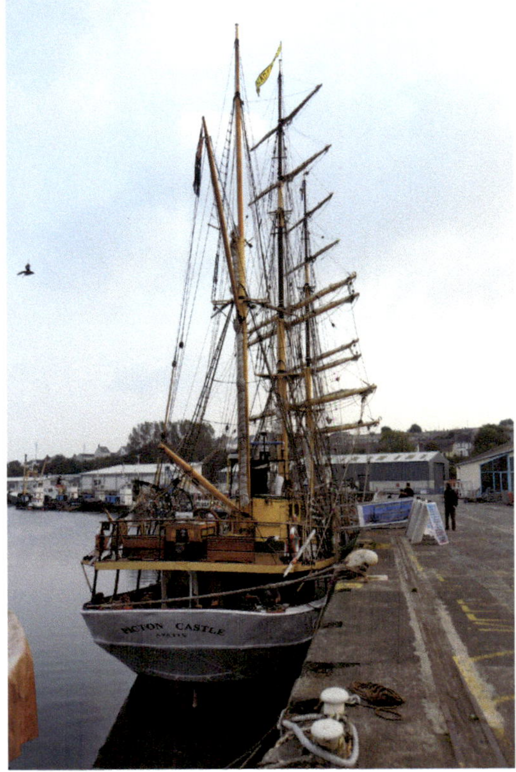

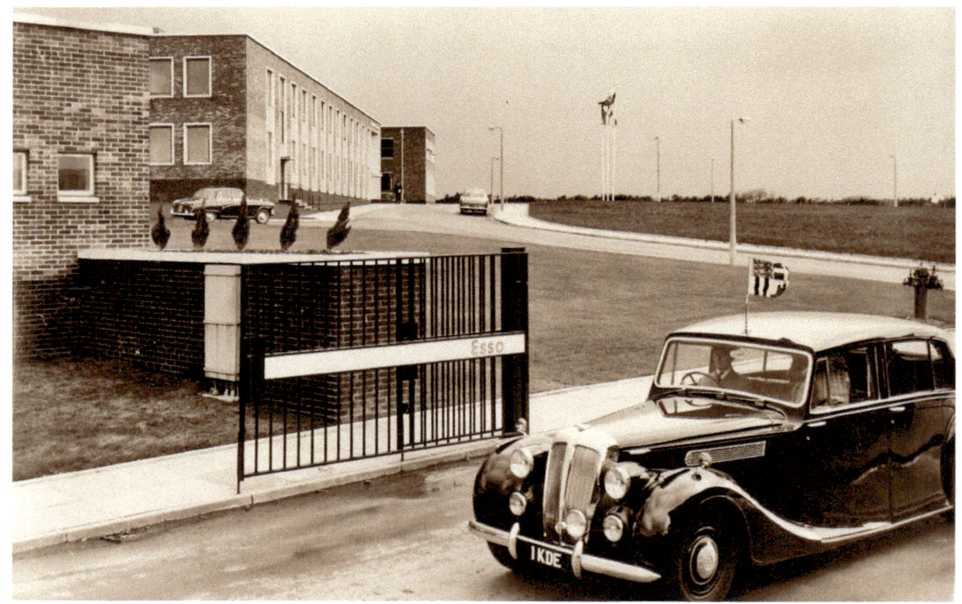

The Esso Oil Company

Esso was the first company to construct an oil refinery on the Milford Haven Waterway. Construction started in 1957 and the refinery was opened in 1960 by the Duke of Edinburgh. The cost was £18 million and the refinery had the capacity to process 4.5 million tons of crude oil a year. A special train brought visitors from London and the ceremony was performed in the impressive company headquarters. The following morning a serious explosion occurred on the Esso Portsmouth tanker moored alongside the jetty.

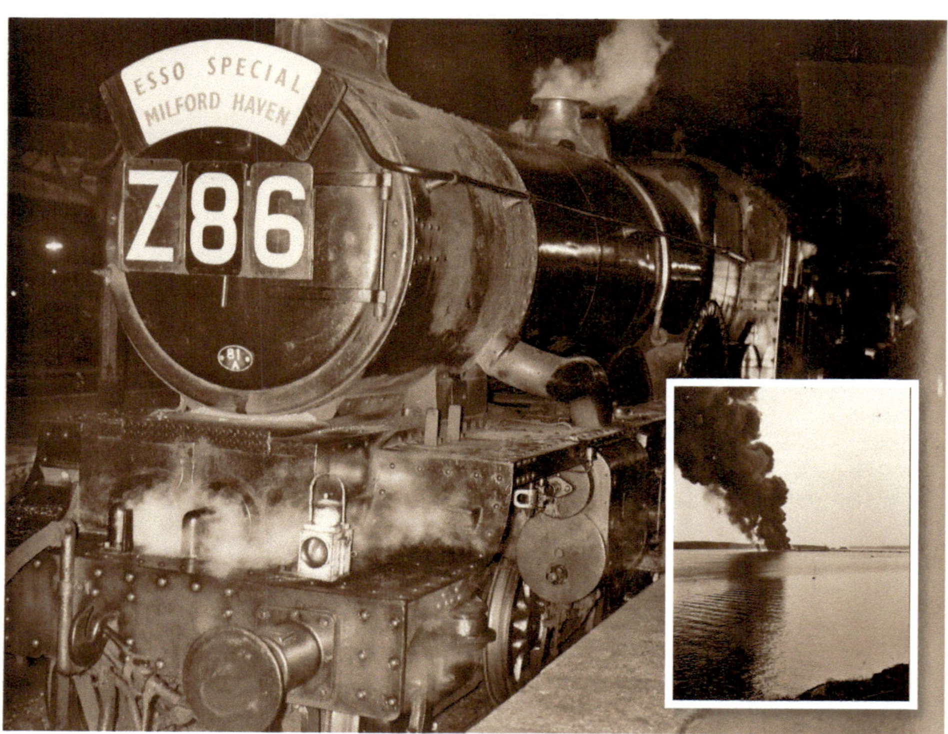

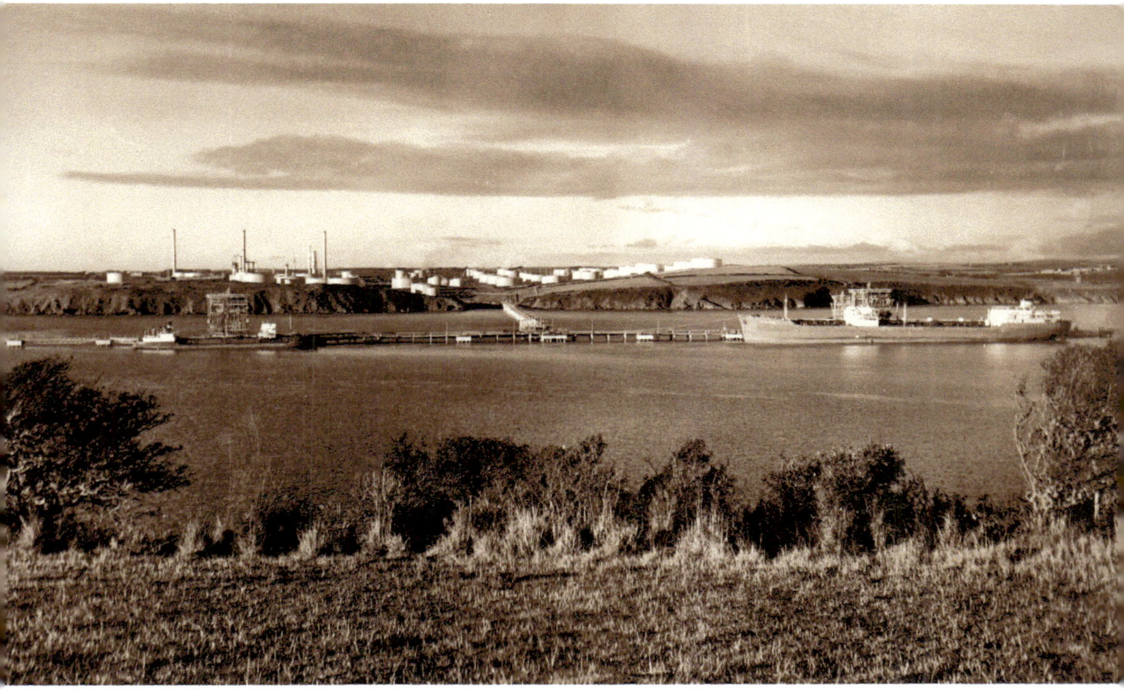

Esso Refinery

This view of the Esso Refinery was taken from across the Waterway at Angle. The refinery ceased to process oil in March 1983. Today, the site has been converted by the owners ExxonMobil into the South Hook LNG terminal.

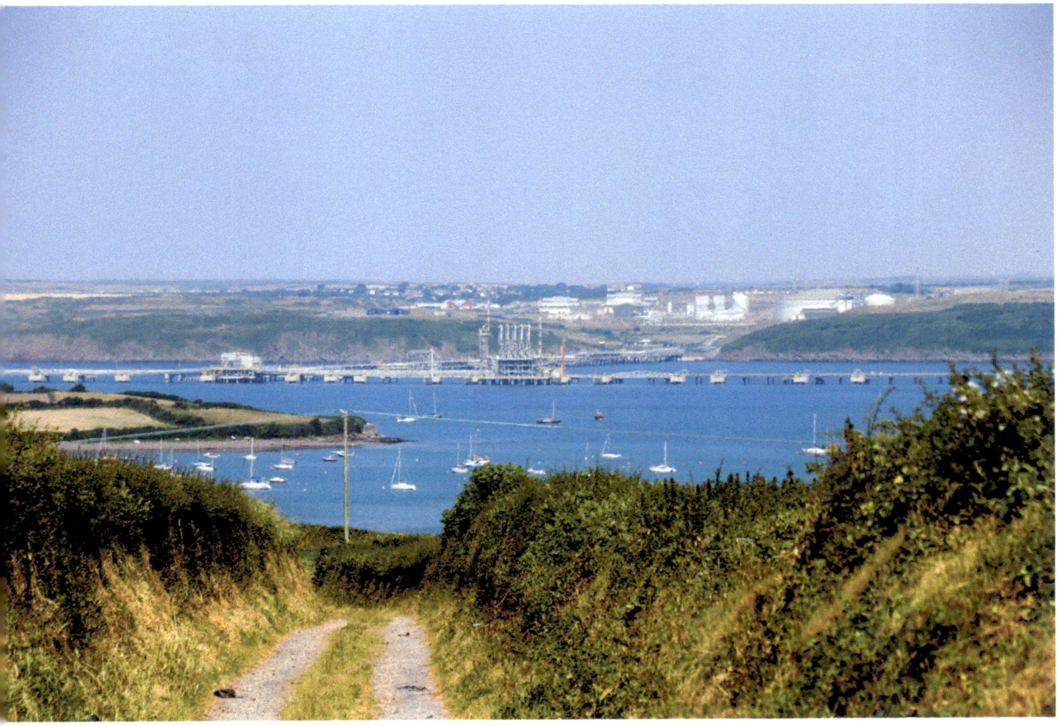